Adaptive Leadership Handbook:

Law Enforcement & Security

Innovative Ways to Teach and Develop Your People

LT Fred Leland

Lt, Walpole, MA Police Department, and Law Enforcement
Security Consulting (LESC.net)

&

MAJ Donald E. Vandergriff, FRSA, MA

US Army (ret.) (Adaptive-Leader.com)

Forward by
Sid Heal, LT LA County Sheriff's Department

D1534283

The views expressed in this book are those of the authors alone and do not reflect the official policy or position of any Department of the U.S. Government.

Cover Image: © Les Cunliffe - Fotolia.com

Forward
Adaptive Decision-Making
Sid Heal

All crises are fraught with uncertainty. While uncertainty must be reduced to the maximum possible extent, it can never be completely eliminated. Accordingly, efforts will always be necessary to deal with the unexpected. Effective leaders are compelled to continually improvise, innovate and adapt to ever-changing circumstances. The most successful leaders are able to both anticipate a change and promptly deal with it. Developing these types of leaders then becomes an imperative.

The concept of adaptive decision-making is best understood as the mental process of effectively reacting to a change in a situation. In the simplest terms, it refers to problem-solving. There are three major factors involved. First, the essence of the concept is a behavior change. Obstinately continuing a course of action despite significant changes in the circumstances is not adaptive even if it is effective. Second, whatever responses are employed must be effective. It makes no sense if they make things more difficult. Lastly, any response must be in reaction to a change of circumstances. Change for its own sake is not adaptive.

Whether leaders are adaptable and to what extent can be attributed nearly entirely to three factors, all of which are present in every instance. The first involves the personal traits and characteristics of a particular leader. Every leader has a unique and infinitesimal combination of knowledge, experience, education, courage, skills, imagination, intuition, ingenuity and other attributes.

These work singly and in combination to inhibit or foster effective reactions. The second is the organizational rules, norms and culture that encourage or discourage adaptive behavior. Organizations that dogmatically punish failure are not conducive to experimentation or exploration.

Understandably, leaders that emerge from this type of environment are reluctant to deviate from norms. The third is the extent that a person is trained to recognize and adjust to changing circumstances. This last factor is particularly important because of the implied potential for increasing creativity, ingenuity and effectiveness by preparing people to lead in chaotic and ever-changing situations.

While much study has been done on developing skills to enable people to "*think on their feet*," definitive methods have yet to be identified. Undoubtedly this is partly because training is only one of the three factors involved.

By nature, some people are more bold and imaginative than others and so they enjoy natural advantages. Likewise, some organizations are more accepting of risk than others and so even leaders with average abilities enjoy advantages over exceptionally endowed people but who find themselves operating under a discouraging or threatening administration. It does appear, however, that training can enhance abilities to adapt, both individually and organizationally.

The most critical aspect for enhancing organizational adaptability is with a nurturing environment. Organizations who routinely encourage and reward creativity, ingenuity and innovation not only encourage such practices among those assigned but serve to attract those who desire to work in such an environment. Of particular note is that simply providing a policy to that effect is, ineffectual. It is only in practice that the culture becomes relevant. The most nimble-minded people are also the most perceptive of hypocrisy and will not miss any disparity between policy and practice. It is with improving abilities in individuals, however, that training appears most promising. Studies of leaders who seem particularly adept in this area reveal two fundamental processes in sequence.

The first is that they have an existing pattern from training or experience, even if only remotely similar, from which to draw upon. They mentally compare the present problem with this existing mental image, which in turn provides insight and ideas of what might work. In other words, they have developed intuition.

The second is they do not accept the idea at face value, but rather conduct a mental simulation which allows them to mentally compare and "test" their intuition with the present circumstances. This mental simulation includes an action sequence in which one state of affairs is transformed and compared with another. In this manner, effective adaptive decision- makers can be best understood to have thought the problem through further than others.

When developing a training program for adaptive decision-making, two principles have proven especially beneficial. The first is to expose students to challenging scenarios simulating those expected to be encountered and which are designed to incorporate a need to recognize and adapt to a change in the situation. These are normally done in one of four ways: moderated discussions, practical applications, decision-making exercises and free-play exercises.

Regardless of the format of the training, the most fundamental requirement is that there is at least one change in a situation sufficient enough to challenge the status quo. As the training progresses and students become bolder, different situations are added and more varieties of change are injected, even to include the bizarre. Each of these altered states widens the scope and deepens the depth of all participants' understanding and serves as experience for other situations in the future, including real life ones. This is because humans naturally seek satisfactory resolutions and avoid actions and decisions that have already proven unproductive. They become experts in a particular problem and setting because they have the advantage of having already thought through the problem — even if it was only hypothetical.

The critical aspect of this training for the students is not just the process but the feedback. Feedback includes input, criticism, suggestions, comparisons and other types of collaborative problem-solving that are a necessary part of human understanding. Especially important is recognizing the need for change because diagnosis has proven to be among the most difficult skills to teach.

The tactical leaders most readily able to adapt are not only agile in thought but deeply immersed in the supporting science. They are fully aware of human limitations and possess domain specific knowledge which enables them to more quickly identify problems. They have developed a wide repertoire of experience from both actual incidents and training. Perhaps most importantly, they remain focused on the end state regardless of problems and setbacks. It is no surprise that despite the worst possible circumstances they seem to be successful more often than not.

*This article is republished here with permission of the author and was originally published in the current issue of "The Tactical Edge," the official publication of the **National Tactical Officers Association.***

About The Author: *Charles "Sid" Heal is a retired Commander from the Los Angeles Sheriff's Department where he spent more than half of his career assigned in units charged with handling law enforcement special and emergency operations. He spent his early formative years on the streets of south central Los Angeles before becoming a team leader on one of the department's six full-time SWAT teams. He continued to rise in rank and eventually became the commanding officer of the Special Enforcement Bureau. He holds three college degrees and two lifetime California teaching credentials and is the recipient of more than 160 awards and commendations relating to his career in law enforcement.*

*In addition to his career in law enforcement he is also a retired Marine Corps Reserve officer with service in more than twenty countries, including four tours of combat in four different wars. He is currently the chairman for the strategy development section of the National Tactical Officers Association and vice-president of the **California Association of Tactical Officers.***

PREFACE

You don't make money off books like ours. You do it because you care and you are a leader. Fred and I care, to the point that we sometimes lose money (and get in trouble from our wives), but in the end, we are paid by the gratitude from law enforcement officers, Soldiers and Marines who say, *"Thanks, what you did for me, made me better."*

We wrote this book because the techniques and methodologies presented in this book work, and what we have seen in most departments, and the military as well, border on incompetence at its worst or at a minimum, the lack of understanding in practical ways, technical problems verses adaptive challenges develop and the relationships among leadership, adaptation and systems work together to reach the outcomes we seek. Today, most training and education is similar to the mass production of the Industrial Age with little substance.

How current training methodologies are used, leads to the most common cause of failure in leadership which is treating adaptive challenges (non-linear and dynamic) as if they were technical problems (linear and static) with technical solutions. What's the difference?

In their book "The Practice of Adaptive Leadership: Tools and Tactics for Changing Your Organization and the World" the authors state, "While technical problems may be very complex and critically important, they have known solutions that can be implemented by current know-how. They can be resolved through the application of authoritative expertise and through the organizations current structures, procedures, and ways of doing things. Adaptive challenges can only be addressed through changes in people's priorities, beliefs, habits, and loyalties.

Making progress requires going beyond any authoritative expertise to mobilize discovery, destroying certain entrenched ways, tolerating failure, and generating new ways to thrive in the climate of chaos and uncertainty." 1

Unlike books from academe that emphasize theories of how it should be, written by very smart people but with little or no practical experience, we have applied these approaches to thousands of police and military personnel; and they work! The results have been shared with us through years of consistent feedback from former students: "This works and made me a better leader" and "Why did we not get this sooner in our careers?"

The problem remains with cultures, in both law enforcement and the military. They are the biggest obstacles to adopting these practices, which align with the latest in learning theory. This has evolved out of the University of Los Angeles' (UCLA) Department of Psychology, headed by Dr. Robert Bjork, a leader in the application of learning theory, as well as exhaustive historical research by Don Vandergriff on what makes the best developed problem solvers in high intense professions.

One only has to glimpse news articles in a budget crisis to know that the first thing cut in a police department, or the Department of Defense, is always training and education. It is often intangible and hard to measure, so why not cut it?

Even when training or education (henceforth "development") is funded adequately, it is almost always done poorly, using out of date methods that we will touch upon in the book. Despite a heavy weight of evidence to the contrary, a belief persists in many departments that the only way to improve is learning out on the streets. We do not dispute that experience is important, but it must be balanced by innovative, demanding and relevant development courses conducted in a fail safe environment that encourages learning.

Data proves that this creates the best personnel be it Soldiers, Marines or Police officers to deal with the growing complex environments they now enter. Long gone is the past, where training was memorizing rote information, and passing was proving you could comply with a mountain of policies and regulations, while remaining safe.

The challenges will remain, and that is why we wrote this book, which is a compilation of what Fred posts on the Law Enforcement and Security Consulting (LESC) blog (http://www.lesc.net/blog), and articles we have written together. It is also based on successful efforts I made with the Army, Marine Corps and specifically, the Baltimore City Police Department 2009-2011, when on the verge of reforming their recruit training; the Baltimore City Council decided other priorities preceded more effective development for its officers. These articles are all based on experiences, both successes and failures, in bringing the best development possible to professions dealing with the most complex problems imaginable - other people.

If what we advocate in this handbook is so good and has such a significant impact on how officers perform on the street, then why is it not common across law enforcement agencies?

Because, it's the culture, stupid!

Cultures are unique to each organization and/or profession. These cultures take shape over time, eventually becoming so entrenched that people resist any change, even change that is positive and valuable to the organization. Many organizations get stuck by the current way they do things, simply because it's the way they have always done it. They resist mainly because they fear losing something such as traditional methods of training, or operating how they have learned and developed over their careers. They fear they will lose control of their influence, their authority or prestige within the organization, and potentially their positions or jobs. Much of this is ego and individually driven and entirely self-serving, just hiding behind a smokescreen of leadership.

The rapidly changing world and evolving threatening challenges demand we become more self-aware and seek trade-offs. This means between traditional methods of training and operating and the uncertainty of ongoing, experiential trial and error the future demands if we are to thrive while handling crisis and conflict. 2 This must be done with an understanding we collectively have a shared purpose, which focuses on winning conflict and crisis at low cost in the moral, mental and physical dimensions which often times takes us outside our comfort zones.

We both know and want to share with readers; it takes hard work, patience and persistence to lead adaptively.

In 2010, while working with the Baltimore Police Department, I heard a senior police officer tell others that the only place to gain experience was on the street, that training was a waste of time. Fortunately for us, he was at odds with the Baltimore Police Commissioner Frederick Bealefeld, who was adamant that the BPD fix the development of its officers, using the latest methodologies.   Sadly after the Commissioner retired in 2012, we heard that our reforms did not stick, and things were sliding back into mass production methods.

I know from now years of friendship, Fred has similar incredible stories of senior police leaders expressing their view that training was a necessary evil, and the ideas that he tried to implement were a waste of time (despite the fact that officers loved and valued the development they received). Their focus was that money could be better spent elsewhere, like on new technology, new cars, radios, weapons, and equipment while personnel's hearts and minds were often neglected leading to disconnected values and beliefs (sounds like the US military as well).

But, even when a department has the money to train, it is used wrongly. A lot of this is the misconception that if you have a lot of money, then it buys you good training. Over the years, we observed several classes of instruction both in the classroom and in the field, on ranges and training environments, where it was evident that the physical facilities were first class, with plenty of material good, but the training still "sucked".

Why?

As we previously pointed out, it is all about culture and a

mentality of not knowing what you don't know. For example; over the last 13 years, learning science and what we know about how the mind learns has advanced incredibly (we have discovered and confirmed more). It has turned what we thought about learning (education and training) on its head. Herein lays another benefit of adaptive leadership, which is to help you observe and take advantage of the opportunities adaptive leadership offers, more frequently than you have before.

If this is also true, then why do our public school systems continue using the "Leave No Child Behind" program is reminiscent of the Industrial Age of mass production. According to experts at learning sciences, such as Dr. Robert Bjork, the approach of mass memorization is the worst way to develop problem solving abilities. The very abilities and traits that our officers must have to deal with evolving threats they encounter on the streets every day.

Through this book we will introduce you to the works of COL John Boyd, USAF, whose brilliant work forms the basis of what we do. Col. Boyd passed on in 1997, but his legacy continues to grow, particularly on how to develop leaders of character to out-perform their opponents. Fred and I have spent a good part of the last decade developing ways to teach people how to practice Boyd's OODA loop (more on this in the book).

Along the way after introductions to putting Boyd's, Sun Tzu and Clausewitz (two other brilliant military (human conflict) thinkers) as well as other's thoughts to practice, we begin introductions to actually implementing these ideas in the classroom along with examples of how they translated to the street. Over the course of the book, these real-world examples compile to actually form a real world Program of Instruction (POI) for a course that was implemented successful in a large police force just a couple of years ago.

We will conclude the book, not with the traditional conclusion that sums up what you have read, but with actual After Action Reviews (AARs) on how all the stuff you just read about was actually put to practice by police men and women in a four week's Sergeant Leader's Course for the Baltimore Police Department. The surveys and AARs conducted, after each, four-week iteration say it all about what we are advocating here, total reform of how our police men and women are developed, so they are more effective "on the street".

Three different officers, those who went through the development methodologies described in the following pages, say it best:

The previous classes, especially in-service seemed to be merely checking the box. "Okay, here is a situation and here is how it was resolved. Study it and know it." I didn't like that approach very much. I enjoy the way we did it this in the [Sergeant's Leader's] course because it was really my plan or decision that failed or succeeded.

BPD courses in the past have been monotonous and boring. The approach in this new course required us to take an interest, make a call, and put ourselves in the shoes of a real leader on the street. I think the class discussions were the best part of the course. We went over alternate solutions for TDGs [tactical decision games], and we had to defend ourselves against criticism. This made me more confident in myself, but it also showed me other perspectives and made me work on dealing with criticism.

Remember, real change is actually evolutionary; small victories through implementation of well thought out ideas, changes cultures over time. Implement the ideas in this book, one step at a time, with the overarching outcome to develop others to carry on what you started. Before that man or women walked out the door on their shift, did you ask *"could I have done more to prepare them for what they may encounter?"*

Fred Leland
Walpole, MA
October 2013

Don Vandergriff
Kabul, Afghanistan
October 2013

Chapter 1
Balancing Efficiency and Effectiveness and Building Cohesive Law Enforcement Agencies

Through the Boyd Cycle is how we process information and make decisions in our day to day law enforcement duties. We utilize this process of observation-orientation-decision and action to see the world around us, orient to what we perceive is going on and then based on this observation and orientation we make decisions and take actions to accomplish certain objectives based on what our goals or intent is. As law enforcement professionals we need to not only understand the Boyd cycle but we need to condition it through training so that we become more effective at applying it on the street.[1]

How are our efforts at becoming efficient law enforcement agencies affecting our ability to effectively execute timely observation, orientation, and decision and action cycles on the street?

Is there a balance to be sought that has room for across the board adjustments to efficient processes, policies and procedures and effective real time decision making utilizing people and ideas?

One of Col. John Boyd's most important insights we need to make a greater effort to understand is, *"Machines don't fight wars, people do and they use their minds."* How this applies to law enforcement is to understand what technologies, processes, policies and procedures work on the street, one must first understand how people think and act in the uncertainty, fear and chaos of dynamic encounters and what creates friction in decision making as a cop interacts with a suspect bent on getting his way or in a crisis situation such as a multiple car accident with mass casualties, a blizzard, hurricane, tornado, or fire etc.[2]

Only with this understanding is it possible to develop technologies, processes, policies and procedures, to serve the street cops needs.

By understanding the needs and dynamics of people (cops) who work the streets, it is possible to design a system from the streets to the courts that advances police departments, efficiency and effectiveness.

Is It Not Time We Robustly Embrace The Philosophy of Decentralized Control?

Considering the types of environments, crises and adversaries the law enforcement officer will probably face on the streets of the future is it not time for a change in the bureaucratic processes to a system that affects individual and organizational decision making and sustaining cohesive departments?

A law enforcement cultural change that embraces fully a philosophy of a decentralized bias for action based upon a high degree of professional trust and confidence between leaders of law enforcement and the led.   This philosophy will provide principles for exercising good judgment in unique situations, not formulas and checklists. Although specific tools i.e. weapons etc. and basic procedures are ingrained through training and repetition, this philosophy advocates adaptability in the application of the techniques on the street.

Policies and procedures must be written in such a way that specifics are left to the cops on the street facing the problem, a bottoms up approach whose vast experience and education will allow him to pick the right solution for the right situation (mutual trust is crucial here).

At the tactical level, an officer will make decisions according to the particular conditions of environment, the adversary or crisis his own resources and the overall mission and intent set by the leaders of the department using his best judgment. Currently, police training centers on teaching specific techniques or habits so they can be repeated in a consistent manner regardless of conditions.

The difference between how we currently train and prepare

versus the philosophy I am advocating is similar to the difference between techniques and tactics. Techniques require inflexibility and repetition, while tactics require flexibility, good judgment and creativity. Officers can only gain the ability to execute this new philosophy with experience and education, stressing free play force on force training brought to a conclusion with clear winners and losers. Keep in mind no tactical concept is an end in itself and that there is more than one solution to a tactical dilemma.

Tell Them What To Think and Do... or Teach Them How To Think and Do?
Our belief about leadership and developing an organizational environment that is supportive and understanding which helps greatly in developing cohesion based on mutual trust, empathy and common experiences as well as self-sacrifice. These attributes greatly enhance both efficiency and effectiveness. To ensure these attributes are more than mere words it is import for leaders to lead daily and not only when a crisis is upon us.

Leadership is an ongoing act not an event driven phenomenon. Meaning good leaders develop their officers on a daily basis so they are ready and prepared when crisis hits, compared to leaders who prepare and educate themselves and then try to puppet master through micro-management their officers dealing with a crisis, creating more uncertainty and chaos.

It is important when setting organizational goals that we focus on identifying outcomes. What is it we expect and officer to do and how do we expect an officer to behave and perform as he/she carries out their daily duties? Once those outcomes are identified develop policy and procedures, rules and regulations, checklists, training programs that focus on balancing efficiency and effectiveness.

Let's talk about balancing efficiency and effectiveness and how it relates to what we do.

Efficiency, is commonly described as achieving maximum productivity with minimum wasted effort or expense.

Effectiveness, on the other hand is described as being successful in producing a desired or intended result (outcome). Efficiency denotes we look at and measure results based on inputs or an opinion or recommendation offered as a guide to action, or conduct such as; policy and procedure or rules and regulations or a checklist to follow.3

Efficiency is an important aspect to policing. We must ensure things that need to be done such as information and evidence gathering, dissemination and documentation in reports, etc., is indeed getting done. However it is important for leaders not to get lost in the efficiency of processes as it breeds a zero defects environment that creates a frontline that waits to be told what to think and slowing down considerably the effectiveness of timely decision making and tactical problem solving.

To be effective in human interaction, we need feedback on the policy, procedures, rules and regulations or checklist we are using. Are they working or not? Feedback or output as it is sometimes called is information gathered and perceived by the user, the cop on the street. The kinds of feedback the officer makes, and the kinds of input the officer on the street accepts, as he interacts with his environment and the people in it, defines the street cops orientation of the situation and effects the decisions and actions he takes.

In this context, it is clear we need to understand the differences between being efficient and effective and balance them accordingly based on the unfolding situation. Efficient policy and procedures must be thought of as a framework based on foundational principles and include room for adaptation, people and Ideas, if they are to be fully effective.

Balancing Our Efficiency and Effectiveness
Let's use something common to every law enforcement agency, *marksmanship training* to explore this a bit deeper. Police

marksmanship training focuses on task, conditions and standards.

The task is to be able to develop individual officers who can safely and efficiently shoot and hit a target from various distances. We do this by teaching stance, draw, grip, sight alignment, sight picture, trigger squeeze and follow-through. The condition this is taught in at most law enforcement locations is still a static range environment, using silhouette targets.4

The standard in most departments is to shoot so many rounds in an allotted amount of time, and includes magazine changes, malfunction drills, different shooting positions, firearms safety rules and to qualify with an 80% score. All, or the majority of law enforcement marksmanship training, and this includes recruit and in-service training for veteran officers, is to qualify an officer in the safe and efficient use of a firearm. And of course this is done in a sterile environment (we mean solely focused on firing of the weapon(s) with no other focus than that on the firing of the weapon).

But is efficiency enough?

Is it enough at preparing young and veteran officers for the threats and problems they may face on the streets? What is the outcome of the current way we train?

We have pushed folks through training with a qualifying score in an efficient way with hundreds of guys a year in Massachusetts alone and thousands across the country. On paper we have efficiently meant the standard of qualification.

The question then comes to mind; does meeting this standard make them effective on the street?

Can they maneuver and communicate with back-up officers, innocent bystanders, victims, and an adversary, assess threats and set up tactically appropriately? Can they shoot accurately when being shot at themselves or under pressure?

Statistics prove otherwise and that 14-20% hit rates are common according to FBI statistics and research of real life gun fights.5

What does effective marksmanship training look like?
There have been some fine trainers in our profession who have realized efficiency is not good enough. They have changed the training methodology to incorporate not only safety and fundamentals of marksmanship but the attributes of self-awareness, *problem solving and threat assessment, adaptability, critical and creative thinking, decision making, tactical skills, social skills, fitness,* etc. This has resulted in more effective outcomes on the street in tactical responses and approaches, assessing threats, tactical decision making and more accurate hit rates when deadly force was used.

One form of this type of training is known as free play force on force training. It involves using those tangible and intangible skills as they will be used on the street to solve tactical dilemmas. There is nothing new here, when it comes to talking about this type of training hell we have talked about it for more than 20 years however most agencies across this country getting this type of training on a consistent basis are few and far between.

Why?
We are focused on, too heavily on efficiently, meeting tangible, easy to measure standards, versus effectively developing officers capable of reaching outcomes. This problem is not based on dishonesty, lack of integrity, or lack of intelligence by us law enforcement senior leaders. The problems are systemic in nature, a complex mix of law enforcement tradition, conditioned responses and institutional responses to the world we live and work in. If we want to continually improve our effectiveness and safety on the street, we must evolve through continued learning.6

We can start by removing some of the rules, procedures and processes that stifle initiative and work together to develop cohesive top down/bottom up organizations that trust one another to execute in all aspects the job of policing requires.
While at the same time develop rules, policies, procedures and

processes in an effort to be efficient, achieving maximum productivity with minimum wasted effort or expense that focus as well on effectiveness, so the street cop is successful in producing a desired or intended result.   This will leave maneuver room for experienced people to use their tactical ideas resulting in cops who become tactical problem solvers making them both more efficient and effective in all aspects of policing.

The outcomes we are looking for in our professions are centered on solving complex and continually evolving problems in our efforts to protect and solve problems in the communities we serve. Now in our strategy to protect and serve we must keep in mind all aspects of the conflicts and problems we face, in their many forms and how cops perform when dealing with these problems. For a law enforcement officer dealing with these problems, this takes an ability of applying numerous critical tasks working in synergistic way in constantly changing conditions.

The leadership climate and training provided to officers must not only focus on efficiently meeting tasks, conditions and standards, it must also include developing the attributes, required for individuals, teams, and organizations to carry out the mission effectively.   I would be willing to bet these attributes and values are in most agencies mission statements and policies and procedure manuals as BOLD typed words! Is it not time we put those words into BOLD action? This is the mission and intent of this book.

Chapter 2
Establishing the Discipline to Train and Invest in Preparedness

"Plan an advantage by listening. Adjust to the situation. Get assistance from the outside. Influence events. Then planning can find opportunities and give you control."
~Sun Tzu1

This chapter is for leaders and frontline professionals willing to assess the situation within their agencies in regards to training, preparation, readiness and response capabilities, who need ideas on how to keep training regular and relevant, at the strategic, operational and tactical levels of your organization, in these tough uncertain and economic times.

To be more successful in performing our duties at the level of professionalism needed in handling dynamic encounters, crisis situations we must train and train often at individual, team, agency and interagency levels. The investment in training to prepare for conflict and crisis situations requires discipline and strength of character. The payoffs of training and preparation are high yield results that save lives.

Are We Truly Prepared and Ready to Lead Under Emergency Conditions?

People that work with and for you make your organization what it is. An investment in preparing them to handle the types of problems they face and hence you face, is an investment in being a more successful organization. Training in my view is "practice" and practice makes us better at what we do, not perfect, but much, much better. I say not perfect and I am often questioned as to why not, PERFECT?

My answer is we will strive to mitigate the effects of crisis, rather than cause or add to a crisis situation. We will work to reverse or reduce the effects of an emergency situation, which will lead to more lives saved. Quite frankly the current state training and preparedness is in at this time, perfection in crises, in the unexpected, uncertain and rapidly unfolding and changing circumstances is still based in the complacency of *"it will not happen here"* and react mode.

The size and scope of the crisis and the sense of chaos and confusion it creates in victims and those responding, leads to information overload and makes developing an adequate response a challenge.

In responding to crises and rendering aid, first responders must constantly assess the changing conditions, and adapt plans to meet these unfolding conditions with an adequate set-up and response to save lives. This assessment includes not only; *"what's happening now"* but it also entails organizing initial responding officers and other first responders in establishing command and control, communications, identifying the threats and the danger or kill zones. This initial assessment and *"set-up"* is crucial to the overall effectiveness of the response and is directly related to the outcome.

If our initial response brings a semblance of control to chaos and helps us realize, get a better picture of what's going on, then a viable response can be initiated quickly based on a sound strategy and effective methods and tactics to mitigate the situation. If we respond out of emotion and take reckless action, then we lose control of the situation and it becomes more chaotic and only leads to more uncertainty and confusion and our efforts spiral downwardly to an ineffective response.

First responder's decision making cycles (OODA Loops) must constantly be updated based on the rapidly unfolding circumstances and the implicit and explicit knowledge they have, which allows them to set up perimeters.

First the inner perimeter or a tactical rally point which is where the tactical decisions get made, contact and rescue teams are established and the initial response is initiated. This happens relatively quickly from seconds to minutes based on the overall situation.

While first responders take action to stop the threat and rescues are taking place and the crisis evolves, additional resources are called in to assist and can take from several minutes, hours, and days to arrive based on the scope and the scale of what you are dealing with. These additional resources may be needed to assist in the tactical response; locating the threats and recue activities or to enhance the overall response with support activities such as: establishing a larger outer perimeter for containment purposes.

Setting up command posts and staging areas who work together getting additional resources needed to assist in mitigating the crisis. This requires even greater coordination and communication amongst the various agencies responding and is also part of this support role and crucial aspect of bringing a successful conclusion to crises.

When crisis happen in the unexpected way they normally do, along with the complacent mindsets we possess as a society, organizationally or individually in relation to conflict and crises, we simply cannot prevent every bad thing from happening despite our best efforts.

But with training and preparation (individual, group, agency intra and interagency wide) we can get much better at how we prepare which leads to more effective initiative driven actions before, during and in the aftermath of crisis situations.

One of the main reasons for my analysis is that preparation and response to crisis situations takes practice and experience to lead, respond to, make decisions and take action, dealing with an emergency event.

It takes discipline and dedication at all levels federal, state, local, organizational, individual and the citizenry learning, unlearning and relearning from each experience if we are to become better at how we work in crisis.

We are nowhere near ready, we are sadly still in the talking stage and must move in a proficient way to the walking the talk stage and preparing first responders law enforcement, security, fire and medical personnel, citizens, etc. through realistic training that prepares them/us for what potentially lies ahead.

Is Preparedness a Game or Something Much More Serious?

You must control your soldiers with esprit de corps. You must bring them together by winning victories. You must get them to believe in you. Make it easy for people to know what to do by training your people. Your people will obey you. If you do not make it easy for people to know what to do, you won't train your people. They will not obey. Make your commands easy to follow. You must understand the way the crowd thinks.
~Sun Tzu2

If I were to ask you about let's say coaching a high school football team for your local high school and told you the only time you were needed to be there as coach, was on game day. That is right no practice during the week, just take the team and win is all we ask. How do I prepare them if I cannot practice you ask? Well sir they have been trained and practiced in their freshman, sophomore and junior years. You will be the varsity coach and the team knows the game and how it's played, all you need to do is set up the game plan on game day and organize your team so they win!

Ludicrous!

How can I be expected to develop the cohesion necessary to put a winning team on the field, without practice, despite their prior training and the three-plus years' experience? Yes it is ludicrous.

Yet this is exactly what we expect of law enforcement, security personnel and other first responders tasked with responding to and winning in crisis situations.

Training initially consists of developing a knowledge base in the basic aspects of the job, take for instance law enforcement. Subjects such as; law and procedures, report writing, patrol procedures, community policing, basic firearms training, some building entry techniques as well as some specialized training in domestic violence, operating under the influence of alcohol, arrest procedures and defensive tactics etc. These are a great base of knowledge to start with and build on, yet therein lay the problem. There is not very much building upon the basics. Most is left to learning via on the job training.

But _what if_ nothing we have ever been taught or experienced is sufficient to the problem we face? Understanding the essence of winning and losing and rethinking our methods of training formally and informally must change. The nature of Conflict has changed, how we think must change, how we prepare must change, how we orient and reorient ourselves in an uncertain environment must change if we are to be successful.
~Ed Beakley Anti-Terrorist and Homeland Security Specialist[3]

The world has changed and conflict and how it's waged is blurred. Crime and terrorism are now linked and actors utilize national, international and transnational networks to implement their strategies and tactics as we have already seen here at home and abroad. The threats and crime trends we deal with are not as clearly defined as they once were and the stakes are higher, much higher than points scored in a game. Our adversaries have us on scattered ground with our resources spread thin and leaving the Homeland open and easier to attack.
This is a dangerous situation, strategically and tactically out of position. We must get serious and invest in preparing our people through training.

Training People an Investment in Preparedness and Frontline Results
To flourish and grow in a many-sided uncertain and ever changing world that surrounds us, suggests that we have to make intuitive within ourselves those many practices we need to meet the exigencies of that world. The contents that comprise "this discourse" unfold observations and ideas that contribute towards

achieving or thwarting such an aim or purpose.
~Col. John Boyd4

Whether we are dealing with conventional or unconventional threats there are indeed lots of similarities and yet still many uncommon factors and uncertainties we must contend with. In the quote above from John Boyd he states; *"that we have to make intuitive within ourselves those many practices we need to meet the exigencies of that world"* Intuitively adapt to changing conditions and respond with sound decisions and appropriate actions.

To be able to channel and leverage that ability to do so takes training at a standard much higher and much more effective than we utilize currently.

I will use the law enforcement training example to compare with my coaching analogy to make my point on the importance of preparing for the unexpected and why it is worth the investment.

The initial training for law enforcement varies by state but is anywhere from 12-26 weeks. Then once graduated from the academy, the officers get anywhere from 8-12 weeks of field training in an effort to help him/her apply what they have learned in basic training to the streets of the community for which they work.

Adding up the basic and field training utilizing the maximum standard, 26 weeks basic plus 12 week field training equals 38 weeks of training.5

From then on, for most in law enforcement, they get 40 hours of in-service training annually to maintain their status or certification as a law enforcement officer. 38 Weeks of training at the maximum standards with one week a year after that throughout a career. Yes there are also specialized training classes but there is only a select few who can attend because of budget and time issues, etc. So for the sake of argument the majority of officers get 38 weeks of basic training.6

Success on the street responding to a wide variety of

situations is expected without mistakes, no fowls or penalties, no being knocked back and out of position. Winning every contact, every engagement is what's expected. In the current system of how and when we train, is this expected success a realistic expectation or is it a smokescreen of rhetoric over substance and talk to appease with little walking the talk that is needed to succeed?

Talk seems to be plenty, but walking the talk is scarce!
In the real world game of life and death shouldn't we be better prepared than a Sports Team on Game Day?

Shouldn't our training and education system be evolving at a rate higher than that of kids or professional athletes playing a game? The answer would seem an obvious yes!
Yet the reality is clearly NO we do not!

High School football teams at the varsity level which is made up of seniors so for the sake of argument let's say they have the 3 –plus (Pop Warner) years. For the sake of my comparison I will take into consideration only the 3 high school years of football.
Practice starts in August and the season usually ends on Thanksgiving day   so that is approximately12 weeks of practice a year which adds up to 36 weeks of practice over a three year period. This practice consists of both physical and cognitive development.

Players must take the knowledge and skills taught and apply them in practice on the field, in actual free-play force on force exercises preparing them for game day.

My question, would you take the coaching job mentioned above in the final year with no practice time and just game day advice and expect to win? Why not? Because you know it is unrealistic to think you can have a winning season without practice or training.

Yet this is only a sport on which there are only so many game plans, responses and outcomes, outcomes that do not involve life and death matters. Most I submit would not take this job because they know success would be a rare occurrence.

What does this analogy have to do with crisis and

preparedness? Sadly too much! Let's take a look.

Law enforcement officers get very little time applying what they have learned in the classroom environment of a training academy.

There is very little free play force on force exercises conducted. In the State of Massachusetts for example; about 40 hours of hands on force on force free play exercises is allotted in training time and this is broken up amongst an academy class of 30-60 recruits. So how much real training time is allotted per student? I think you would agree, nowhere near enough. The high school kids playing a game get more hands on training than those who protect our homeland.7

Football is easy to train because, in the end it is a monotonous game with a defined set of permutations, and a limited territory. Police work has unlimited number of permutations, unlimited territory, and unlimited complexity.

Yet if football practice time was cut and the win/loss column was in the negative, people in that team's community would be up in arms complaining and a mass effort would be sought to re-instate the full program so the kids could prepare and have a fair shot at winning! I would be willing to bet there would be some first responder in that group of upset parents leading the charge to implement the full program of full practice and game day coach.

Why then do we expect our first responders, responding to emergency and crisis situations to do so without even as much realistic training as a high school football team, when so much more is at stake? Have we even considered the thought, pondered the thought for even a few minutes at what's required of those responding to violence on our streets in our schools and across this country? Have we thought about the uncertainty and unexpected nature of the calls for service responders are handling.

How about the violence that effects the psychological and

physiological processes of the human body in high stress situations, and hence our abilities to make decisions and take appropriate actions under pressure? We call it choking in sports when someone or a team fails; *"it happens under game pressure... give him time, more practice and the athlete or team will perform better!"*

We call it a screw up in the business of protection, safety and crisis response and look for heads to roll because we expect flawless responses. Yet we are given very little, *"less"* than a sports team effort to train and prepare. Have we as a profession or as a society considered this? I do not think we have. Because if we did, we would be, much more understanding as a society, as leaders in these professions, of what's required.   There are psychological and physiological responses to dynamic confrontations and the effects on cognitive and physical abilities handling crisis. We would invest more in preparing (training/education=developing) our people for the realities they face.

It is simply insufficient to have harmony and coordination across agency and interagency bounds in crisis, without training at all levels (organizational philosophy, strategy, tactics, methods and techniques, equipment, leader development) to ensure the proper knowledge and skills are acquired , understood and can be applied in chaotic and uncertain circumstances.

In their book; *America's Army a Model for Interagency Effectiveness*, Generals Bradford and Brown state *"If leaders fail to act to common purpose, the best "new," however capable, will not produce results in the fight. The product must be teamed capabilities where for example, leaders at all echelons realize the necessity of developing effective team leadership, shared vision, shared trust, shared competence, and shared confidence, despite inevitable personnel turbulence."*8

When we join the team, in the serious game of protection, we do not... jump into the water to make a splash... we jump into the water to make a difference, a difference in people's lives in their time of need. Our score card is life and death, making a difference starts with looking at the facts and recognizing the TRUTH and then with strength of character PRESS ON! Do what's right!

Communicating the Truth

Tiger, one day you will come to a fork in the road," he said. "And you're going to have to make a decision about which direction you want to go." He raised his hand and pointed. "If you go that way you can be somebody. You will have to make compromises and you will have to turn your back on your friends. But you will be a member of the club and you will get promoted and you will get good assignments." Then Boyd raised his other hand and pointed another direction. "Or you can go that way and you can do something - something for your country and for your Air Force and for yourself. If you decide you want to do something, you may not get promoted and you may not get the good assignments and you certainly will not be a favorite of your superiors. But you won't have to compromise yourself. You will be true to your friends and to yourself. And your work might make a difference." He paused and stared into the officer's eyes and heart. "To be somebody or to do something," In life there is often a roll call. That's when you will have to make a decision. To be or to do, which way will you go?
~Col. John Boyd, TO BE or TO DO? 9

The above quote is not an excuse, but a fact that we in the protection and security game know all too well is true, and I put most of the blame squarely on our profession. Leaders tell community members what they think they want to hear. We tell folks we are prepared when we know damn well we are not anywhere near fully prepared. It is often sighted we do not want to spark panic or unrest; we do not want to be alarmists.
"Alarmist!" "Malcontent!" "Sour grapes," "Oh, he is pissed because he did not get promoted!"
These are typical responses to those who push for change or

reform, but I ask if we in the homeland security and first responder professions do not inform and alarm the folks, then who does? Do we wait for the next explosion or gun shots or do we try our best to inform the communities we work in and for of the potential dangers out there and ask for their vigilance and support? The answers to me seem rather obvious! We must do something and train to make a difference.

In law enforcement we just do not share information very well within the community. There are exceptions and in those departments that do make the effort to share, we see success at bridging this gap and developing more support from society. Most people react in a positive manner when they hear the truth about the situation and its time the training issue comes to the forefront.

Communication within organizations is critical as well. Communications in regards to the strategic, operational and tactical arenas must be discussed openly within an organization. Intelligence must be passed on. Where we think we are weak and need more training has to be discussed and approached in an open dialog if we are to ever move forward and inspire initiative in those frontline personnel who respond. A leader, however skilled, must rely on the performance of his men and women for success. They are on the ground and closest to the adversary and must be able to act on their own initiative.

If they fail, the leader and community fail. If they win, the leader and the community also win. We must as a whole invest in preparedness and the training necessary to do so.

What is the Investment and How Do We Get It Done?
In a world of limited resources and skills, individuals and groups form, dissolve and reform their cooperative or competitive postures in a continuous struggle to remove or overcome physical and social environmental obstacles. In a comparative sense, where skills and talents are pooled, the removal or overcoming of obstacles represents an improved capacity for independent action for all concerned. In a competitive sense, where individuals and

groups compete for scarce resources and skills, an improved capacity for independent action achieved by some individuals or groups constrains that capacity for other individuals or groups. Naturally, such a combination of real world scarcity and goal striving to overcome this scarcity intensifies the struggle of individuals and groups to cope with both their physical and social environments.
~Col. John Boyd10

Am I talking about money? Yes it will cost money but that's not the focus of this chapter. When I talk investment I want to discuss how do we raise the bar, and get the most out of our leaders in developing frontline personnel as well as what training methods do we use at accomplishing this goal that helps control costs and yield high payoff that results in performance and execution under pressure or crisis situations?

Formal Training
This is the most expensive form of training and the most time consuming as it takes and officer(s) off the street and out of service as they in most cases travel outside their jurisdiction to attend. The cost of the class itself is not the major expense, the cost of overtime, multiplied by the number of officers attending is where the funds are drained.

Formal training is beneficial when based on priorities and the climate (crime trends and problems) of your jurisdiction. It is also designed to build a basis of knowledge in a vast array of topics and critical skills related to the profession. It seems to be the most prevalent way we utilize to training our personnel, yes it is necessary, but is it the only way to train personnel?

Formal training also takes place within organizations although even less frequently than stated above. The training process usually consists of firearms training and other physical skills development in the high liability areas of our professions.
Roll-call training is another area of formal training in short bursts of 20 to 30 minutes at the beginning of or sometime

during the shift. This type of training does not cost money because it's being done on down time during a working shift. It is however a high yield method of training as leaders can focus on specific problems in their jurisdictions and on their perspective shifts. The problem here is not many supervisors are willing to take the time and extend the effort to do so. Mindset shift is needed here because the benefits are great and easily justifiable.

Chapter 3
Methodology to Enhance Learning, Education and Training through Experience

"You have strengths and weaknesses. These come from your position."
~Sun Tzu1

On the Job Training-Conclude with the AAR

By on the job training I do not mean you show up for work and fly by the seat of your pants and hope things work out as they should. No what I mean by on the job training is that you learn from every experience and focus on the lessons learned to make yourself better at the job. This can be done by encouraging supervisors and individual officers to constructively critique performance.

An example, I respond to back up an officer on a domestic violence call. When I arrive there is a second back-up officer arriving directly behind me. I observe the first responding officer on the front door steps and the subject is being handcuffed showing no signs of resistance. The secondary back-up officer got out of his car very quickly and walking at a pace that was almost a run to the front step where the subject and contact officer were.

As the secondary officer ran up, I said *"relax, relax, think and cover him"*. However, he was over-focused on getting there. The cover officer began a pat down and no resistance was shown. As the cover officer searched, the first responding (contact) officer stood nearby and maintained control of the subject. The search conducted was quick and when contact was made with an item in the right front pocket, the officer asked, *"Was that a set of keys?"*

The subject responded *"yes it was keys"*. The officer continued on and they then sat the subject in the back seat of the patrol car for transport.

Both the contact officer and the cover officer were young officers with two-years on the job. As soon as the subject was secure, I called the two officers over and told them, "Ok guys we are conducting a patrol car AAR [After Action Review], what did you miss?" "Nothing!" "Ok!" "When you searched the subject what did you miss?" They both responded, "I cannot think of anything." I went on, "Let's try again, when you searched you asked the subject if he had..." The first officer immediately responded, "Oh yes! Keys, he said he had keys in his right pocket". I replied, "Did you verify they were keys?" "No I did not," the officer said lightly. "What should we do?" I asked. "Take them out and check" they responded. "Absolutely" I replied.

I continued AAR, with a second lesson when I asked, "Who was the cover officer in this scenario?" "I was LT," the officer who conducted the pat down exclaimed. Then, I went on with, "What's the cover officer's job?" The second responding officer who became the cover officer responded with, "The answer is to keep an eye on surroundings and to be an extra set of eyes for the contact man to ensure his and everyone's safety."

Then, I asked further questions, "While you were searching the subject under arrest what role did you take over?" He responded with, "I became the contact officer and should have stayed back and watched and only act if danger presented itself." I continued, "What was my role as the third guy on scene?" The cover officer replied, "LT you were the cover guy as well."

I kept asking questions to keep them thinking while I had their attention, "Did you consider that before you conducted a search or did you just react without thought?" Honestly, he replied, "I just reacted." I then summarized the AAR with, "Is this, how you want to approach calls or should you have a mental plan, some strategy that will assist you in your performance whatever your role?" I went on, "Should you communicate this to other officers on the scene?"

"A plan is much better than not thinking and we should

always communicate to one another so we are all on the same page," the officer explained. I closed out the AAR with "OUTSTANDING! You got it...Learn, adapt and focus the next time..."

This incident is a simple one and it ended with keys indeed in the pocket, but the lessons learned by the two officers will stick with them and quite frankly will stick with me as well. The point is that this presented an opportunity, over just a few minutes to conduct an AAR with the two young officers. Not doing the AAR was a missed opportunity to develop adaptability, but also not prepare the officers for a worse situation. The consequences of the keys being a knife or some other weapon would be a lesson that could leave us with another named engraved in stone. Every time you take advantage of an opportunity to learn through an AAR, both student and teacher (leader, supervisor) benefit from the experience. Keep in mind the roles of teacher and student can be reversed and a leader can learn lessons from the frontline as well if he is open-minded and willing.

Yet we do not take advantage of the OJT opportunities through effective AARs that present themselves. We must change this and be willing to lead and be led when you make the mistake that is pointed out. These lessons are too powerful to be ignored.

Tactical Decision Games

A highly effective method of education that develops rapid decision making is a tool called the tactical decision game (TDG) or decision making exercise (DME). This is a critical tool of MAJ Don Vandergriff's training methodology with the military. More importantly, he uses this tool as a basis on teaching others how to use the art of facilitation to evolve adaptability.

He writes about it in his book *Raising the Bar*. He has achieved great results in using these games to develop decision makers who will demonstrate adaptability in combat. He has received great feedback from those serving overseas in combat to the benefits of the TDG's in creating decision makers performing for high stakes and under high pressure.2

Tactical decision games are situational exercises on paper representing a snap shot in time. A scenario is handed out that describes a problem related to your profession (law enforcement, security, military, business, etc.). The facilitator sets a short time limit for you to come up with a solution to the problem presented. The TDGs can be conducted individually or in a group setting. As soon as time is up, with the facilitator using *"time hacks"*, an individual or group is told to present their course of action to the rest of the group.

What you did and why? Justifying your actions to everyone else!

It is important that individuals or groups working together are candid and honest in their responses. You're only fooling yourself to do otherwise. The lesson learned from the TDGs can make you more effective and safe in the performance of your job. The time to develop the strength of character and the courage to make decisions comes here, in the training environment. Mistakes can be made here that do not cost a life and valuable lessons are learned.

The key here is the facilitator/instructor ensures responses are brought out and lessons are learned from the scenario. This can be done while working. I know because we have used them on my department and I have used them training security companies. It takes some effort, but can indeed be done.

The TDGs are effective at developing decision making in the field. In the few years we used TGDs in the Walpole police department and during the daily grind of the four week Sergeant's Leader's Course for the Baltimore Police, officers went from the initial thought of what are we doing this for? To getting involved and discussing strategy and tactics necessary to resolving the problem faced in the TDG setting.

This evolved to applying what was learned, to the street under pressure. Tactical response and approaches to calls, communications, utilization of tactical basics such as;

contact/cover principle and cover and concealment, approach strategies, perimeter containment and overall officer safety improved greatly utilizing these short scenarios.

Knowledge of laws and policy and procedure improved by utilizing decision making exercises to fit legal and policy questions.

This simple tool works and works well. I use the term simple tool but, make no mistake, its work implementing and conducting these exercises. Developing scenarios and insuring appropriate lessons are learned takes thought and innovation to insure proper training is taking place. The instructor/facilitator needs to understand his job, is to draw out answers, not give them out. I must emphasize this point because I have made that mistake in conducting the exercises. The goal in using TDGs is for the facilitator to guide the students, who are the "decision-makers" and "innovators" give answers, not for the instructor to give the answers, directions and create followers; we have enough of that in our professions already.

The TDGs are about developing individual, initiative driven frontline leaders who can make decisions that meet the mission of the agency. *TDGs are used to teach leaders how to think and to train and reinforce established ways of doing something, such as task training. The techniques can be traced back at least to the Chinese general and military theorist Sun Tzu, who was advocating their use more than 2,500 years ago.*[3]

Decision Making Critiques/After Action Reviews

The decision making critique (DMC) or after action review (AAR) is another critical component to developing decision makers. The AAR is conducted after the decisions are made and actions taken.

During the AAR, the group candidly discusses events and decisions amongst the group (all ranks) involved in the incident to bring out lessons learned. The facilitator keys on two aspects of the incident, was the decision made in a timely manner?

What was the rationale of the individual or group in making their decision? What is important in an AAR is that the player justifies in their own words why the made the decisions they made during the course of the game.

We have used these methods and the powerful lessons that are learned from reviewing and critiquing a crisis situation you were actually involved in is a better than most formal training you can get. Why? Because you were there and experienced the circumstances first hand and then sat down and discussed the strengths and weaknesses of the response. From these lessons learned comes recognition of patterns, changes in patterns (anomalies) and adaptability is developed. This reinforcement stimulates initiative driven decisions and actions and continued adaptation to new threats and problems.

After Action reviews help develop communication, trust and unit cohesion and helps in a team approach to developing best practices in a variety of situations. A key component to remember in conducting both TDGS and AAR is a candid open dialog, in an effort to learn. Anything less and you are only fooling yourself.

Conclusion...Are We Ready?
If individual, organization and interagency effectiveness is what we are truly looking for we must take what we know about ourselves, our organizations and the problems and threats we face, including knowledge of those criminals and extremist mindsets that threaten our society and way of life. This assessment should bring about questions, who is more serious about success, us or them?

- Who is doing more to prepare, us or them?
- Who is actively utilizing and developing new ideas to out think and out smart and out maneuver the adversary, us or them?
- Who is utilizing people, ideas, information, intelligence and technology and creativity at a more successful rate,

us or them?
- Who has inspired individual initiative in their followers, us or them? Who is prepared for game day, us or them?
- Who is committed to win? Is it us or them?

Any given Sunday is game day for a kid's game and they come prepared and committed to play and give their all to win.
Any given DAY at any given TIME could be our game day and the stakes are much, much higher. Are we truly prepared?
Think about it deeply and honestly because *"how you think about the future determines what you do in the future!"*

*"Invest in preparedness, not prediction...I will never get to know the unknown since, by definition, it is unknown. However, I can always guess how it might affect me, and I should base my decisions around that...you always control what you do, so make this your end." ~Nassim Nicholas Taleb, The Black Swan; The Impact of the Highly Improbable*4

Chapter 4
Adaptability on the Frontline... and "Bottom-Up" Leadership

This chapter is based on an article written in 1999 by USMC Commandant GEN Charles C. Krulak titled: *"The Strategic Corporal Leadership in the Three Block War"*, which is about decisions being made at the lowest level within an organization if we truly want to seize the initiative dealing with changing conditions. In GEN Krulak's articles focus is on the military and the United States Marine Corps. I see it applying to the law enforcement and security professions as well as any other organization where time critical decisions are needed to be successful. This is my attempt to show how it applies in our mission in protecting the homeland.1

It's a Friday night and the call goes out, respond to a particular location (single family dwelling house) for an 18 year old male threatening suicide with a gun. The dispatcher states, "I received the call from the mother of the subject who says her son does indeed have a gun and is emotionally distraught over the break up with his girlfriend." The sector car is a single officer unit and a back-up car with a two-man unit is sent to resolve the situation.

Your shift supervisor and lieutenant are in a staff meeting, and you were told not to disturb them. The meeting was to discuss budgetary issues and the possibility of cut backs and possible layoffs.

You arrive at the location and the back-up unit pulls up directly behind you. The house is located off a busy road and set back 100 yards on a few acres of wooded land, the house is quiet and there is a vehicle parked in the driveway. You have dispatch run the car's license tag.

You quickly get out of your patrol car and start to walk towards the front door, but are called back by the back-up officers who remind you this is an emotionally upset and armed person.

You discuss a plan of action with the group that's focus is on getting the person to come to us. You voice your concern of the mother whom you believe is inside and the team needs to go in. Back-up officers remind you no violence has occurred as of yet and that forcing the situation could create more of a problem by the escalation of violence. They also remind you that negotiation in these types of circumstances is the best option and usually very successful. You agree and then position members of the team opposite corners of the house using cover in an effort to contain and gather more information about the situation.

You get the phone number to the house and place a call to the house. The 18 year old man tells you he has lost his girlfriend and life is not worth living. As you continue to talk with the young man, back-up officers are notifying additional resources such as a medical and response team.

Your conversation continues, and you are told by the young man his mother is not home. The mother is at a friend's house a couple towns away. You have dispatch confirm this and it is verified that his mother is not inside, and she is responding to the scene, according to the friend she just left and is 10 minutes away. You tell dispatch to get hold of mother via her cell and have her instead go to the station. Later, you're informed she agrees to do as instructed and is on her way to the station.

You continue your conversation with the young man and talk him back to reality by sharing a story of your past relationships when you were his young age (tactical communication). After five minutes on the phone conversing, the young man says he will put the gun down and come out. You tell him to wait your instructions and he agrees.

You then notify your back-up he has agreed to come out and that you will be directing him out the front door and that he is leaving the gun on the table inside. You reconnect with the young man and tell him to follow your directions exactly and he agrees. He comes out the door as directed and complies.

He is taken into custody and transported to the hospital where he is to be evaluated.   From call to conclusion is only about 8 minutes, a successful resolution to a potentially deadly situation.

This scenario is similar to many that have been conducted in the real world of policing and security in recent years and represents the likely types of unknown and high risk situations law enforcement responds to. It also represents the enormous responsibilities and pressures which are placed on our young informal leaders (cops and security officers on the street).

The real life scenario described above, "Tactical Response and Approach to Suicidal Person" is fictional in the sense of my description of how it was handled based on an AAR of the situation and lessons learned.

This is what really happened:
The officer walked to the front door and knocked on it while two back-up officers watched and made no effort to correct the potential dangerous tactics. It was resolved safely based on luck, not skill. Numerous cops have been injured or killed responding in a similar fashion. Why did you not offer tactical advice to a fellow officer clearly putting himself in danger?

When asked "Why?" the responses were numerous, "we are not his boss", "it's not our job to tell another patrol officer what to do", "we did not want to interfere", "he is a cop, he should know what to do", "where were his bosses?" "It turned out fine didn't it?"

At first reading these responses you might think these are cops who do not care about their jobs!
I wish that was the case the problem would be easy to fix! All of these guys are good cops. I know them and their work. But they are wrapped up in the culture of the profession, which is based on a negative form of leadership, a mechanistic, directive in nature, top down autocratic approach also known as, micromanagement.

This style of leadership breeds the individual perception of not interfering with a brother or sister officers methods of operation.

It's his call, his responsibility and he and he alone is responsible for his actions. And dare I say the political correctness of not making waves even if it's good or lifesaving advice! NONESENSE! We are all accountable for each other's safety. Hell that's the meaning of BACK-UP!

Let me digress.

This attitude stems from a negative organizational culture which gives the perception to frontline personnel, "do nothing until you have permission to do so or do not get involved unless it's your call or are assigned to do so." No thinking, no communication, no adaptation. This is a failure in leadership in not creating and nurturing a cohesive environment. When leadership fails bad things happen. A lot of times we get lucky but when luck runs out the equation usually involves serious consequences.

The orientation formed in this real life example (fictional option of response) based on the lessons learned in an after action review, was a group of three acting as one, sharing thoughts and ideas and adapting to the situation. That's what brought a safe resolution: three separate assessments, channeled into one resulting in good decisions. This is the type of organizational culture we want in our departments.

A Change in Culture, Top down and Bottom up!
There can be no true problem solving without decentralization of control and individual initiative.

To change from a culture of *"tell me what to do to one that breeds and nurtures creativity, innovation, adaptation and time critical decision making,"* we must move, really move from centralized control to a decentralized form of leadership. We have been talking about decentralized control in policing for years now, since the onset of *"community policing"* initiatives. True! But that's the problem we have been "talking about it, and that is all."

We need to be practicing it.

Get beyond the talk and walking the talk if we truly want to see results that meet the challenges we face in policing. Yes there have been some organizations in law enforcement who have taken this approach seriously and the results show the value of frontline decision making. It takes constant practice to master these cultures! The action taken by leadership needs to be more than written mission statements and words. It takes action, action over time through learning, education, and training. Not just in the formal sense but in the real world sense of learning from everything we do at all levels of the organization and throughout the community on a daily bases.

This takes a mindset shift as to how we lead or as John Boyd talked about in his discourse on winning and losing, destruction and creation. Destroy our old ways of thinking about leadership which is based on *"Taylorism"* (manufacturing and management model based on the theories of Frederick Taylor of getting things done from the Progressive era (1890-1920)) and deterministic outcomes. This method works when time is plenty and risk is low, while the experience of your workers is low.[2]

The world we live in is often probabilistic, complex, and uncertain and things happen unexpectedly, risk is high and time is critical in the dynamic encounters law enforcement responds to. These types of situations require adaptability on the frontline and hence *"Adaptive Leaders"* as the modern strategist Don Vandergriff would say, *"frontline personnel the key to solving conventional and unconventional problems and threats."*[3]

Cops or patrol officers on the street work individually or in small groups making decisions and solving problems daily with little or no supervision. These are the folks who solve the problems. These are the folks there in the moment, when bad things are happening and a solution is needed.

They must know they are free and empowered to make

decisions. Supervisors are not always right there. They are often assigned to another seemingly more serious call or some specialized duties that takes them away from their primary responsibilities of overseeing things as they happens on a tour of duty.

This is even more the case in small to midsized organizations.

A leader is accountable for actions of frontline personnel whether they are on scene or not, so it is imperative that leaders train and prepare those on the frontline. Leadership accountability comes from our preparation and the continued education, learning and developing of frontline decision makers. NOT from standing over them directing them, or written policy and procedures, or checklists on how to perform in a given set of circumstances. A leader does not have to be on every call, it is impossible to be on every call. It is just not necessary if you prepare your frontline people effectively and development is an ongoing process. Train and Trust FRONTLINE Personnel! They will get it done and done right!

Leadership's role is to develop individuals who understand and practice integrity, courage, initiative, decisiveness, mental agility and personal accountability. These fundamental qualities must be aggressively cultivated which in turn allows for an atmosphere of adaptability at the lowest level, on the street. "I am here now in the situation that requires a decision…" I AM EMPOWERED, SUPERENPOWERED TO DECIDE and ACT! Frontline personnel must know this is what leadership wants and leadership must support it!

Don Vandergriff in his book *Raising the Bar Creating and Nurturing Adaptability to Deal with the Changing face of War* describes "adaptability" as: *"the process of adjusting practices, processes, and systems to projected actual changes of environment, e.g. the situation or the enemy. It also includes the creation of innovative organizations, doctrine, systems and training concepts as demanded by the environment, allies and the enemy.*

And finally someone who is adaptive can think of solutions to *problems in chaotic, unpredictable situations that are based more on intuition than on analysis, deliberate planning and doctrine."*4

Adaptability comes from training in all the dimensions of conflict mental, moral and physical, decentralized control with strict individual, organizational and community accountability.
This involves lifelong learning of all involved and takes more effort than what the culture of policing requires now out of its leaders and frontline personnel. This requires the same out of the community as well. All working together, truly working together ""walking the talk" of progress and innovation if solving our problems and dealing with threats is truly the goal.

Yes, it rocks the boat and takes us out of our comfort zones, but the results of giving power to the frontline to make decisions leads to insight, imagination and initiative and speed of action. Action depends on understanding this. You will be pleasantly surprised by the results achieved.

"We love the term 'adaptive leaders' and 'innovation' as long as they do not rock anybody's boat."
~Franklin C. Spinney5

Chapter 5
Handling Dynamic Encounters: Go Get Him, or Set Him Up To Get Him... With an Adaptable Response

Some have described and compared police encounters as either static or dynamic. It's my view that there is no such thing as a static police encounter. All encounters whether they progressively evolve over a longer period of time or erupt rapidly in a short period of time, without warning, are all dynamic. Time is moving forward, circumstances changing and the ability of responders to adapt to the ongoing circumstances is always critical.

"Mastering speed is the essence of war. Take advantage of a large enemy's inability to keep up. Use a philosophy of avoiding difficult situations. Attack the area where he doesn't expect you."
*~Sun Tzu the Art of War*1

In handling dynamic encounters, the phrase "time criticality" is often discussed. In this discussion there is often a miss-conception that to put time on your side, you must force the issue or, force the subject into action and always advance your position by moving forward. Speed is the essence of conflict, but speed does not always mean moving fast physically. It means preparing so you are in a position of advantage, which gives you time, hence speed.

Sun Tzu's definition of speed is often misconstrued and shown through quick responses such as; doors being immediately kicked in upon arrival. You see knee jerk reactions to the report of a single gunshot and immediate entry made without knowing any more than the fact that a gun went off. You see it in tactical responses and approaches to various calls for service where the possibility of danger exists.

You also see it in responders traveling at high rates of speed across cities and towns or running as fast as they can into an office, in an effort to get to the scene quickly. No thoughts taking place, no observing, orienting, deciding and acting as to how you will approach, "just get there" is the apparent goal.

The responders end up in the driveway or in a room without any critical thought to potential violence being an outcome. They want to force the issue. Individual responders approach rapidly in circumstances where it's clearly understood (or should be) the adversary has the advantage and are not actively engaged in deadly actions. Or worst case from my observations, respond in circumstances where not much thought at all has gone into who does or does not have the advantage, they just GO GET HIM!

I understand adrenalin and emotional responses, to high risk encounters. After all, our entire goal is to protect those we serve from harm and in an effort to do so we responders feel an overwhelming urge to rush. I have been there and responded emotionally myself. The problem is rushing in recklessly, when its un-necessary, creates more of a problem instead of, solving the problem. This problem is reinforced because we have succeeded in a lot of these situations and have mistaken "good luck" for "good strategy and tactics."

Rapid response and forcing the fight are viable options in our professions. There is a time and place for the strategy and tactics of dynamic response. They are not the sole options. Sometimes action required is holding a position, or backing off a decision, when circumstances change from active to inactive. The focus on this article is not to solely criticize our responses but instead to shed some light on the 2,500 year old premise of knowing when to press the fight and when not too, so we gain the strategic and tactical advantage.

"Victory comes from knowing when to attack and when to avoid battle."
~Sun Tzu, the Art of War2

"Go Get him" verses "Set him up, to get him"

The first question that must be asked in deciding what type of response is necessary in the types of situations, law enforcement respond to, should be, and "is Immediate Dynamic Action Required?" If lives are in "imminent" jeopardy, then the answer is yes. If it is they are in danger but there is no imminent threat to life, then the option may be a non-dynamic scaled response. For a safe resolution, in either scenario the circumstances do demand immediate action. That immediate action does not necessarily mean immediate physical or face to face conflict. If there is no clear imminent threat of loss of life do not force conflict but do not be passive. How do we take action if we are not face to face?

John Poole in his book *Phantom Soldier* states:

That action must do two things:

1) *further friendly strategy, or*
2) *attack enemy strategy*

*By attacking enemy strategy, victory can often be won before the battle starts.*3

To further friendly strategy in a progressively unfolding set of circumstances where there is no *"imminent threat"* to life or serious bodily harm, we can prepare for and handle unforeseen circumstances by:

- Establish command and control
- Gathering information (Environment and Individual(s))
- Keep everyone informed
- A clear mission intent is known by all
- Position entry/arrest teams (2-4 man response teams (SWAT))
- Position an over watch
- set up perimeter containment and security
- Prepare to negotiate
- Prepare to adapt to changing conditions

To further the friendly strategy it is important to note that the overall commander "TRUST" subordinates team leaders to make decisions. Place individual teams, in positions of advantage of their choosing and allow them to act when, from their position they see opportunities present themselves or, the situation suddenly escalates to that of imminent threat to life or serious bodily harm.

Oftentimes there is no time to seek permission to take appropriate action. This is critical to seeking the advantage, and why we must have prior training and trust established in an organization. This lack of trust and thus an inability to adapt, is why we see a lot of law enforcement responses go bad. Obviously communication and continued updates of changing conditions throughout response teams is paramount.

Putting the friendly strategy in place allows us to "attack the enemy strategy" by containing and or confusing him. His options are few, and time, in most cases is now on our side. We can now as long as conditions do not change to life threatening status, use tactics such as communication and negotiation in an effort to subdue the adversary. The subject may simply see he has no options and give up, or impatience may put adversary in a disadvantageous position, we can exploit to gain advantage.

If the situation does change rapidly, our preparation and holding back allows adaptation and transition to an appropriate action quickly, to gain advantage and control. Sun Tzu in the Art of War said, "If it is not in the interest of the state, do not act. If you are not sure of success do not use troops. If you are not in danger, do not fight the battle." The employment of strategy in an effort to subdue the enemy without fighting is achieving the best possible results at the least possible cost.4

The following is an example of a scaled response to potentially dangerous set of circumstances.

I am looking for a distraught young man who threatened suicide. In this process I checked the surrounding neighborhood for signs of the young man to no avail.

There is a large park in the neighborhood so I parked my cruiser and got out on foot to take a look around. In the park I was approached by a woman and her young child who pointed to an area of the park about 500 yards away. She said 'I just saw a man with a knife throwing it at trees'. "It's important to note we had just had a murder in the park about a month earlier that shook the small community I work for."

She described the man as about 5' 9" 165 pounds, brown hair around 30 years old. She also said he was mumbling incoherent words and appeared "drunk."

I was in full uniform and as I approached. I noted a section of trees and brush, not very thick but did offer some concealment. I approached quietly through this area and put myself in a position to observe this man. I observed the knife in his hand, him throwing the knife at the tree, retrieving it and throwing again. I noticed a bicycle with a six pack of bud light bungee corded to the bike rack and an open beer on the ground next to the bike. The subject occasionally gulped from the beer. I also noted he was unsteady on his feet and believed him to be somewhat highly intoxicated.   I said to myself we have potentially dangerous situation here, man with knife, highly intoxicated, with unusual behavior of throwing a knife at the tree repetitively, in the park, at the time of a recent unsolved murder.

Because of the clandestine approach, I was given time to make decisions, call for back up and set up a tactical clandestine response by two back-up officers and wait till we were positioned advantageously. The officers and I had time to confer and decided we would wait till he tossed the knife at the tree and then approach him tactically.

We did and initially the subject on seeing us looked at the knife and then slowly processed his options, it appeared, from his facial gestures and overall body language, and realized that he was out numbered and offered no resistance. We placed the subject into protective custody.

He had nothing to do with the murder in the park nor did he have anything to do with the original suicidal youth that put me in the area in the first place.

I often ask myself what would have, could have happened if I decided in full uniform to just walk up to this guy from 500 yards away, in clear view, allowing him the opportunity to observe me and make his own plans. I do not know for sure what that outcome would have been.

I do believe however the fact that we took a clandestine and tactical approach—controlled the time issue—and outnumbered him 3-1 had a great impact, even in his state, on his deciding to comply with our demands peacefully.

This scenario and response seems, rather obvious. But, look around you at fellow officers, or check the officer down memorial page and you can clearly see that these, most basic tactical concepts—that have strategic impacts—are not being used consistently by responders. They put themselves in bad positions because they want the situation resolved and resolved now! The results of such actions are paid at too high a cost, with loss of life.

Some other examples where we could use better tactics, whether a person is armed or unarmed, and is in some form of conflict that we must bring resolution to, are:
-    Mental illness
-    Distraught family members
-    Physically isolated
-    Armed not actively engaged in imminent life threatening actions

Dynamic Responses
You must use total war, fighting with everything you have. Never stop fighting when at war. You can gain complete advantage.
"To do this, you must plan your strategy of attack."
~Sun Tzu, the Art of War5

A situation turns dynamic when a person puts lives at risk. The protection of life is our priority, always. If the circumstances change or we are suddenly put into a spontaneous set of conditions where life is threatened then, dynamic responses are required. Action is now the critical component to seizing and maintaining the initiative. The tactical decisions you make will determine outcome of the situation. In this case you must react and put a "mental plan" into action to stop the threatening circumstances. The plans you develop and decisions you make will be based on implicit information and tactical judgment.

Your knowledge, training and experience as well as the equipment you have will need to be considered in your decision making options.

Here is another example of a robust (dynamic response) to potentially dangerous set of circumstances. The call came that a man with a sword was trying to get into the house to kill his father. We all responded rapidly to the address in question and the first arriving officer reported the subject had left and was headed towards his own home about 2 miles from the incident location.

The officer reported the subject was armed with a Japanese short sword and had tried to stab his father, who was somehow able to keep him out of the house. The screen to the door was sliced and stab marks were in the door from the sword. Important information relayed from the officer at the scene told the story of a man in an emotionally/chemically induced violent state.

While in response to the suspect's address, a detective radioed that he was out with the subject in the driveway of his home. Upon arrival, the subject was in the car on the passenger's side with his wife behind the wheel and child, in her arms. The suspect was shouting at the detective who had the subject held at gun point.

The detective was positioned on the driver's side in an attempt to get the wife and child out of the car, who were too scared to move.

Another officer and I immediately approached the passenger side. We both kept our guns holstered as we knew the detective had us both covered. The sword could not initially be seen but both his hands could, and they were clear at the moment. We opened the door and immediately took the subject, who struggled and fought, off his feet to the muddy ground and controlled him physically and then handcuffed him. The Japanese sword was in the car between the seat and the console.

The intuitive decision in the heat of the moment was made to act and control the situation by taking this suspect into custody. We believed that due to his emotionally charged state—he had already attacked a loved one his father—that the potential harm to his wife and child outweighed the option of waiting him out. My gut feeling at the time was that he was indecisive, yet still emotionally charged and unpredictable. The opportunity to take control was presented by the situation in the car. This intuitive feeling was based on the circumstances at the time. We acted upon intuitive judgment based on the current condition taking place at the moment, without harm coming to anyone.

I have often thought this case over and asked would it have been a better option to wait and negotiate? As in most standoffs negotiation can be very successful, but this set of circumstances was still unfolding. The subject was emotionally charged and not thinking clearly. He was confused and caught off guard by the detective who initially located him. We arrived seconds after the detective and while positioning ourselves, quickly conferred and then approached, as part of a plan.

Allowing the subject time in this scenario, I believe would have given the initiative to him. The Japanese sword was in the car, but not in his hand. It would have only taken a fraction of a second for him to regain control of the weapon.

This meant that his wife and the baby would have been in imminent jeopardy of death or serious bodily harm.

In an AAR afterwards, we all felt that the critical analysis in this particular set of circumstances warranted a robust dynamic response.

Some other examples that require dynamic responses are:
- Spontaneous attack or ambush
- Suddenly come under attack (Progressive turned Dynamic)
- Active shooter who is, or in the process of shooting victims
- Hear screams with shots fired
- Screaming do not hurt me, do not kill me
- Violent crimes in progress (life in imminent jeopardy) subject takes tactical advantage
- So called routine, better referred to as unknown risk circumstances turned life threatening
- High risk car stops
- Alarms with evidence of a break
- Arrest and detainments
- Responding to calls for service
- Domestic disturbances
- Field interviews and street encounters
- Etc., etc., etc.

It is my experience and from research, that law enforcement professionals all too often needlessly rush, using dynamic responses, in circumstances where a non-dynamic (scaled) response would clearly better our position of advantage. We have to reconsider the way we do things in an effort to keep ourselves and those we protect, safer when responding to situations. If an individual is no longer in position to harm others then the conditions requiring high risk intervention has changed and a more scaled, cautious solution should be pursued.

We should depend upon our complete knowledge of the circumstances, combined with our knowledge of conflict, strategy and tactics and seek the advantageous position.

How we set up and take advantageous positions, our responsiveness and ability to transition to the changing conditions and our ability to attack the adversaries' strategy and maneuver him to an advantageous position for us are keys to success. A thorough understanding of all this will enable us to gain the advantage and if at all possible win without fighting. It is important to understand we are making decisions based on the ongoing circumstances and not on yesterday's approach. Use your experiences to help you read the situation via your observation-orientation-decision and action cycle (The Boyd Cycle) and adapt to the present moment conditions. The circumstances we respond to are dangerous.

In the heat of battle, it is difficult to curtail emotions and slow the process down. In my opinion the vast majority of circumstances require just that, slowing down—this is controlling time as well and setting the conditions.

We must have presence of mind and develop individually, the ability to read the situation. The response is obvious to some circumstances, and others not so. For certain, all conflict is ridden with uncertainty, chaos, disorder, confusion and is unpredictable. To know when to use non-dynamic verses dynamic tactics is a skill that takes practice and time to develop. Your intuitive sense as to what's happening can be enhanced through available time, to gain deeper knowledge of the situation. Even a few seconds, a fraction of a second, can make the difference between a good or bad tactical decision.

So whatever time you have available take it. While responding gathers as much information as you can, think about the possible problems and quickly run them through your mind with plans to handle them. Think about proper approach and basic tactical concepts such as cover, concealment that can give you the advantage of time through a clandestine approach. Time critical, speed, does not mean rush into a reckless response; it means get the time advantage through information gathering and preparation and positioning.

Next time you hear the term *"time is of the essence, we have to do something!"* Just what is that *"something"* we should be doing? Is it "GET HIM" in a blind emotional rush into circumstances forcing an issue? Or, should it be "SET HIM UP TO GET HIM" a strategic and tactical response that puts us in a position to win? There is a time for each type of response. Knowing the difference, controlling emotions (mental calmness) being flexible and able to adapt to changing circumstances and make good decisions, in dynamic encounters is the key to successful and safe resolutions.

Chapter 6
Evolution of Strategy and Tactics to Ongoing Deadly Action "Active Shootings" and Operational Art

An **active shooter** is defined as ... *an armed person who has used deadly physical force on other persons and continues to do so while having unrestricted access to additional victims.*1
The vision most law enforcement officers have when it comes to an active shooter is one or two people with guns moving through a building, randomly shooting anyone in their path. Active shootings are often thought of as taking place in a public place, such as a school where kids attend.

Sandy Hook Elementary, Westside Middle School, Thurston High School, Columbine High School, Virginia Tech, the Amish school house in Pennsylvania and many other schools, universities and campuses have been victims of an active shooting incident. The fact that many of the offenders are children themselves, combined with intense media attention, cements the idea that active shooters take out their rage on schools.

Unconventional Methods of Attack
The fact is that an active shootings can take place in any environment—in the streets, as in the case of gang related violence or cornered criminals in an effort to gain the advantage; at the workplace, often by a disgruntled employee; at a shopping mall, perhaps by a kid who lost his girlfriend or job,; even in nursing homes, hospitals and neighborhoods. Also locations that have high security that appear to reduce the risk of this kind of threat have been victimized such as; NASA and the recent Navy Yard shootings in September 2013.

We are witness to a worldwide evolving threat from highly trained active shooters.

Terrorists have used small arms and small unit swarming

tactics at luxury hotels, restaurants, train stations, community centers, cinemas, police headquarters and other public locations. Recent examples include the coordinated attacks in Mumbai, India and the premeditated shootings at Fort Hood, Texas and the gangs and narco-terrorists on the Mexican border.2

The North Hollywood shooting in 1997 is yet another example of a conventional crime turned unconventional, when an armed confrontation between two heavily-armed bank robbers and the LAPD. It started when the robbers were engaged by LAPD officers while leaving the bank they had just robbed.3

Some had a difficult time describing the Beslan Russia school siege and massacre in 2004. It was a siege, a hostage situation, a terrorist act and an active shooting situation. It is also underscored how an adversary can use a combination of tactics in an effort to disrupt our response and delay our actions.

How should we handle adversaries who use small arms, small unit tactics and multiple techniques converging on multiple targets from numerous directions in a single incident? The answer lies in our dedication and discipline to prepare and train for these incidents.

It is imperative that we use our capabilities to the fullest: awareness, strength of character, information and intelligence gathering, decision-making abilities and tactical skills. Using them in combination is essential to successfully combating any active shooting situation. It is critical that we penetrate the decision making cycle of an adversary to soften his resolve, disorient his mental images, disrupt his operations, and overload his system so he either stops his actions and complies or is disrupted by the terms of law enforcement.

An active shooting can a take place anywhere, any time. And the types of active shooters vary greatly in their levels of sophistication, planning, preparation and training and their commitment.

In a study conducted by the law enforcement training company Hard Tactics researcher William Barchers, concluded that:

The faster a shooter is confronted, the higher the probability of event resolution with minimum loss of life. The group studied 40 active shooting incidents. Seventeen incidents were resolved by the shooters themselves, with the shooter ceasing his attack and committing suicide, or attempting to do so. In at least three cases, the shooters ceased their attacks when verbally confronted by someone they knew. In the remaining cases, the shooters were overcome by physical confrontation by the intended victims.

*One of the most important facts to emerge from this study was that of the forty studied incidents, only six were resolved by police. We must continually learn-unlearn and relearn from past incidents and then adapt the science and art of tactics to the unfolding circumstances.*4

Time and Failure to Adapt: the first enemies of law enforcement

Time is often the enemy of law enforcements in the case of an active shooting because initially the shooter dictates the tempo. Most active shootings begin and end in 8 minutes. The Mumbai terrorist attack carried out by 10 men in 5, 2 man teams lasted over 60 hours and left 195 people dead and 295 wounded.5

Because of this fact we in law enforcement must not only focus on the standard training, diamond and T-Y formations and moving towards the guns. We must employ superior situational awareness to read the scene, recognize the pattern of what's going on and channel our ability to think on our feet. The elements of a strategic and tactical mindset include observing our environment; orienting to climate of the situation; making good sound implicit decisions; and taking action to solve the problem. We solve the problem by applying *what we know* to the situation at hand, known as *"operational art"*.

Following the Columbine incident and criticisms of the law enforcement response in that case, many learned that *"setting up a perimeter and waiting for SWAT to arrive,"* while deadly action is taking place, is unsound strategically and tactically. The lessons learned here and from many other incidents have reshaped law enforcements thoughts on proper tactics in handling violent ongoing deadly actions.6

Most law enforcement officers could tell you exactly what's expected of them when responding to an active shooting situation. Go to the location of ongoing deadly action, wait shortly for back-up 1, 2 or 3 other officers form a diamond or T-Y formation and then march to the sounds of the guns and stop the ongoing threat. If there is shooting going on, keep moving towards the sound of the guns, engage the threat and stop it. There are documented cases where this tactic has worked well in resolving conventional *active shooter situation* and are viable tactics under the right conditions.

Those conditions being, one or two people, not highly trained, armed and actively engaged in shooting innocent people. Our training in the conventional active shooting response can and does work with these conditions present.

The traditional 4 man diamond formation, which most in law enforcement have trained in, has been adapted due to the time/risk factor and the numbers killed in these tragic incidents. The 3 man (T –Y formations), 2 man and even 1 man entries are used to engage the conventional active shooter. There is often no time to wait for SWAT and patrol officers must respond. Often times we have to adapt standard tactics (science) with know how (art) to be effective in stopping these threats.

This means each cop on the street or patrolling a city, town, university or campus, a security officer on a post or military personnel defending the country abroad must possess more knowledge in understanding conflict and its resolution.

They must mast the individual and small team skills to launch successful operations dealing with conflict and violence inherent in an active shooting situation. Applying this knowledge, connecting strategy and tactics, is operational art and is the often missing link in law enforcement responses.

Preparation for initiative driven tactical response

The first question that must be asked in deciding what type of response is necessary in the active shootings, law enforcement responds to, should be "is immediate dynamic action required?" If lives are in "imminent" jeopardy, then the answer is yes. If it is "they are in danger and no imminent threat to life exists", then the option may be a non-dynamic scaled response.

Action must do two things: (1) further friendly strategy, or (2) attack enemy strategy. By attacking enemy strategy, victory can often be won before the battle starts.

Putting the friendly strategy in place allows us to "attack the enemy strategy" by containing him. His options are few, and time, in most cases is now on our side. The subject may simply see he has no options and give up, or impatience may put adversary in a disadvantageous position, we can exploit to gain advantage.

Reading the Scene

It's crucial for the first responding officers to take up positions so that they get eyes on the objective in an effort to read the scene. The information they gather is critical and must be communicated to oncoming responders so that the initial tactical set up is in an area with the least amount of risk involved to responders. They should keep in mind not to only look at the scene from their perspective but from the adversaries as well.

First responding efforts can be done quickly and should focus on:
  - Reading and understanding the environment
  - Reading and understanding the climate of the situation (What's going on?)

- What tactics will work in the current situation? (use insight and innovation)

THIS IS TWO-WAY STREET *"FRIENDLY & ADVERSARIAL"* **(both: Observe, Orient, Decide and Act)**

Dynamic Encounters

Some have described and compared law enforcement encounters as either static or, dynamic. It's my view that there is no such thing as a static law enforcement encounter. All encounters whether they progressively evolve over a longer period of time or erupt rapidly in a short period of time, without warning, circumstances surrounding law enforcement encounters are all dynamic. Time is moving forward, circumstances changing and the ability of responders to adapt to the ongoing circumstances is always critical.

In responding to dynamic encounters the protection of life is our priority, always. If the circumstances change and we are suddenly put into a spontaneous set of conditions where life is threatened then, dynamic responses are required. Action is now the critical component to seizing and maintaining the initiative. We must now set the tempo with fluid initiative driven action with our focus being to stop the ongoing threat. To do so we must know both the art and science of tactics and how to apply this knowledge to the unfolding conditions.

Tactical response and rescue teams

The team whether it consists of 1, 2, 3 or 4 men should be made up of tactically savvy people. Officers, who possess the 5% mindset, and know the tactical concepts to utilize and have been trained to an effective level, will be the most effective in using these tactics.

An understanding and ability to apply the tactical formations, such as the diamond formation, which is used to move to and from, or across danger areas or down hallways in schools and office buildings and consists of 4 people, the point man who focuses on the front, the right and left cover men, who focus on the right or the left, specific to their position and then the rear guard who focus on the rear. All communicate and engage threats in their area of responsibility.

The T-Y formation is commonly used with 3 members in the team. The T–Y formations are used for the same purpose as the diamond, rapid movement, good observation and ability to engage adversary. All formations offer their own strengths and weakness mostly centered on fields of fire and tactical movement and clearing rooms and intersections (T, L and cross) encountered in a building.

Two-man tactics are commonly used by law enforcement in active shootings. One officer and back up is the most prevalent tactical team in policing, although, movement of two men in a tactical way, is not consistently taught in law enforcement. This must change. In a two-man team, contact cover is done by both with each man being responsible for 180 degrees of their area. Again verbal and non-verbal communication is critical to ensure safety and effectiveness.

One-man entry is a controversial entry technique and it's only used as a last resort in engaging ongoing deadly action. It's obvious to see the disadvantages in going it alone in an active shooting situation although when the deadly action is taking place on the part of the adversary and the lone officer is positioned at an advantage the need to enter and take action may be the only way to stop the threat. It's imperative that the lone officer be capable in his tactical ability to engage alone.

The focus of these formations is to enhance rapid movement to the threat and maintain security through collective observations. Keeping in mind where, you may individually and/or collectively have to move once the threat is engaged.
The focus of effort is movement in these formations to get you in a position to effectively stop the threat.

As the numbers in the tactical response team gets smaller the work load becomes much more difficult as there are fewer eyes on the surroundings. It is important to adjust your pace as the situation and your manpower dictates. Speed is often times gained by positioning verses an over exaggerated sense of urgency. Keep this in mind.

Room Clearing

Coordination and setup is an important consideration in room clearing and is facilitated by your team movement and proper approach and evaluation prior to the setup.

Observation of doors, how they open and close? Is the door centered on the room or is it on the right or left side of the room?

The answers to these questions dictate the technique you will use for entry. The goal is positioning to observe as much as you can before entering. In many instances before entering a room as much as 80% percent can be cleared visually before stepping off into a room. Utilize the various cornering techniques as the situation dictates. Team members are *"reading"* each other, flexible and responsive to the dynamics of the situation. Superior situational awareness and timing are necessary!

Rescue teams

Rescue teams are teams used as a follow on to rescue downed and injured victims. The tactical response team's focus is on the threat and they do not stop for victims. Injured victims are the rescue team's responsibility.

There are a couple of different ways Rescue teams are used. Some advocate waiting to send in rescue teams once the threat has been stopped. Others advocate soon after the tactical response teams enter and clear a section, rescue teams are sent in as a follow on unit who actively rescue while the adversary is still active.

In short it comes down to training and preparation. Is your rescue team tactically trained? If so using as a follow on to rescue the injured while response team is actively engaged is a viable option. If EMS is not tactically trained then rescue should wait till the threat is stopped.

Communication Considerations

When we respond to a critical incident it's important to quickly establish you are on location and have command and control. This allows others responding to know someone is present on the scene, and that you can communicate the situation, identify danger or kill zones and set up the perimeter in an effort to isolate and contain the situation. You must quickly put an adaptable plan together and communicate this plan. This communication puts everyone involved on the same page and helps to bring order to the chaos.

Now when talking about tactical communication it's important to understand that this does not mean we are constantly on the radio relaying our every move. This *"over talking"* on the radio or elsewhere causes more chaos and disorder. Remember our goal is to bring order to disorder, not add to it. What communication does mean is that you calmly; clearly and concisely relay critical information in a timely manner. Your every thought does not need to be coming over the radio! I know it's somewhat human nature under stress, to want everyone to know everything, but resist the urge and just communicate what's critical.

Responding units should stay off the radio and allow the person on scene and in the best position to relay critical information. Most communication at an active shooting should be bottom-up. The frontline is in a position to make observations, direct others and take action. Command should trust their responding personnel and be on the listening end of communication and support frontline units. If trained and prepared properly the frontline will relay critical information up the chain so command can organize needed resources.

Remember, climate is contagious; panic leads to more panic, as calm leads to more calm. Adapt to the situation; do not let the situation adapt to you.

Time for "Unconventional Tactics"

Law enforcement actions must evolve as well if we are to first detect and prevent these actions from taking place. When despite or efforts a violent ongoing deadly act does unfold we must be capable of dealing with it successfully by

penetrating our adversary's moral-mental-physical being to dissolve his moral fiber, disorient his mental images, disrupt his operations, and overload his system—as well as subvert, shatter, seize, or otherwise subdue those moral-mental-physical bastions, connections, or activities that he depends upon—in order to destroy internal harmony, produce paralysis, and collapse adversary's will to resist.7

This requires insight, innovation and initiative and law enforcement using unconventional strategy and tactics as our adversaries have.

Conflict is a clash between two complex adaptive systems. Who wins?

He who adapts faster wins. And you can only do it by thorough preparation.

Our goal in responding to ongoing deadly action is to first and foremost to protect life. We do this through superior situational awareness which enhances or understanding of the environment and what's going on, so we can interact, adapt and position ourselves at the advantage, apply various tactics that work in stopping the threat and in protecting the innocent lives in jeopardy, which is the goal of our strategy.

Chapter 7
Unconventional Tactics for Unconventional Threats

"In tactics, the most important thing is not whether you go left or right, but why you go left or right."
~A. M. Gray1

Tactics is the art (understanding the strengths and weaknesses of your people and of your opponents and applying this differently to every situation) and the science (the technical aspect of understanding your equipment and its abilities) of winning engagements and conflicts. Tactics refers to the concepts and methods we use to accomplish a particular objective. The essence of conflict has been defined as a struggle between two hostile, independent, and irreconcilable wills, each trying to impose itself on the other, or a "clash" between two complex adaptive systems! This *"complex adaptive system"* is a, walking, talking, submitting or confronting, interacting and isolating, persuading and forcing, running and gunning, thinking and acting, disrupting adversary(s).2

Tactics is not a thing, but a process, especially a mental process. It's a way of doing something. It is not just a certain type of attack or defense; it is also why you chose that particular attack or defense. Tactics is not just your decision; it is how you come to your decision, your method. This implies that tactical judgment and calculated risk taking is necessary in our approach to solving complex violent encounters, with armed and dangerous adversary(s). It also implies using a unique approach and doing something unexpected by the adversary, considering the specific adversary, time, risk level and place.3

Keep in mind the unexpected tactic chosen may be conventional or unconventional. Just because a certain method/tactic has been around for a while does not mean it cannot be used in an unexpected way.

Tactics are both science and art not in what to do, but in HOW TO THINK! We should not respond without knowing and understanding the "WHY" behind the way we respond. This is an important aspect of tactics for all law enforcement officers to understand, especially those on the streets who deal with the complex problems and make the critical decisions found in every community.

Adversaries we encounter also have a say in the outcome of engagements. This is a fact that we often forget when we respond and deal with calls and crisis at the street cops' level. Adversary's train and prepare i.e., Fourth Generation Warfare techniques and methods is where we are evolving when it comes to potential threats. *New generations of terrorists and criminals, both at home and abroad, are also pursuing innovations as a result of the information revolution.*4

We are already seeing this methodology taking place with gangs, organized crime, drug cartels and even the untrained. Remember Columbine and the 17 -18 year olds who had set up a secondary location with an improvised explosive device to disrupt the response system; or conventional criminals using unconventional methods such as; the armed robber, using a hoax or real explosive devices in one location as they rob a bank or business in another. Mumbai India is a powerful example of this at work. A small 10 man terrorist team split up into two-man teams and spread out and swarmed over this city. They killed hundreds and wounded more while keeping the city of Mumbai at bay for over 60 hours as those tasked with dealing with the crisis remained confused and hesitant in how to respond to such an attack.

They are organizing into loose, transnational networks that allow for increased coordination and cooperation among dispersed groups and individuals who are able to stay securely separated in case anyone is caught and incriminated.

For example, inside the U.S. some leaders of the sprawling radical right in the United States subscribe to a doctrine of "leaderless resistance" that can motivate "lone wolves" to commit violent acts entirely on their own account.5

There's a growing power of small units, groups, and individuals who are able to connect and act conjointly by adopting network forms of organization and related doctrines and strategies and technologies. These cases speak to the rise of "swarming" as a mode of conflict. In the future, we shall have to learn to fight nimbly against an array of armed adversaries who will likely do all they can to avoid facing us head-on in battle.6

Adversaries of the future will use elusiveness by mobility or concealment, and systems disruption through targeting multiple locations to test our emergency response systems. Superior situational awareness through planning and use of technology is part of their methodology and stand-off capability, by blending in or utilizing surprise to set up in an attempt to establish and maintain the tempo of conflict will be part of this as well.

P.I.N an Adversary

TRAINING...GOOD REALISTIC and INNOVATIVE TRAINING is a critical factor in the ability to think and act under pressure. It has always been important (although not focused on enough in law enforcement) and the need for it is even more necessary today as threats and those who threaten continue to evolve. Law enforcement must continually evolve their tactics as well. Short of actual experience, there are innovative training approaches that can better prepare law enforcement officers for all type of threats.

Then questions become common after experiencing several various training methodologies such as TDGs: What techniques work and which ones fail? When do we use 4 men, verse one, or, two or three man concepts verses SWAT techniques?

The all-important "WHY?" we choose a particular technique must be explored as well.

We have been researching and experimenting in training with *swarming tactics* also known as converging tactics and whether or not this type of technique has a place tactically in our response to an ongoing deadly action "active shooter," multiple adversaries or multiple target situations. Two great resources we used are John Arquilla and Dave Ronfeldt *Swarming & the Future of Conflict* and Sean J.A. Edwards, *Swarming on the Battlefield Past, Present and Future.* Both resources are from RAND, National Defense Research Institute and cover the history of swarming tactics, how the methodology is used, the command and control structure necessary for successful swarming operations and the tactics strengths and weaknesses.7

SWARMING is described as engaging an adversary from all directions simultaneously. The technique is nothing new. Alexander the Great and Genghis Khan use the techniques to outwit and outpace lager and more highly trained adversaries. Can we in law enforcement, when we encounter dispersed and maneuvering adversaries combat it; defeat it with this type of response? Will this type of technique work for the first responders, the street cops responding to ongoing deadly action where minutes if not seconds weigh heavily on the death and injured count?8

For example, instead of responding and massing at side 1 of a location under attack and entering as a group, 4-man diamond formation and then move to contact to stop the threat, the first responder enters solo and back-up responds to side 2, and enters, then next responder enters on side 3 and then side 4 (*not necessarily in that order*).

In other words we respond and engage the threat by dispersing and then converging on the threat, cutting off the shooter(s) mobility and hence his access to more victims until we stop the threat. Or another option is we mass on side 1 for example, enter and then disperse and converge on the threat?
In several ongoing deadly action active-shooter workshops we conducted with police departments; we experimented with this technique and found it to be an effective response.

This workshop was all force-on-force, free play exercises

workshop using Sim-munitions, with the enemy or opposing forces free thinking (non-scripted). The swarming/converging tactic allowed those responding options to **progress** towards and engage the adversary quickly from multiple directions *interrupting* and *cutting off* the adversary's **ability** to move about and **accessing** victims at **will**.

We found this approach **confuses** and **neutralizes** an adversary, at least momentarily, and long enough to change the tempo, allowing responders to gain the advantage and stop the threat. Converging from multiple directions towards and adversary disrupts adversarial plans and actions as they become surprised. Their decision making process slows down as they attempt to figure out "what's happening."

In the training, adversaries (full time law enforcement officers roll playing as the red team) were stopped by an officer converging from another direction with deadly force as the adversary(s) became engaged with a responder from another. Once the adversary(s) became aware the technique was being used (we ran the exercise several times), the adversaries (red team) became prepared but still confused as they attempted to attack and defend simultaneously, as responders converged on their location.

Another positive factor we found is when you respond and converge from multiple directions, you also cut off possible escape routes, and you encounter victims and potential victims quicker.

This allows responders to quickly point out evacuation routes for those attempting to escape or cover/lockdown positions as uncertain circumstances may dictate.

You may also encounter downed seriously injured victims quickly. You can either make a mental note of their locations for rescue reams and emergency medical treatment when the threat is stopped. Or you can communicate the location to tactical emergency responders (TEMS) (something we need more of), as you continue to maneuver towards the threat. This requires superior situational awareness and rapid threat recognition.

Tactical judgment is crucial as you attempt to separate a friendly victim from a potential foe.9

There is heightened risk to responders as they enter solo and maneuver through the environment alone but the circumstances in an active shooter type situation warrant a rapid and evolving response. Crossfire or friendly fire concerns is another risk in using swarming/converging tactics, but this is always a concern in any evolving tactical situation and is prevented through ongoing training and cops who think and maneuver tactically and possess the critical skills necessary.

The level of training (currently not enough) most police departments give their officers, the 4-man diamond formation, 3-man 2-man techniques, present the same problem once contact with an adversary is made, does it not? Communications is also a crucial factor when using swarming/converging tactics. Explicit communications are critical as you maneuver and progress to locate the adversary(s). Once an adversary is engaged, implicit communications to coordinate fields of fire is even more crucial. This implicit communication and tactical judgment can only be obtained beginning with tactical decision games, then moving to free play force-on-force training that creates and nurtures cohesiveness, trust and adaptability under pressure.

With training and adaptive leadership, we are more than capable of employing this method. In my view, it's an option we can we apply to an ongoing deadly action, situation, where we have the element of surprise. Surprise, not in the fact that we are coming or are there, but instead, surprise in the methods we use, as the adversary knows we are coming.

Training full spectrum street cops, those officers responding to the scene first, will be the key in accomplishing this. I feel we must explore this more deeply as an option especially for police departments with smaller numbers of officers working the street.

"Knowledge must be so absorbed into the mind that it almost ceases to exist in a separate objective way."
~Carl von Clausewitz10

Interaction with your adversary(s) allows you to gather actionable information to utilize in your efforts to solve whatever strategic and tactical problem you face. Information you have gathered only becomes actionable if you have the ability to take what you know and apply it in a way that accords with the circumstances and your overall intent. You must always keep in mind that it is impossible to control exactly how the adversary(s) will respond to your actions. So the goal is to control the adversary's mindset with both direct and/or indirect action which takes thinking and adaptability.

Insight and imagination is needed to adapt tactics and apply them in an innovative way to the particular problem at hand. The ability to apply these attributes in a violent encounter puts you in a position of advantage. You can then seize the initiative on your terms.

You control the tempo of things with interaction--moving in, tactically loitering, communication, deception, force options, etc., and focus your efforts to prevent or resolve the problem.

This is known as "operational art" a much needed concept to explore and understand if we are to connect our endgame (strategy) with how we play the game (tactics).

Winning deadly engagements requires knowing many things, including an understanding of the environment, the climate of the situation, psychology, physiology, decision making, combative skills, firearms skills, leadership and the overall mission or intent. In an engagement all these factors combine in a synergistic way and require interaction with your adversary(s), fellow officers and the community. Tactical Options and knowing how and when to apply, along with the "WHY" we have chosen a particular tactical options is the key.

Chapter 8
Harnessing the Street Cops Wisdom and Taking Whole of Conflict

"Hear counsel, and receive instruction, that you may be wise in the days to come." Proverbs 19:201

In 2012-14, there have been great discussions by experienced law enforcement professionals taking place on active shootings. The discussion hit a vast array of factors surrounding active shooting situations such as does the title we give the topic "ACTIVE SHOOTER" cause confusion in the ranks of responders and how we respond?

What tactics should we be using 4 man, 3 man, 2 man and even 1 man entry techniques?

What if we have multiple subjects or multiple targets, then what?

Do we respond differently based on our adversaries ability and if so how?

Does the size of your department matter, if you're from a small town or a large metropolitan area, do tactics change?

These are all great questions and responses in a back and forth dialog to help reshape our thinking in an age where threats are evolving at a faster rate than in the past.

In the discussion I noted a healthy sense of searching for the right answer as to how to handle, but at the same time I sensed an unhealthy search for one way of doing it. This search for a tactical procedure that fits every type of possible scenario surrounding ongoing deadly action is an obstacle to effective responses to dynamic encounters. This got us thinking about the policies and procedures. This leads to the checklist driven world of law enforcement with its linear, canned response approach. That is part of the problem in delivering an effective full spectrum response to the vast array of problems and adversaries we face today.

The Ever-changing Pace of Conflict

To meet the ever changing pace of conflict we must change our attitudes and training methods to that where we focus on teaching street cops how to think instead of, what to think. Cops must be able to arrive on scene, gather information as it's unfolding through all their senses and come to some judgment or orientation as to what is going on. Cops must be trained to a superior level so they can do adapt on the fly under the stress of unfolding circumstances and then make decisions and take actions to resolve the situation with the least amount of risk to all involved.

Action taken based on the circumstances could require a vast array of methods depending on the judgment made while reading the scene. In reading the scene the officer must consider all factors including the perspectives of others (innocents, adversary(s) and friendly). The street cop must make a judgment and adapt a response by taking the whole (holistic) and not by checklists. Taking whole as described by the ancient strategist Sun Tzu is:

Know yourself and know your enemy. You will be safe in every battle. You may know yourself but not know the enemy. You will then lose one battle for every one you win. You may not know yourself or the enemy. You will then lose every battle.[2]

Taking the holistic approach is about knowledge and not just information that we have stored in our brains. Just knowing information is not good enough (technical and skills). Instead we must be able to apply individual and collective knowledge in a tactical way on the street. This ability comes from hard work individually and organizationally and learning from both direct and indirect experiences and using both rational and intuitive abilities in making decisions. Obviously considering time and risk factors!

Harnessing the Street Cops' Wisdom

Street cops handle by far the vast majority of dangerous situations on the street, yet they receive the least amount of training in ways that teach them how to frame and solve complex problems (adaptability). This must change in our profession if we truly wish to deal with the serious problems we face more effectively and win on the moral, mental and physical realms of conflict. To harness the wisdom the street cop has, we must learn from their experiences in circumstances where they win and lose on the street. There are numerous lessons to be learned with either outcome, and we must take it upon ourselves to leverage these lessons if we are to become effective full spectrum cops delivering full spectrum responses.

This ability to learn, unlearn and relearn is crucial combined with the *adaptive leaders* who understand their role in creating (consistent training) and nurturing (inspiring, influencing) decision making from the bottom up. Correct decision making on the frontline—the street—where the circumstances unfold in real time are critical every time a cop walks into an unfamiliar situation. Adaptive leaders continually develop their cops. They know leadership is a day to day thing not an event driven thing, and they take the time to develop their subordinates. They take advantage of down time, roll call, on the street to critique lessons learned. They listen to the experience of others including subordinates in this effort to learn themselves. This all creates the cohesion necessary to adapt on the fly to any situation.

This approach is applicable in any type of operating environment but especially so when facing the complex problems of policing, car stop, domestic disturbance, robbery, neighborhood problem or dealing with today's transnational crime or terrorist action or any ongoing deadly action.

It is often more difficult to identify the weaknesses of today's emotionally disturbed or high stressed person, criminals, criminal gangs and terrorists, and a greater challenge to find ways to exploit them. However, the reality of our current conflicts shows that finding creative ways to defeat an asymmetrical threat is essential for our street cops.

It is vital that street cops understand the long term consequences of their immediate actions.

This requires the ability to operate within the framework of their higher command or what's known as *"Commander's Intent."* This intent constitutes the long term contract between senior and subordinate. Ethical conduct and adherence to the Rules of Engagement (ROE), the use of force, are always part of the Commander's Intent.   This serves to emphasize the often strategic-level consequences of actions at the lowest levels. In other words we must walk the talk of decentralized control if we are to truly raise the bar and develop full spectrum cops who are more than capable if we free them up to adapt to unfolding conditions and make necessary decisions.

Harnessing the street cops wisdom takes both training and building upon every experience building commitment and self-confidence, strength of character in street cops making them effective full spectrum responders with the ability to *take whole* the factors of conflict and violence enhancing our abilities to decide, detect, deter, disrupt, disengage, prevent and resolve any situation with interaction, insight, innovation and initiative. We have many street cops in our ranks more than capable so let's harness and use their abilities, their wisdom, to get the job done!

"Adapt strategically to diminished circumstances by devising new ways of coping with old and new enemies."
~ Edward N. Luttwak[3]

Chapter 9
Interaction, Insight and Imagination, and Initiative... The Building Blocks of Police Operational Art

The essence of winning and losing is in learning how to shape or influence events so that we not only magnify our spirit and strength but also influence potential adversaries as well as the uncommitted so that they are drawn toward our philosophy and are empathetic towards our success.
~Col. John Boyd1

Operational art in the world of conflict is the link that synergistically connects strategy and tactics. Conflict is a clash between multiple complex adaptive systems trying to impose itself on the other. As previously discussed, conflict can turn violent or it can be resolved peacefully. Our strategy as protection professionals is to impose our will on the adversary. To do so we must use our ability to interact with our adversary who is an independent and animate force with its own objectives and plans. Interaction helps you control the dynamics of the situation on your terms.

Superior situational awareness and ongoing interaction such as communication, negotiation, tactical movement both overt and covert and tactical set up will help reduce uncertainty and open up opportunities for us to use our insight and imagination to adapt tactics to an evolving situation and seize the initiative. This ability to use insight and imagination and apply knowledge through initiative-driven interaction with our environment, and the *climate (what's happening?)* of the situation, considering both adversarial and friendly situation and their effect on the moral, mental and physical dimensions of conflict is known as operational art.

Strategy and tactics is both art and science.

When we learn tactics we learn in a way that builds off of

certain ideas and principles that have been used in engagements throughout history. Police tactics are based on military tactics with the obvious adaptation by police to the civil side of keeping order and solving problems. In the end tactics are methods we use to help us win the numerous types engagements we find ourselves in. Interaction is a tactic or methods used to help you gain control.

Winning requires knowing many things, including an understanding of the environment, the climate of the situation, psychology, physiology, decision making, combative skills, firearms skills, leadership and the overall mission or intent. In an engagement all these factors combine in a synergistic way and require interaction with your adversary(s), fellow officers and the community. Interaction with your adversary(s) allows you to gather actionable information to use in your efforts to solve whatever strategic and tactical problem you face.

Information you have gathered only becomes actionable if you have the ability to take what you know and apply it in a way that accords with the circumstances and your overall intent. You must always keep in mind that it is impossible to control exactly how the adversary(s) will respond to your actions. So the goal is to control the adversary's mindset with both direct and/or indirect action which takes thinking and adaptability.

Insight and imagination is needed to adapt tactics and apply them in an innovative way to the particular problem at hand. The ability to apply these attributes in a violent encounter puts you in a position of advantage. You can then seize the initiative on your terms.

You control the tempo of things with interaction--moving in, tactically loitering, communication, deception, force options, etc., and focus your efforts to prevent or resolve the problem. This is known as *operational art* a much needed concept to understand if we are to connect our endgame (strategy) with how we play the game (tactics).

Everything man is and does is modified by learning and is therefore malleable. But once learned, these behavior pattern, these habitual responses, these ways of interacting gradually sink below the surface of the mind and like the admiral of a submerged submarine fleet, control from the depths. The hidden controls are usually experienced as though they were innate simply because they are not only ubiquitous but habitual as well.'
... The only time one is aware of the control system is when things don't follow the hidden program. This is most frequent in intercultural encounters. Therefore the great gift that members of the human race have for each other is not exotic experiences but an opportunity to achieve awareness of the structure of their own system, which can be accomplished only by interacting with others who do not share that system...
~Edward T. Hall2

Learning, unlearning and re-learning is the core of adaptation, and adaptation is the crux of operational art. Adaptation comes from understanding these key attributes and how to apply them. They are the building blocks to applying a sound operational art. Skills plus attributes equal readiness!

Definitions of attributes that apply to operational art:
Interaction-when two people or two sides interact they have an effect on one another. This effect can through tactical savvy allow us to exploit our adversary's decision making process and open up opportunities for us to seize the advantage and gain control.
- Insight-is the ability to observe and orient intuitively to openings or advantages given up by our adversary and then see how we may adapt the science of tactics in an artful yet skillful way to the unfolding conditions.
- Imagination-is the ability to form mental images of the necessary tactics and how they apply to the ongoing situation in accordance with our strategy. Imagination enhances decision making!

- Initiative-All action in conflict, regardless of level, is based upon either taking the initiative or reaction in response to the adversary. By taking the initiative, we dictate the terms of the conflict and force the adversary to meet us on our terms. The initiative allows us to pursue some positive aim even if only to preempt an adversary's initiative. It is through the initiative that we seek to impose our will on the adversary. This is the action phase!

An example:
You respond to a residence along with two other officers for a domestic disturbance. On your way to the location you interact and communicate over the radio with dispatch gather information that is pertinent to your response considerations.

You learn it's a verbal altercation between husband and wife and that the husband is drunk and that the wife wants him out.
You know that domestic violence calls of a verbal dynamic can turn to physical violence quickly. Understanding the sense of urgency, we set up a tactical response and approach. You and the two responding officers interact beforehand and agree the best approach will be to rally at a location down the street from the particular address and approach the scene on foot.

As you approach you can hear shouting coming from the house. You continue to evolve your plan where one officer will take the 1 and 2 corners of the single family home and the second officer will take 3 and 4 corners of the building as you engage the husband and wife. Once you determine by looking covertly through a window there are no weapons and that it is indeed just a verbal altercation, you call out to the husband and wife who immediately stop shouting at one another and welcome you in. You hand signal the officer at the 1 and 2 corner to be your cover man and he takes up a position inside as well. He then calls for the 3 and 4 corner man to enter and assist in gathering information from one of the spouses.

In domestic situations, it is usually best to separate the

auguring couples so emotions are quelled.

This three man team interacting and using collaborative insight and imagination with one another has allowed them to safely approach, separate and contain the subjects and gather more information. This information gathered has allowed them to make a determination as to what action to take. They decide that no criminal act has occurred but have talked the male subject into leaving for the night and to stay with a friend, who will meet him at the station.3

The male subject is intoxicated but is not falling down drunk, and he asks for a favor. *"Can I go out and close my shed doors before I leave?"* You agree, but decide to walk with him as a safety precaution. As you step out the back door you notice the yard is a mess there is junk everywhere in the back yard.

You and the subject continue to speak as he walks toward the shed that you can see and the doors are open. The subject walks inside and reaches up on the counter and slugs down another beer contained in a coolly. You tell him to show some respect and he bows his head humbly and apologizes for the disrespect. As he starts to close the shed doors he asks you what you think of the four foot saw blade he has hung on the shed door. You look and ask, *"Where the hell did you get that from?"* He tells you he found it on the side of the road one day and that he just loved the damn thing.

You begin to get a funny feeling inside telling yourself that this guy is up to something. He seems to be stalling and talking about foolish things that most people would not talk about knowing they were being forced out of their own home for the night. He closes the shed doors and begins to walk back towards the house when he suddenly stops and asks you, *"Do you mind if I straighten up the back yard?"* He begins to bend down and reach for a 2X4. In an instant your gut is screaming "why does he want to clean the yard now," the same yard that looks like it has not been cleaned up in the past 20 years? You move in and place him in handcuffs. He offers no resistance. His stay with a friend to sober up has now become a stay with the police.

This is an example of *operational art*. There are flaws in judgment such as, *letting him go to the shed in the first place*. The point is not about being flawless, because flawlessness is rare in conflict and violence. We can easily ask the question, *"What would have happened if you told him you cannot close the shed?"* Would this have escalated the situation? Would you been more prepared at that point inside with no room to maneuver? The point is did our awareness level and the interaction with our adversary open up opportunities for us to adapt? The answer is yes it did. Opportunity opened up to both sides as interaction will do. Risk goes up when we interact with an adversary.

There is always give and take, move and counter moves when dealing with conflict. Your awareness level must be superior when you are interacting with an adversary. Did we see opportunities and then use our insight and imagination to seize the initiative on our terms? Yes we did. In the end no struggle or assault took place, nor did he make an overt act to assault. Although my insight and intuition says he was most definitely thinking about it.

A honed Boyd Cycle will give you insight as to what's happening. You will recognize signs and signals, patterns of behavior that make sense or seem out of the norm allowing you to feed off and understand the unfolding circumstances. Through experience, you will develop a *fingertip feel* for *operational art*, which you can nurture only through hard work. The lessons learned allow you to use interaction, insight, imagination and initiative driven tactics to the situation at hand and winning on your terms.

Pressing down the pillow refers to one's efforts to let the head of one's opponent rise. In battles based on martial strategy, it is taboo to let your opponent take the initiative, thus putting yourself on the defensive. You must try at all costs to lead your opponent by taking complete control of him. During combat, your opponent intends to dominate you as much as you want to dominate him, so it is vital that you pick up on your opponent's intentions and tactics so as to control him...

According to the principle of martial strategy, you must be able to control your opponent(s) at all times. Study this point well.
~Miyamoto Musashi4

Chapter 10
Critical Decision Making Under Pressure

Decisions in rapidly changing dangerous circumstances are made at times without thought. I have heard and even uttered the words myself, "I didn't think about it." I just acted." "We just did what had to be done."

Can that be true?
Can those of us involved in extreme situations where life and death are at stake actually make decisions without thinking, without analyzing options, intuitively? The answer is clearly yes.

Dr. Gary Klein in his research of cognitive development talks about making decisions under pressure in what he describes as "Recognition-Primed Decision Making". What Klein found working with the United States Marine Corps, Emergency workers and Businesses across the country, was, *"It was not that the commanders were refusing to compare options. I had been so fixated on what they were not doing that I had missed the real finding: that the commanders could come up with a good course of action from the start. That is what the stories were telling us. Even when faced with a complex situation, the commanders could see it as familiar and know how to react."*[1]

Klein *says "the commander's secret was that their experience let them see a situation, even a non-routine one, as an example of a prototype, so they knew the typical course of action right away. Their experience let them identify a reasonable reaction as the first one they considered, so they did not bother thinking of others. They were not being perverse. They were being skillful. We now call this strategy recognition-primed decision making."*[2]

The Recognition-Primed Decision Making model fuses two processes Klein says, the way decisions makers size-up the situation to recognize which course of action makes sense, and the way they evaluate the course of action by imagining it.

Now it is important to keep in mind that decisions evolve with circumstances some decisions are made simply with more time to decide and others require quick if-then thinking to achieve results. The focus here is how to prepare ourselves to do those rapid decisions that needs to be made under pressure.

Law enforcement and security personnel at times make decisions with very little information available and even less, time. This time criticality is because either rapidly changing circumstances that unfold unexpectedly and spontaneously allowing little time to decide or an individual officer is locked into a complacent mindset his Boyd Cycle is turned off, misses critical information unfolding progressively and is caught unprepared. Decision making in both cases is made more difficult due to little information being picked up on and processed.

Law enforcement and security officers find themselves in these types of situations all too often. If not prepared through training, education, experience and backed up by strong character leadership time critical decisions do not get made and the advantage goes to the adversary.

To gather and process the incoming information in rapidly changing circumstances requires judgment and decision making without all the facts.

*Actually due to intuition built through experience we gain situational awareness, meaning there is a lot of information an experienced decision maker uses, it was just not available to us in earlier stages.*3

To pick up on this information the signs and signals, we must have our individual Boyd Cycle "Turned On!" The Boyd Cycle (OODA-LOOP) is both a subconscious and conscious act, of observation, orientation, decision and action cycles we use in our daily routines to make decisions. Through repetitive and innovative training it becomes second nature.

Col. Boyd explained a person in a conflict; any conflict must **observe** the environment, to include himself, his adversary, the moral, mental and physical situation, potential allies and opponents.

He must **orient** to what it all means, "what's going on" which is part of the ongoing process throughout the situation. Orientation involves the information observed, one's genetic heritage, social environment and prior experiences (birth-present) that forms our picture of the situation. The results one forms during the orientation phase must be **decided** upon and an attempt made to carry out the decision, he must **act**.4

Driving a car combines mental and physical skills is an example of this decision process. While driving we make hundreds of subconscious and conscious decisions as to what other drivers will and will not do based on the signs and signals they display and take action accordingly in most cases.

If we *observe* a turn signal or brake light come on in front of us, we *orient* on it and make a conscious *decision* to slow ourselves or turn safely. Then we *act* to do so in an effort to avoid accidents. This also keeps traffic flowing.

If something happens unexpectedly and we observe and absorb the information, we make intuitive subconscious decisions and take decisive action as in swerving to a safe part of the road or stopping quickly to avoid the hazard. If we are not paying attention, having a spirited conversation, dialing a cell phone or distracted in some other way, problems arise, near misses, accelerated stopping and accidents occur. Why? There is a break in a properly running Boyd Cycle and we miss critical information.

The driving example combines cognitive and physical abilities which are necessary to be successful at driving. Yes there are accidents, deaths and seriously injured, but when you consider the number of cars on the road and the daily activity taking place in cars we are damn good at combining these cognitive and physical skills.

Why? Because we do it all the time, every day and this translates into experience at picking up the obvious and subtle signs giving us situational awareness while driving that translates into very good conscious and subconscious decision making.

This driving analogy is important to look at because it shows the correlation between doing and developing experience, using both our cognitive and physical abilities in carrying out our daily tasks—it becomes second nature. This directly relates to what we in law enforcement and security do in carrying out our duties day to day. It also shows the importance of continuous training (driving everyday) and its effect on developing this ability in those who deal with crime, crime problems and dangerous encounters. Where both implicit, and explicit information is utilized in, solving these types of problems.

Our goal should be to harness the ability to develop the cognitive decision making process with the physical skills required in both progressive and spontaneous circumstances and refine the necessary methods through experience and apply it accordingly based on the environment and current circumstances. The first step is a shift of mind that intuition is not magic, not some strange force that comes from some unknown mystical location. That indeed intuition comes from a fine tuned senses, leading to a rapid decision making cycle developed through tough and continuous development through decision making exercises.

Intuition is defined as the way we translate our experience into action. Our experience lets us recognize what is going on (making judgments) and how to react (making decisions). Our experience enables us to recognize what to do and we can make decisions rapidly and without conscious awareness or effort. We do not have to think through situations in order to make a good decision.

Recognition-Primed Decision Making can be enhanced through training and through understanding that conflict is time-bound competition based on observation, orientation decision and action cycles.

Recognition-primed decision making is guided and controlled through tactical judgments based on your individual perceptions as circumstances unfold. What Col. John Boyd called, "Implicit guidance and control."

The late Col. John Boyd in his work stated that conflict is time competitive observation, orientation, and decision and action cycles. Boyd's decision making cycle has been proven in its ability to give the upper hand, the clear advantage to the one with the fastest O-O-D-A cycle. The OODA loop had to be implicit in order to be made rapidly enough to outpace our adversary and win. Again these decisions are made based on the individual involved experience, background as well as training and the new information presenting itself via the unfolding circumstances.

The word implicit is used throughout Boyd's work. I understand it as tactical judgment and intuitive decision making. This type of decision making is necessary in an effort to deal with and resolve crime and violence we in law enforcement and security are facing. There is no time in dangerous rapidly unfolding circumstances, for contemplation and analytical decision making. By the time you stop and contemplate, ponder an idea and come up with a solution, it may be too late.

The real world of crime and violence is not a class room or boardroom model, where there is time to strategize and take hours, days and weeks to come up with a plan. It is clear we must recognize forming patterns and respond guided by implicit information if we are to be successful. This is not to say we do not use explicit information gathered when the time and information is available. There is a balance between explicit and implicit information.

We do our homework and gather information in accordance with what is unfolding at the time. This is both an art and science developed by education, training and experience... It alludes to the critical importance of understanding conflict and the strategy and tactics essential in resolving it...

What's not clear is understanding, and how we explain intuitive decisions. Why is being able to explain decisions important? The obvious answer is so those who sit in review of our decisions understand how and why a critical decision was made.

So that the citizenry, who participate in review boards and sit on juries have a better understanding how we use tactical judgment to decide.

So those in leadership positions within our professions and those who conduct investigations into events surrounding decisions, frontline law enforcement and security professionals make. In the heat of the moment, our decisions are thoroughly investigated, fairly. Not just with the available physical evidence, provided at the scene of an incident, but taking into account how conflict unfolds and how individuals process information and perceive circumstances as they unfold.

This knowledge as to how we process information and make decisions is so critical to understand and consider if justice, is to prevail. The most important reason is so that the individuals in law enforcement and security can deal with the aftermath of an incident through understanding that decisions made on the fly, in rapidly changing circumstances do not match the analytical models.

Analytical models are done when there is plenty of time. This allows for an analysis and synthesis to take place in the static environment of a classroom or in a living room watching a media report of the circumstances. The man in the arena has only time to read and pick up on important subtle signs showing danger and act. It is clearly a different process that physiology shifts us from a frontal lobe conscious thinking, analytical being, to a mid-brain subconscious instinctive reaction responding through operant conditioning to meet the challenge or threat.

In the world today explicit and clear answers are expected after a response, even if it is a use of force situation, an officer handling a suspicious person or a response to a natural disaster to save lives. How do we explain what we did not "think about" so others understand?

Intuition, implicit judgment appears simple to understand but is not an easily acquired skill. The words intuition and implicit almost imply "there is something missing. This term implies an unscientific or haphazard approach. In conflict one plus one does not equal two but we live in a world where there is an explicit answer to every situation. Yet in the real world of conflict that is not the case. You put two people together who disagree and you cannot predict what's going to happen, let alone the conflicting individuals get so angry they decide to get physical or worse deadly.

In conflict there are chaos, uncertainty, disorder, and friction that confuse and slow the decision making cycle down. You cannot predict exactly what's going to happen next, because there are things going on that you cannot see or hear for example; the numerous thoughts going through your adversaries mind:

"I will do what I am asked," "I will not do what I am asked," "I will escape," "I will fight," "I will assault," "I will kill," "I will play dumb until...," "I will stab," "I will shoot," "he looks prepared I will comply," "he looks complacent I will not comply," etc.

Remember your adversary has his own objectives and plans as you do and they combat one another, thereby creating conflict! In conflict 1+1=? Pause to try and figure out (analysis) what's happening or gather more explicit (precise) information and it could be over with unfavorable results. Therefore the needed tactical judgment or implicit, guidance and control.

The problem arises when our judgments in the heat of the moment amongst all the chaos, uncertainty, disorder and friction were perceived as unreasonable or wrong by others. We respond with what we perceived as happening based on the unfolding circumstances was not, after all is said and done, accurate. Our judgment was wrong! What you thought was a gun... was a wallet, or cell phone. Who you thought was the suspect was an innocent bystander. This is worst case scenario. However in this worst case scenario we could still be justified in our actions based on the circumstances.

What about the body language that you observed that showed signs the citizen was becoming anxious and you were fearful of assault. You take initiative to control the situation and the citizen responds by becoming physically assaultive. You take control with reasonable physical force, a complaint is filed and you are now under investigation for excessive force. What about the citizen who verbally abuses you while in your professional capacity and you strategically decide to raise your voice and use verbal manipulation to gain control, which you do. Again you're facing a complaint investigation.

How are these examples explained appropriately? How does the lack of understanding by ourselves and those who sit in judgment of us, as to how we make decisions, affect our in the moment, under pressure decision making? Why is it important to understand and be able to explain it? How and who do we train so there is a clearer understanding of the decisions we make, for all involved? How will all this enhance our ability to perform under pressure and become better intuitive decision makers?

Chapter 11

Explicit verses Implicit Information: It's Role in the Process

In previous chapters we discussed the Recognition-Primed Decision Making, the Boyd Cycle and the importance of training in the development of the decision making process. In this second part I want to answer some questions. What is implicit and explicit information? How we make decisions based on one or the other, or a combination of both types of information we receive?

I also want to answer the question how does our lack of understanding of conflict and decision making affect our decisions in the real world while under pressure? How do we explain these decisions after they are made to all affected by the decisions we make (leadership, citizenry, organization, juries)? How and who do we train and educate so there is a clear understanding of the decisions we make? Finally how will this educational process enhance our ability to perform under pressure and become better decision makers?

In the law enforcement and security professions most of the little training conducted surrounds physical skills training. Training focuses on firearm proficiency, how to swing and block with an impact weapon, use oleoresin capsicum (Pepper Spray), defensive tactics and handcuffing techniques. A small portion of time is spent talking about use of force decisions and filing appropriate reports as to the action taken by officers.

Although there have been great strides in bringing new training techniques such as Redman suits, Sim-munitions and range 3000 simulators to combine the physical and mental realms of conflict. While this training is excellent, it is just a small part of the overall conditioning that must take place in the preparation of our profession. This type of response training is called conditioned response. It is a specific training for a specific reaction, and while it is important, does not fully prepare people for complex situations.

Decisions are made in two ways as we exposed in earlier chapters. They can be done through analytical thought when time is plenty and the circumstances allow for a detail analysis and synthesis of gathered explicit information. Or, they are also made intuitively under pressure when time is critical and only implicit information can be gathered to resolve critical incidents. To understand how we make decisions it is important to understand the nature of how we gather explicit and implicit information as well as how we combine them in making decisions.

Decision Making and Explicit information
Rapid decision making is essential to the law enforcement and security officer. An officer who is unable to make a timely decision puts himself and those around him in danger. Most of us are brought up to make decisions after careful consideration and contemplation. "Think before you act!" "What were you thinking?" Didn't you think it through?" are words we have all heard from parents, teachers, co-workers, bosses, internal investigators and review boards throughout our lives, when our decisions come into question.

There has been extensive research on the topic of cognitive development. One of the models in decision making has been develop by research and transformation and implementation into a usable model is the Adaptive Leadership Methodology (ALM) developed by Donald Vandergriff and his cadre in teaching new leaders in the Army ROTC program.

ALM has been accepted by the Army with the United States Military Academy at West Point rewriting the lesson plans in its Department of Military Instruction (DMI) following the ALM model. In his book Raising the Bar: Creating and Nurturing Adaptability to Deal with the Changing Face of War, Vandergriff describes methods of decision making the first The Military decision Making Process, he describes as the classical or analytical approach:

"The MDMP is a very good example of an analytical decision-

*making process; it is the first of two primary decision making models."*1

Analytical methods such as the MDMP are formal problem solving techniques. (Vandergriff, 2006) *"The U.S. Army's MDMP is a modification of the French Army's misinterpretation of a German Army Decision-making training approach in the late 1800s. In the U.S. Army's model, the decision-maker uses an analytical decision making process to reach logical decisions based upon a thorough analysis of the mission and situation."*2

*"The MDMP as well as other analytical decision-making models use the same basic problem solving methodology."*3 An example of this is the problem oriented policing, problem solving process SARA: ***scanning***-identifying the problem; ***analysis***-learning the problem's causes, scope and effects; ***response***-acting to alleviate the problem; and ***assessmen***t-determining whether the response worked.

The SARA Problem-Solving Model is employed by most law enforcement agencies and provides techniques for identifying the elements of the problem; techniques to support the search for the underlying causes of the problem; and techniques for the development of the most effective strategy to address the problem.   The final phase of the model highlights the requirement to assess the final results and to determine if the response was effective. The SARA model is widely applicable to problems faced by many neighborhoods and has produced excellent results for hundreds of communities across the United States. It establishes a collaborative, systematic process to address issues of community, safety, and quality of life.4

This approach is very good when you have the time for gathering, pondering and analyzing. Explicit (precise) information is gathered, reviewed, analyzed, and discussed by a collaborative group of police, business owners, and community members.

Decisions are made as to what strategies and tactics to utilize then a plan is developed and put into action which is under constant assessment by all so adjustments can be made to make the plan effective. The key here is there is "TIME" to get explicit and detailed information and walk through the process to achieve desired results.

Explicit decisions are needed if you are trying things or experimenting to resolve these progressively evolving problems of the community. Intuitive decisions are not needed exclusively to resolve these types of issues because time is available. A big factor in this type of problem solving and the need for explicit information is it gives time to develop trust amongst the group which is sometime lacking in communities and a problem for rapid decision making.

Rapid Decision-Making and Implicit Information

When the focus has turned to critical decisions that need to be made and time to make decisions is critical such as; use of force decision making. Most decisions must be made intuitively and rapid based on implicit (understood) information or tactical judgment based on the patterns we have learned from experience (birth-present) and the new information we are gathering, analyzing and synthesizing in the rapidly changing circumstances. This leads us to a second type of decision-making.

*The second type of decision-making model is a naturalistic or heuristic model.*5

Experience has much to do with this method of decision-making. There are three key steps inherent in heuristic decision-making: experience the situation in a changing context, recognize the pattern of the problem from personal knowledge and experience, and implement a solution. Although this is commonly used decision-making approach, heuristic and naturalistic models for decision-making have only recently come into prominence in decision-making literature.6

Security and law enforcement officers use the rapid decision-making process by recognizing the signs and signals of crime and danger intuitively or through what we in the protection professions call our sixth sense. Our sixth sense is intuition based on, experience. *"Intuition is how we translate our experiences into action.i"*

Again I will use the car analogy as an example. It is a freezing cold, snowy night and the roads are covered with snow and ice. You are traveling at 40 mph on a narrow curvy road. Your mindset is on getting home after a long shift. As you come into a sharp corner your vehicle begins to slide out of control. As you feel your heart rate pick up and hands lock onto the steering wheel and foot goes to the brake automatically due to the fear of and avoidance of an accident.

Your experience is you have lived in this wintery environment your whole life and have driven the icy, snow covered roads countless times before. Your intuition kicks in with "this is BAD!" You intuitively release or pump your foot on the brake, steer towards the direction of the slide and drive through the problem to safety. When you're once again safe then your heart rate comes back down to normal and breathe a sigh of relief. The conscious mind comes back and gives you a scolding for being complacent and driving too fast for the conditions.

*"Experience is a reliable guide when it is relevant to the contemporary and future operating environment and missions, and when it's filtered, processed and stored in the brain using enduring principles and useful, reliable thought models. When key elements of the operating environment, opponents, technology and missions change rapidly, how experience is translated into intuition is even more important."*6

Failure to use rapid intuitive decision-making in circumstances where it is required can be deadly. We must take slices of important information, called pattern recognition, make decisions and take the best option if, we are to survive dangerous and deadly encounters.

I have used the following scenario in training for 8 years. It is a tragic example of when decision-making is indecisive.

A young officer with about 1 year on the job observes a motor vehicle for speeding on the highway. The speed of the vehicle was approximately 98mph. The officer pursues the vehicle as it gets off the highway to secondary roads, the offender does not appear to be trying to escape, just traveling at such a speed he does not see the pursuing officer initially, the vehicle eventual pulls over, in a remote area. It is important to note this is a remote area of the country and back-up is a long way off at least 20 miles.

Once stopped, the officer and the traffic violator exit their vehicles. The violator, a male in his fifties walks towards the officer. The officer says "good morning sir" and they exchange pleasantries. The officer observes the subject has his hands in his pockets and tells him, "Sir take your hands out of your pockets." The subject asks, "Why?" "Take your hands out of your pockets sir," the officer demands again. The subject in a display of complete frustration, anxiety, non-compliance and contempt, starts to do what I describe as an Irish gig in the middle of the road all the while telling the officer; "here I am, here I am, shoot my F#$%ing ass!"

This behavior continues for 30 seconds, and then the subject approaches the officer exclaiming; "I am a F@#$ing Vietnam combat veteran" as a struggle ensues. The subject is struck by the officer's impact weapon, only to walk away towards his vehicle and open the door. All the while the officer is ordering him to "get back", "get back," "sir, get back" "sir get back here to me!" The subject is standing at the operator's driver's side door leaning inside while retrieving something. The officer is keeping his distance and giving orders to get back. The officer notices the subject has a long gun (M-1 carbine) in his hand and orders him "sir, put the gun down." He radios for back up and continues to tell the subject, "Sir, put the gun down, put it down now sir!" The subject shouts back an emphatic "NO!"

The officer continues several more times to order the subject to put the gun down, and then they exchange shots. The subject fires suppressive fire to keep the officer at bay while moving to avoid the officer's shots and closes the distance (the subject displays knowledge of tactics having likely served in the Army or Marine Corps). The officer and subject continue to exchange gun fire until the subject's rounds finally strike. While the young officer is struck, he continues to order the subject to put the gun down. The officer continues the fight and hits the subject center mass, but the subject is able to reload his firearm. After the subject has reloaded, he continues to shot and move and kills the young officer on the roadside. He then walks towards his personal vehicle shouting "mother f@#$er!"

In the end 60 rounds exchanged—33 by the subject and 27 by the officer–the Subject hit the officer a total of ten times and the officer struck the subject once. The young officer involved died at the scene. The subject escaped and was apprehended the next day.7

I use this video for training, and it has a powerful effect on me and law enforcement and security officers. This incident is a catalyst for my research on decision making.   The lessons are plentiful, but I focus on the decision-making. Keep in mind the review of this incident is for learning lessons and in no way is meant to dishonor the memory of a fallen brother officer. It could be one of us and any given day due to lack of decisive decision-making.

In my view this incident was about decision making or lack thereof decision making, despite all the physical aspects of conflict that unfolded.   At the core of this incident was not making decisions and seizing the initiative. This is an example of where rapid intuitive decision making could have, should have and would have ended in the favor of the officer. Why? What made him indecisive and therefore ineffective in this case?

Take a look at this fact; from the time the rifle was first seen to the first round being fired was 30 seconds.

30 seconds does not seem like a very long time, but in a hostile situation that is a lifetime. It is important when reviewing this incident and the decisions involved that the viewer is not getting lost in the gun fight. It should have never got that far. Let's break this down so we can see the

importance of understanding the decision making process based on experience gathered in this line of work, and discussions from the previous chapters in this handbook.

The subject was stopped for speeding, once stopped he exits his vehicle, which whether you agree or disagree with, is common practice known as a walk back in this part of the country. Once the conversation ensues and the request for the subject to remove his hands from his pockets ends in a diatribe of unusual behavior i.e. Irish gig in roadway, shouting "here I am", "here I am", "shoot my f@#$ing ass!", it turns to an assault on the officer. After which, the subject walks away. Intuitively, the officer's mind should have been screaming "BOLD action is required" as soon as the signs of unusual behavior began.

Bold action translates into several options,
1) I cannot handle this guy alone, he is too strong. I must disengage and regroup with back-up.
2) I can handle him physically, and I must use reasonable and necessary force to control the subject. I must act now and choose one of the two options before the situation escalates out of control (i.e., gun appears).

Then the subject walks to his vehicle, retrieves, readies a rifle and after several orders to put the weapon down, refuses and assaults the officer with lethal force.

Again bold action is required:
1) Close the distance rapidly with the Subject while he is in the process of readying the weapon, and if he does not comply, deadly force would be reasonable and necessary.
2) Seek cover and engage with deadly force.
3) Drive into, the non-compliant tactical advantage seeking and escalating to the imminent threat of deadly force subject.

4) Disengage from the suspect to a safe cover location remembering rifle verses pistol gives advantage to the subject. Continue to monitor with available resources, insuring public safety. Then a more detailed explicit plan can be implemented.
5) Why was the officer indecisive?

We will never know for sure, what the young officer was thinking but, I have listened to various responses from veteran officers involved in trying circumstances. They list: poor training, liability concerns, no leadership backing, no community backing, never thought it would happen to him (complacency), reluctance in taking a human life, being disciplined for using force etc.

These are few of the most common responses I have heard and discussed as factors surrounding indecisiveness. What Klein and Vandergriff have discovered through hundreds of observations of and the study of decision making in complex environments, is that people fail because they have not been prepared properly for this situation. What we consider as conventional training does not fit the bill.

The training aspect we will discuss below but the other responses listed as factors in indecisiveness are all part of what's known as friction-"*Everything is very simple in war, but the simplest thing is difficult.*"8 In the decision making aspect of conflict, any unthought-of, unresolved issues or concerns will slow the decision making cycle down, in an attempt to analyze these issues in the midst of a crisis situation, causing an overload of the senses and indecisiveness.

Under pressure and the survival stress response, kicks in. An automatic response takes place, shifting thought, from the frontal lobe (analytical thinking) to mid-brain (intuitive thinking).

According to Vandergriff "it is not automatic, just faster, and conditioned through doing many complex scenarios none of which were the same (each followed by constructive feedback sessions called AARs."9 A high stress situation causes chemical changes in the brain that cause you to think and act differently than when under normal conditions.

Most of those involved in traumatic situations give little or no thought to their behavior; they instinctively do what their experience has programmed them to do, through education, training and preparation. In this scenario it appears as though the young officer is over thinking the issue, and hence he is confused and indecisive. He was unable to adapt in time to take effective action.

The ability to adapt to changing conditions in rapidly changing conditions and seize the initiative requires the ability to think on your feet. *"Adaptability is an effective change in response to an altered situation. Adaptability is not speed of reaction, but the slower, more deliberate processes associated with problem solving."*10 This is where the observation and the ongoing process, orientation phase of the Boyd Cycle come into play.

The young officer in this case should have been making the observations via all his senses including intuition, obviously he was seeing everything unfold, but he failed absorb the information effectively and orient to the magnitude of the threat unfolding in front of him. This caused a form of paralysis when the survival stress response instinctively kicked in. You might ask, "If it's instinctive, why did he not do something?" The answer is he did not because he was not trained properly in rapid decision making (It is the responsibility of both the individual and his or her organization to prepare them).

I do not attribute the officer's indecisiveness to complacency in this case, because he initially appeared alert and aware by ordering the Subject's hands out of pockets in attempt to gain some semblance of control. Once the circumstances went outside the normal training of what he had received, he could not decide.

This problem rests not with this young, conscientious and brave officer. It rests with the culture of the institution he worked for. Out of date training is prevalent in the law enforcement and security professions.

Let me remind you, that there remains a place in our profession with what we call training. But, to just depend on it, puts us decades behind of what we now know about learning.

We should do all we can to learn from this incident and others like it, in an effort to evolve and adapt our approach and response strategies and tactics. Training in decision making, specifically deciding under pressure should be a staple of training for all law enforcement and security officers.

The Winning Combination Gathering Explicit and Implicit Information

In the heat of a rapidly changing set of circumstances where risk is high it is imperative we process information implicitly via the Boyd Cycle if we are to gain the edge and seize or regain the initiative. We also discussed situations where risk is low and time is prevalent for gathering detailed information and thoughtful analysis over time in an effort to implement whatever plan we wish to fit the circumstances or problem we are facing.

We talked a lot about the use of implicit information and rapid decision making and how there is no time for analytical processing of information. That is true in the spontaneous and unexpected circumstances our duties sometimes put us in. But what about when you're planning a dangerous mission, a high risk warrant services if in law enforcement or a response to an individual who may be potentially violent in the workplace if you're a security officer? Neither case has the individual involved forced anything dangerous and TIME is on your side.
In this type of situation you can take time and do a thorough background and intelligence investigation to learn all you can about the individual in question.

After gathering and analyzing the information collected, you can notify the proper authorities such as law enforcement and employers in an effort to prepare a plan and intervene based on current practices. In law enforcement, you can take precautions as well by calling out a highly trained response team. They are better equipped and prepared to handle the type of service required.

You can put a detailed plan deciding when and where you want to execute the plan into action.

You can put all the right personnel in the right places before implementing any action. You can prepare by doing your homework and gathering all the explicit details.

Once in place and the plan goes into action, and contact is made, the implicit side of the equation is back at the forefront because good plans should actually resemble the study biology instead of an engineering problem. In biology successful organizations evolve, while those who don't die. In engineering everything is linear leaving little to chance. For over a century, the U.S. military and law enforcement approached problems as if they were engineering problems, when in fact, it is more like biology.

Organizations and how they solve problems should evolve. The preparation and planning cannot take into account the silent evidence, the thoughts and motivations going on in the mind of an adaptive individual with his own ideas and plans. Personal development needs to include training in the Boyd Cycle using several approaches talked about in this handbook. This leads to situational awareness and adaptation as long as the plan is allowed to evolve. So you must be prepared to adapt to the changing circumstances, only in this case will you have all the tools and personnel on scene and ready to take whatever action is necessary based on the subject's response. This is the combination of explicit and implicit information gathering and both decision making models in an effort to give you every advantage in setting up the environment and individual for your success.

You can do this on the fly in a variety of circumstances by slowing down and thinking while in route to domestic violence or an alarm call. Use the time in route to the call for "if/then thinking" as it relates to your approach strategies such as; park down the street a few hundred yards and approach on foot to the alarm or domestic. You will be amazed at what more explicit information you can observe to improve your orientation of what's going on.

We take too many "tactically troubled" short cuts in this profession and pay with the loss of life. Give yourself the advantages and set yourself up to respond. Let's stop mistaking good luck for good tactics and harness every possible way to adapt, learn and evolve in our abilities to make better decisions and hence more tactically savvy techniques that give us the edge we need.

Chapter 12
Creating and Nurturing the Decision Making Environment

Complexity of Decisions

We discussed the Recognized Primed Decision Making and the importance of understanding and employing the Boyd Cycle to process with implicit and explicit information in earlier chapters on critical decision making. Earlier, we used several examples of where and how this applies to the everyday work we do. We also discussed two ways we process information analytically, when there is plenty of time and the risk is lower, as well as intuitively made decisions when time is scarce and risk is high. This leads to an understanding that critical decisions can be complex especially in environments where conflict and competitive minds collide.

We often after a decision is made, struggle to explain our responses appropriately. Decision makers have problems articulating their decisions and actions. And those who review the decision, struggle to understand the action. This leads to unnecessary suspicion from investigators and frustration on the part of the decision maker. This fact creates problems in the individual decision maker, making future decisions, as well as effects the whole organizations decision making capabilities, why?

There is confusion, uncertainty and mistrust over what is a good or bad decision. Officers are often told they made a bad decision, are disciplined over it and told to *"get out there and handle it right the next time."* No explanation as to why the decision was bad or how he/she may do it better, just get out there and do what's right! This is unacceptable and creates a risk adverse culture. Then, this creates unnecessary friction. In turn this slows down of the decision making cycle, which is both dangerous and leads to an ineffective organization. Not acceptable in professions where life and death are part of the mix.

We must seek more knowledge and understanding of how conflict unfolds and how we make decisions, if we are to be more effective at making and reviewing them. How we handle our officers after their decisions are made is critical to the long term health and effectiveness of our law enforcement organizations.

We use *Complexity theory* in an effort to understand the dynamic nature of conflict and decision making.

Briefly put, complexity theory postulates how complex systems are capable of generating simple patterns, and conversely, how simple systems are capable of displaying complex behaviors.[1]

We must have some understanding of complexity theory and how it relates to the complex nature of humans and human behavior in competitive environments, if we are to explain or gain understanding and comprehension of the environment, behaviors and events around us. "What's happening now?"

This definition of complexity fits perfectly in the world of law enforcement and security where rapid decisions making is necessary to fulfill our obligations to protect and serve the community or organization. To perform a decision in a competitive environment or, to understand what happened, if you are reviewing or investigating the circumstances surrounding a decision, you must take into consideration that conflict is a complex phenomenon full of uncertainties, and a vast array of other problematic factors that cause friction and slow decision making down. That small change in the individuals, the environment and in the situation itself can produce significantly larger outcomes, like winning or losing, life or death.

I want to focus on how we can effectively create an environment of good decision makers. An organization must develop sound decision makers in an environment that includes ongoing development through innovative training and the nurturing of strong character. Strength of character is the bedrock of rapid decision making.

Training

One of the best resources I have read on the training and leadership aspects of developing rapid decision making is Don Vandergriff's book, *Raising the Bar: Creating and Nurturing Adaptability in the Changing Face of War*. Vandergriff has spent years researching and fine tuning his methods of learning and education in the United States Army. His leadership model called Adaptive Leader Methodology (ACM) in Chapter 3 of the book is for developing rapid decision makers. It is now being accepted by the U.S. Army, specifically at the United States Military Academy at West Point New York in the Department of Military Instruction as well as U.S. Army Cadet Command and in the U.S. Marine Corps Infantry Officer Course and the Expeditionary Warfare School. After all is said and done, what we do in rapidly changing circumstance is to think on our feet, "Adapt"! 2

*"Adaptability is defined as "an effective change in response to an altered situation. Adaptability is not speed of reaction, but the slower, more deliberate processes associated with problem solving."*3 To be effective on the street you must be able to process information under pressure quickly but deliberately.

Through continual development with varied scenarios and constant feedback from mentors, peers and instructors, people learn to pick up on signs and signals that signify change is taking place, and then be able to respond accordingly.

The type of development Vandergriff speaks of enables an individual to synthesize multiple courses of action faster in a given situation, and then pick an appropriate one, then act on it. This is the orientation part of Boyd's OODA loop, and it is the most important part. Once an individual orients on the key aspect of what they have observed, then, decide and act parts become easier and less stressful.

Vandergriff discovered after years of watching hundreds of

students, the more tactical decision games they did, accompanied by good AARs, the better they handled real world situations (this is based on continual feedback from his students in combat and in dangerous policing situations).

To meet and deal with the types of crime, crime problems, conventional and unconventional threats we face, we must develop and nurture mutual trust and strength of character with in our organization and community to make effective decisions, especially decisions under pressure. "Raising the Bar" describes key characteristics of adaptive individuals. Which I agree is critical to possess if we are to be successful and change the internal and external culture which affects how we respond and deal with the serious issues we all face.

Vandergriff's approach develops adaptability in leaders focusing on five areas:
(1) **Intuitive**-this enables rapid decision-making without conscious awareness or effort
(2) **Critical thinker**- the ability to achieve understanding, evaluates viewpoints, and solves problems
(3) **Creative Thinker**-equally important, called fingerspitzengefühl or the feeling in the tip of one's fingers (Napoleon called it a "gut" feeling)
(4) **Self-Aware**-an understanding of one's own strengths and weaknesses
(5) **Social Skills**-the ability, to assess people's strengths and weaknesses, the use of communication skills, and the art of listening.4

These characteristics are critical to being a good decision maker and adaptive individual. The characteristics listed above, have been talked about in the law enforcement and security professions for years. Let's develop and etch them at the forefront of our minds by conducting valuable training and setting high standards that focus on these characteristics.

As mentioned above there have been efforts made in the area

of cognitive/physical training which use force on force role plays, Sim-munitions and simulators all great tools to enhance this effort. At the heart of all this training, or as Vandergriff says development, is the ability for instructors to facilitate the after action review after each event.

The problem we face in law enforcement and security is that the vast majority of officers do not receive the training due to budget constraints, short staffs and the nature of what we do (little time available), creating a shortfall on this great training reaching everyone who works the street. But the biggest obstacle to this type of development is cultural. Once again a *mindset shift* is needed in how and when we train to develop these characteristics and skills necessary. But, surprisingly, as advanced as Vandergriff's model appears to be, it requires little resources, just very good instructors who understand its principles and how to teach within the framework of Boyd's OODA loop.5

Mindset Shift... Take Advantage of Time!

Col. John Boyd described conflict as "time competitive" observation, orientation, decision and action cycles discussed above in previous chapters. These time competitive cycles should also be considered in preparation for future encounters, taking advantage of available time on shift to train and develop decision makers.6

Most agencies do not spend the time or money on training frontline personnel. Those agencies that do, send their personnel to training send them to a one day, two day, or week long training classes that use out of date methods of learning, i.e., *competency theory* focused on short term memorization presented using power point lectures etc. These types of training classes are good for short term measures of memory. According to Dr. Bjork, Dean of UCLA's department of Psychology and the leading learning expert, it does not promote long term continued learning.

The problem here is, two-fold
    (1) Training is conducted with outdated learning models
    (2) In most cases you cannot afford to send enough personnel to get an organizational benefit from the training.

If your agency can afford it, and send everyone, you can only send, once, with no follow-up. Problem with this is, the skills learned; perish quickly due to lack of conditioning through repetitive training. The benefits of cognitive and physical training are perishable, so if we are to be successful in creating and nurturing these skills it takes repetition and constant work if there is to be any real long term benefits.

The *"shift of mindset"* comes into play when changing a culture. There are numerous examples of how this shift in culture can occur, such as taking advantage of downtime during a working shift, such as roll call, to train. Extend roll calls or guard mount time by 15-20 minutes, use uncommitted time on the shift to conduct a mini-training scenario with TDGs. Another aspect is doing it during physical training. Vandergriff has written an entire annex in a handbook on how to develop adaptability while developing the physical aspect of our profession.   Yes, some of this development is still up to individual initiative!

Creating Decision Makers with Tactical Decision Games (TDGs)
Highly effective method of training that develops rapid decision making is a tool called the tactical decision game (TDG) or decision making exercise (DME) or the tactical decision exercise (TDE—as it is called at United States Military Academy's Department of Military Instruction). This is a critical piece of Vandergriff's training methodology with the military. He has achieved great results in using these games to develop decision makers who will demonstrate adaptability in combat. As we pointed out earlier, Vandergriff has received great feedback from those serving overseas and on the streets as to the

benefits of the TDG's in creating decision makers performing for high stakes and under high pressure.7

Tactical decision games are situational exercises on paper representing a snap shot in time. A scenario is handed out that describes a problem related to your profession (law enforcement, security, military, business, etc.).

The facilitator sets a short time limit for you to come up with a solution to the problem presented. The TDGs can be conducted individually or in a group setting. As soon as time is up, with the facilitator using "time hacks", an individual or group is told to present their course of action.

What you did and why?
It is important that individuals or groups working together are candid and honest in their responses. You're only fooling yourself to do otherwise. The lesson learned from the TDGs can make you more effective and safe in the performance of your job. The time to develop the strength of character and the courage to make decisions comes here, in the training environment. Mistakes can be made here that do not cost a life, while valuable lessons are learned.

The facilitator/instructor plays a pivotal role to successfully implementing TDGs. Their job is to insure responses are brought out and lessons are learned from the scenario. This can be done while working. I know because we have used them on my department and I have used them training security companies. It takes some effort, but can indeed be done.

The TDGs are effective at developing decision making in the field. In the few years we used TGDs in the Walpole police department, officers went from the initial thought of what are we doing this for? To getting involved and discussing strategy and tactics necessary to resolving the problem faced in the TDG setting. This evolved to applying what was learned, to the street under pressure.

Tactical response and approaches to calls, communications, and use of tactical basics such as: contact/cover principle and cover and concealment, approach strategies, perimeter containment and overall officer safety improved greatly employing these short scenarios.

The introduction of decision making exercises also improved an officer's knowledge of laws and policy and procedures.

This simple tool works and works well. I use the term simple tool but, make no mistake, its work in implementing and conducting these exercises, particularly learning the art of facilitating. Developing scenarios and insuring appropriate lessons are learned takes thought and innovation to insure proper training is taking place.   The instructor/facilitator needs to understand their job, which is to draw out answers, not give them out. I must emphasize this point because I have made that mistake in conducting the exercises. The goal is to make students and subordinates to discover the answers. It is not to create followers.   We have enough of that in our professions already.

The TDGs are about developing individual, initiative driven frontline leaders who can make decisions that meet the mission of the agency. *"TDGs are used to teach leaders how to think and to train and reinforce established ways of doing something, such as task training. The techniques can be traced back at least to the Chinese general and military theorist Sun Tzu, who was advocating their use more than 2,500 years ago."*8

The decision making critique (DMC) or AAR is another critical component to developing decision makers. The AAR is conducted after the decisions are made and discussed after student responses. This is where the instructor/facilitator again draws out lessons learned from the group critique. The facilitator keys on two aspects of the TDG, was the decision made in a timely manner? Secondly, what was the rationale of the student or group in making their decision? It is very important that they defend their rationale or reason for making the decision in their own words. As Vandergriff continues to drill into students that attend his workshop, *"it is not about the tactics but the decisions"* when facilitating the discussion of a

TDG.

I have been asked how often you conduct the exercises. Keep in mind that the benefit of developing rapid decision makers comes from constant conditioning, but varying the conditions and situation each time.

Like anything else conditioning comes from repetition, but unlike task training (rote memorization), repetition means constantly changing the conditions while focusing on the five aspects of adaptability mentioned earlier. Realistically in an environment that has no specific training unit, and the person in charge of training has multiple tasks such as running daily operations, in charge of investigations, scheduling and frontline supervisory responsibilities, it is challenging. It is worth the effort to conduct these exercises. Here are some examples as to how a multi-tasking, understaffed agency can reap the benefits of conducting TDGs and developing adaptive personnel.

In our environment with shifts it's tough to do TDGs daily, although it can be done. If it gets demanding and busy on the shift you "ADAPT" and handle the necessary call for service, then when things slow down get back at the TDG (we now always have one ready "opportunity training"). The method used in my department was 1 game per month, 12 training evolutions that were not taught elsewhere with numerous lessons learned, from each TDG. The training objectives and lessons learned, did improve decision making and the tactical mindset of officers with just 12 TDGs conducted. There was a significant difference in responses to calls and how they were handled.9

How to conduct TDGs
Here is an example of a TDG.

It is 1AM. You receive a dispatch reporting that a prisoner escaped in a marked police unit with a fellow officer's gun. The suspect is a female emotionally disturbed prisoner who was returning after an evaluation from the hospital transported by a fellow officer.

Ten (10) minutes later it's reported she has shown up at her sister's house that has custody of "her" child. She kidnaps her own child and shoots and kills the sister's family dog. She leaves the scene and comes into contact with a fellow officer responding to the location.

She drives at a high rate of speed towards this officer, hits the driver's side door, officer jumped from and shoots at her but misses. She continues to flee, crashes the car and then flees on foot with her child.

A search is commenced for 5 hours when she suddenly reappears in town, on the street, pointing the gun at police and her child who she is holding in her arms. She begins to laugh and taunt and makes statements "I will shoot you" and points the gun at those around, including her child and the news media that is on scene. From a car length away, you begin to negotiate. She then states I have ruined my life. You are fixing to work a murder suicide.

You then give instructions to your students focusing on "how do you handle this situation?" Or, "What do you do now officer? You have 30 seconds, begin!"

When the 30 seconds are up you pick individuals to give their responses. Get them up in front of the room (add a little pressure) and have them explain what they did and why. Do this individually with each participant. When all have completed get them as group to talk and critique each response. You will be amazed at what learning takes place.

You can also do these in a group setting when time is tight. Just give the group the scenario and begin a discussion as to how it's handled. This is again Adaptability, changes do to "time" constraints, and we get the lessons in. Our jobs are about change and adapting to those changes. Take advantage of the time you have to better prepare for the dynamic encounters we are faced with.

Our goal should be to do more of this type of training. To take advantage of any down time available to get a TDG in, when staffed with appropriate numbers of properly trained instructors (minimum 1 per shift) you could easily do a game a week (52 per year) which would be, much more beneficial to all, individuals and agency. Take advantage of actual calls and the lessons learned from them by utilizing After Action Reviews, which in my mind is TDG in reverse.

You actually made decisions and resolved the problem (real world lessons). There is no more valuable training evolution than to take an actual situation you experienced and break down the lessons learned and adapt the lessons to a future response. The TDGs work and work well at developing decision makers and enhancing knowledge from past training.

To bring the training program to an even higher level of learning programs of instruction should use the method explained above, to build experiences, which turn into pattern recognition.

The program of instruction Vandergriff describes, consists of four primary pillars and includes the use of:
   (1) A case study learning method
   (2) Tactical decision games
   (3) Free play force on force exercises
   (4) Feedback through the leader evaluation system.10

This complete comprehensive program of instruction, unify the approaches above in accomplishing learning objectives, which include
   (1) Improving one's ability to make decisions quickly and effectively
   (2) Making sense of new situations, seeing patterns, and spotting opportunities and options that was not visible before
   (3) Becoming more comfortable in a variety of situations
   (4) Developing more advanced and ambitious tactics

(5) Becoming more familiar with weapons capabilities, employment techniques, and other technical details.11

Start with the case studies and TDGs and build upon the program to develop the best decision makers we can. From TDGs, you move into force on force training environment, but all are followed by a facilitated AAR. The cost of not doing so is too high!

Mutual Understanding Community/Protectors: Training Those We Serve

An important piece of decision making is the necessary element of being able to explain our decisions. Explain them to folks in the community or organization who may not have a good understanding as to how we decide under pressure.

In this chapter we discussed intuitive decisions based on implicit information gathered in high risk, little time available scenarios. We understand it, we know what we did and why, but still we have a difficult time explaining it to the world sitting in review from behind the desk in a safe environment, with plenty of time, analyzing the circumstances with an analytical mind. And explicit answers to our decisions are sought.

Why do we have this problem and how do we make those who do not do, what we do, understand? Perceptions and orientation of what we do is based as Boyd has stated on, past experience, genetic heritage, cultural traditions, and unfolding circumstances. People see things, as they, view the world. Based on what Boyd has stated here in regards to how we orient (perceive) the world.12

Can we expect the citizens, to understand and make an appropriate judgment of our actions if most of their perceptions, of what we do come from, the abstract world of media, news, movies, television and print?

If our actions are based on something they heard that has never been disproved or they have never experienced, how do they begin to understand it, in a way that the silent evidence (thought process, decision making, survival stress, etc.) is considered in the process? Again the process should be training and being more open and honest as to, what we do and why we do it.

As a community and a law enforcement organization we say we want to see and get to know our officers, yet if they stop, get out of their cars and have a conversation with someone, they are seen as goofing off and not working. If they are seen in their cars parked on the roadside or in a parking lot conducting surveillance or traffic duties again the inference is, they are goofing off. These examples seem and are simplistic, yet they result in complaints, complaint investigations and at times, reprimands of individual officers. Officers in turn begin to see the community, whether a city or town or the occupants of a facility, they protect, as fickle minded.

The community sees officers as out of touch. Leadership, community or organizational, get wrapped up in the politics of this and in short a great divide is formed which leads to distrust on both sides. This is a sad reality for those on both sides of the coin which in the end leads to poor results.

To do the job at hand protecting and serving, it is pretty much understood that the community as a whole, must work together with law enforcement. To do this there must be a better understanding of what each other's role is and that role is mutual. The community wants to be safe, and law enforcement's objective is to make it that way. We are on the same page. So how do we get to the same paragraph on the page?

Training, education and learning is the key to closing this divide. This is nothing new. It's been written and talked about in the law enforcement realm for more than 30 years.

Although the foundation of experiential learning goes back centuries as Vandergriff explains in his research expounded upon in his article "From Swift to Swiss Tactical Decision Games and Their Place in Military Education":

*"In the late 1700s, Pestalozzi developed his theory that students would learn faster on their own if allowed to "experience the thing before they tried to give it a name." TDGs were used to sharpen students' decision-making skills and to provide a basis for evaluating them on their character."*13

I find it both fascinating and alarming us (law enforcement and security professions), are just recently beginning to conduct this type of training that's been around with documentation that it works and works well. A question of character and lack of knowledge seems to be the answer as to why we are not?

In fairness there has been a multitude of training classes on community oriented policing and problem oriented policing across the nation on the topic of building community trust. But not much of this training focuses on decision making under pressure in for example; use of force situations.

Where training the population in use of force decision making has been conducted as in the LAPD program, there has been great results in bridging the divide between protection professionals and the community. It is a process of communicating and sharing information on both sides of the spectrum to help each understand what's expected and how we go about doing our jobs effectively.

We must continue to bridge this gap between protector and the citizenry by agencies offering more of this training, such as citizen's police academies, working with community groups, schools and things like Local Emergency Planning Committees (LEPC). These groups all educate in their area of expertise, not to make experts, but to gain an understanding of what their goals and objectives are and then what methods are utilized in making decisions to help in understanding.

In the law enforcement and security fields we would put citizens and community leaders in circumstances we handle and have them role play them out. Or use TDGs to give them a feel for the types of decisions we make. Simple methods of education and learning, to bridge this gap which is critical if we want those to understand what it is we do and how we make decisions under pressure. This result in the community as a whole interested and involved and helps all understand the job we perform as well as the risks and consequences.

Adapting to the changing conditions is what makes a true professional. Doing things the way we have always done them is fool hearted and unprofessional. On the other hand change for the sake of change is just as fool hearted. Effective change is meeting the challenges that lie ahead and prepare all for both conventional and unconventional problems and threats. It takes strength of character and leadership, leadership from frontline personnel, mid-level supervisors and administrators, as well as community and local government leaders to reach these goals.

Leadership Roles in the Decision Making Process

The main component in the development of good decision makers falls on the individual and individual efforts. Yes, but the climate for this development comes from the top, in leadership. To achieve the results sought after, if we truly want to call ourselves professionals and prepare for the challenges we face in the future, leaders must LEAD. It is the Leader's role, to create and nurture the appropriate environment that emboldens decision makers. Leader development is two way, it falls on the individual, but the organization's leaders must set the conditions to encourage it.

The aim of leadership is not merely to find and record failures in men, but to remove the cause of failure.
~W. Edwards Deming14

"Leadership can be described as a process by which a person influences others to accomplish an objective, and directs his or her organization in a way that makes it more cohesive and coherent."15 This is the definition we should subscribe too.

However, all too often I have had both frontline personnel and mangers tell me that this cannot be done. This type of training and developing initiative driven personnel will cause more problems for departments and agencies in dealing with liability issues and complaints because control is lost. I wholeheartedly disagree with his sentiment.

The opposite is indeed the effect you get. This is not a free reign type of leadership. Matter of fact if done appropriately it will take more effort and time on your part as a leader, because you will be involved. Your training program will be enhanced and the learning that takes place unifies your agencies and all the individuals in it. How? Through the system described above which develops "mutual trust" throughout the organization because the focus is now on results. The "how to" is left to the individuals and the instructors. But a culture must exist to encourage what the Army calls outcome based training.16

Mutual trust (unity) in turn allows individuals to think and innovate when solving problems, because they know it is what's expected. It's known by all, they will be held accountable for their actions good and bad. And those leaders will be there standing with them in the aftermath of a good or bad decision and that everything will be done to learn from and adapt the lessons too future operations.

If we expect frontline personnel to go out and deal with dangerous circumstances and resolve them, they must be insured leadership will be doing all they can do to develop, nurture and stand behind decisions made. Also be willing to except responsibility when things go wrong. The world we work in is complex and chaotic yet in the vast majority of situations we handle without drastic or tragic results. This is done with "very little training" in decision making.

However in the less than one percent of the time for example a law enforcement officer uses force, leadership fails in backing an officer's decision. Why? We could write another article on, politics, lack of knowledge in conflict, an unwillingness to take a stand on behalf of the decision maker, unwillingness to correct an obvious problem they observe.

If you take on a leadership role, then you must LEAD and have the strength of character to do what needs to be done in creating the appropriate environment. The single most reason for failure is to make a decision, "We will not get backed by our bosses!" These words are uttered not from the 10%, but from those who do care about what they do, yet feel for whatever reason they will not be backed after they have done what they have sworn or are duty bound to do in their efforts to resolve conflicts.

A leader's role is to inspire others to complete the mission, whatever the mission is. It's to develop unity and focus. It's to hold themselves and others accountable for actions taken, rewarding good decisions and learning from and if warranted disciplining for bad decisions.

This must be done fairly with integrity leading the way or we will not be prepared for the problems and threats that we will face. A leader's role is to reduce friction in decision making of frontline personnel. Try it, I guarantee you will relish the benefits and results.

Chapter 13
Exploring Situational Awareness

OODA Loops: The Explorer Mentality...And Recognizing Patterns of Behavior

Col. John Boyd explained that a person in a conflict must **observe** the environment, to include himself, his adversary, the moral, mental and physical situation, potential allies and opponents. He must **orient** to what it all means, "what's going on" which is part of the ongoing process throughout the situation. Orientation involves the information observed, one's genetic heritage, social environment and prior experiences (birth-present) that forms a picture of the situation. The results one forms during the orientation phase must be **decided** upon and an attempt need be made to carry out the decision, and finally, he must **act.**

Anticipation can be the key to winning, but if anticipation is based on yesterday's situation it can be deadly! Never anticipate the outcome unless it's based on the current situation. It is great to anticipate trouble but anticipation of the outcome of any encounter should be based on clear sight and cool minded orientation as to what's going on!   All situations we respond to are unknown risks so we must be constantly vigilant. Your Boyd Cycle must be fluid! It is important to understand both the science and art of tactics and how to apply what we know to the current circumstances.   Fighting today's battle with yesterday's tactics could be deadly! 1

The Butcher Knife: a Lesson on Anticipation

You are an officer assigned to handle an emotionally disturbed person threatening suicide according to a person who called dispatch.

The location and assailant are known to you and with whom you frequently interact with for the same type of problem.

You arrive on scene, park out front, get out of your patrol car and begin to talk with the woman allegedly in emotional distress. She tells you she is fine and that she did not need police services.

After your assessment, you felt she was OK and not a threat to herself or someone else, so you cleared the scene. No sooner than you leave, the previous caller, a friend of the woman in distress, called the station and stated the victim was indeed in emotional distress and had lied to the cop and that she was going to kill herself. Again you think, "this type of behavior is a normal pattern for this location."

You go back to the location and in route you call off back-up stating *it would just be another transport to the hospital!* You go to the door which is open and begin to speak with the woman who is now very angry and animated. She shouts that she does not want to go to the hospital. You continue the conversation in an attempt to persuade her to go. You step inside the crammed apartment kitchen (approximately 8ft by 10 feet).   In the kitchen, you position yourself with a refrigerator to your left, a kitchen table to the right (with just enough walking space between the two), and a kitchen counter behind you making it difficult for you to move freely. As you talk with the distraught and angry woman, she reaches behind her back, lifts her shirt, and quickly draws a large knife, removes it from its sheath and thrusts it towards your chest. You are shocked and surprised at what's happening, but you quickly grab the knife hand, sweep the woman off her feet and to the ground. She continues to struggle, and you use several strikes to get her to stop and regain control.

Given this situation, what would you have done?
- Would you have waited for backup prior to entering the apartment verses calling it off?
- Would you have taken a different tactical approach and response?
- Would you have considered less lethal options, did you have a choice?

- Would you have used deadly force?
- If so, are you confident with the use of your firearm?
- Did your positioning and close proximity to the subject negate even considering your firearm?
- What did you miss here?
- What part of *situational awareness* allowed you to think that this situation was going to end the same as it always does—with an uneventful transport to the hospital and the woman evaluated.   After all it was routine and within the normal patterns of behavior you experienced every time you have responded to this case.   Why only minute or two later was her response different?
- This time why did she decide to try and kill you?
- More importantly, why did you believe it was going to be business as usual?
- And even a more critical question, do you understand the **WHY** behind the tactics you choose to use or are you just trying to force the square tactical technique you learned into the round chaotic shaped, tactical situation?
- Do you realize tactics has as much to do about thinking as it do about the physical application of the technique?

As A.M. Gray, the 29th Commandant of the Marine Corps says; *"In tactics, the most important thing is not whether you go left or right, but why you go left or right."*2

In the end the officer in this *real life scenario* fulfilled the number one rule in law enforcement. **"He went home at the end of his shift!"** All too often this is where the learning ends, a cop comes out alive and we rightfully celebrate the victory.

But what about the lessons in recognizing patterns of behavior and their opposites or anomalies?

How would the explorer mentality and situation awareness have changed this situation and reduced officer created jeopardy?

What might the answers to these questions mean to our responding to and dealing with the host of crisis we must deal with in the future?

Would you continue to use the same tactics and followed the same procedures?

What would you do differently if you decided to continually explore and learn throughout the tactical situation verses anticipating the same old outcome?

Direct experience with deadly force situations is extremely limited even in the most active law enforcement officer career, so we must take advantage of the opportunity to learn from each and every experience. How do we apply these lessons to shape or influence events so that we not only magnify our spirit and strength but also influence potential adversaries?

We also need to win over the uncommitted so that they are drawn toward our philosophy and are empathetic toward our success?

Do we not owe it to ourselves, those we care for and those we serve to learn the most from each experience?

Recognizing Patterns of Behavior

The first quality for a commander is a cool head which receives a just impression of things; he should not allow himself to be confused by either good or bad news; the impressions which he receives successively or simultaneously in the course of a day should classify themselves in his mind in such a way as to occupy the place which they merit; because reason and judgment are the result of the comparison of various impressions taken into just consideration.

~Napoleon 3

It is said we recognize things through the rule of opposites. We understand day as compared to night, happy as compared to sad, failure from success, and peace from war and safety from danger. From the great book, *The Gift of Fear* by Gavin Debecker, I remember a scenario that illustrates this rule of pattern recognition and the rule of opposites.

A Repair man comes to the house to fix an item. What about

his behavior is favorable (meaning his intentions are on the job at hand) or what about his behavior is unfavorable (meaning he may have other things on his mind)? Recognizing patterns of behavior and then their anomalies is critical to survival.4

Here are some for you to consider as the repairman makes his house call.

Favorable:
- Does his job and no more
- Respectful of privacy
- Stands at appropriate distance
- Waits to be escorted
- Keeps his comments to the job at hand
- Mindful of the time-works quickly
- Doesn't care if others are home
- Doesn't care if others are expected
- Doesn't pay undue attention to you

Unfavorable:
- Offers to help on unrelated tasks
- Curious, asks too many questions
- Stands too close
- Walks around the house freely
- Tries to get into discussions on other topics; makes personal comments
- No concern about time; in no hurry to leave
- Wants to know if others are home
- Wants to know if others are expected
- Stares at you

If you are away from home and out working the street, which attributes would you want loved ones to observe in the repair man visiting your home? The answer is rather obvious as it is very apparent as to which behavior does and does not fit the context of the situation. This simple lesson in recognizing patterns of behavior and the rule of opposites is a survival mechanism we should all etch in our minds not just for the repair man but for our street encounters as well.

Officer safety and effectiveness is hinged on knowledge and understanding. This knowledge and understanding is what we call *situation awareness* which is our ability to collect, correlate and store data in a fluid, dynamic environment, accurately predicting future events based on this real time data collection so we may decide and act accordingly. In other words we observe, orient, decide and act based on the unfolding and current conditions and what we believe these unfolding conditions mean.

The Boyd Cycle (OODA-LOOP) is a reflection of the decision and action cycles that are used in making decisions throughout daily encounters. These cycles can result from subconscious and conscious acts of observation and orientation. This means we must always be looking, exploring for behavior, to include conversation that doesn't fit the context of the contact. This includes not only the overt furtive gestures often described in training. It also includes words and or actions such as: verbal tone, phrases that make no sense, micro facial expressions and non-verbal gestures that are incongruent with the circumstances. This is also includes any other outside obvious or subtle factors that may dictate changes in the circumstances making them more dangerous. They also include ones that allow you to observe and orient to an opportunity to seize the initiative and gain voluntary compliance or physical control. Close observations and continually exploring the situation is paramount to making winning decisions and taking sound actions in dynamic encounters.

Situation awareness means possessing an explorer mentality
A general never knows anything with certainty, never sees his enemy clearly, and never knows positively where he is. When armies are face to face, the least accident in the ground, the smallest wood, may conceal part of the enemy army. The most experienced eye cannot be sure whether it sees the whole of the

enemy's army or only three-fourths. It is by the mind's eye, by the integration of all reasoning, by a kind of inspiration that the general sees, knows, and judges.
~Napoleon 5

In order to effectively gather the appropriate information as it's unfolding we must possess the explorer mentality. We must be able to recognize patterns of behavior. Then we must recognize that which is outside that normal pattern.

Then, you take the initiative so we maintain control. Every call, every incident we respond to possesses novelty. Car stops, domestic violence calls, robberies, suspicious persons etc. These individual types of incidents show similar patterns in many ways. For example, a car stopped normally pulls over to the side of the road when signaled to do so. The officer when ready, approaches the operator, a conversation ensues, paperwork exchanges, and the pulled over car drives away. A domestic violence call has its own normal patterns; police arrive, separate involved parties, take statements and arrest aggressor and advise the victim of abuse prevention rights.

We could go on like this for all the types of calls we handle as each type of incident on its own merits, does possess very similar patterns. Yet they always, and I mean always possess something different be it the location, the time of day, the person you are dealing with. Even if it's the same person, location, time and day, the person you're dealing who may now be in a different emotional state and his/her motives and intent may be very different.

This breaks that normal expected pattern. Hence, there is a need to always be open-minded, alert and aware, exploring for the signs and signals of positive or negative change in conditions.

In his Small Wars journal article "Thinking and Acting like an Early Explorer" Brigadier General Huba Wass de Czege (US Army Ret.) describes the explorer mentality:

While tactical and strategic thinking are fundamentally different, both kinds of thinking must take place in the explorer's brain, but in separate compartments. To appreciate this, think of the metaphor of an early American explorer trying to cross a large expanse of unknown terrain long before the days of the modern conveniences. The explorer knows that somewhere to the west lies an ocean he wants to reach. He has only a sketch-map of a narrow corridor drawn by a previously unsuccessful explorer. He also knows that highly variable weather and frequent geologic activity can block mountain passes, flood rivers, and dry up desert water sources. He also knows that some native tribes are hostile to all strangers, some are friendly and others are fickle, but that warring and peace-making among them makes estimating their whereabouts and attitudes difficult.6

The metaphor of the *early American explorer* fits policing and the complex problems we face on the street daily. As we search for peaceful outcomes to the situations we encounter numerous unknowns despite the similarities, in the types of incidents and crises we observe day to day. Standard operating procedures, policy and procedure practices are all very useful when we have standard problem and things go as we plan but what happens when things deviate from the standard and go outside the normal patterns? Here is where we must rely on resilience and adaptation, our ability and knowhow. Experienced people using their insights, imagination and initiative to solve complex problems as our ancestors, the early American explores did.

As we interact with people in dynamic encounters, the explorer mentality keeps us in the game; it keeps us alert and aware. The explorer mentality has us continually learning as we accord with a potential adversary and seek to understand his intent to the best of our ability. An officer who possesses the explorer mentality understands that an adversary has his own thoughts objectives and plans, many which he cannot hear, such as:

"I will do what I am asked," "I will not do what I am asked," "I will escape," "I will fight," "I will assault," "I will kill," "I will play dumb until...," "I will stab," "I will shoot," "he looks prepared I will comply," "he looks complacent I will not comply, etc."
The explorer never stops learning and is ever mindful of both obvious and subtle clues of danger and or cooperation.

The logic the explorer must follow is one that will exploit the potential for a successful crossing to the far ocean within the country the expedition is traversing, based on an understanding drawn from partial clues only. This is choosing a strategic logic or rationale to decide what short-term concrete ends are achievable, reflect progress and allow the expedition to learn how to make even more progress. Whatever his strategic rationale of the moment, it is only as good as his current understanding. It is inconceivable that any strategy of ways and means he could formulate at the outset would not require extensive revision as he progressed and learned more about the country. (Assuming he was not capable of easily overpowering all known and unknown potential difficulties – a very rare case, indeed.)
~Huba Wass de Czege, Brigadier General US Army, Retired 7

Strategic rationales for tactical actions are only good for the short term until they can be discarded and replaced by knowledge learned as a result of interacting with the complex environmental system you find yourself in. The environments are similar yet very different and in constant flux. Those we deal with could be hostile, friendly, and/or indifferent.

The explorer's journey into the wilderness, into the unknown is also a purposeful journey of learning. In fact, effective explorers are always improving their scouting. And the expedition's maps (plans, tactics, techniques, policies and procedures) are constantly in adjustment. They evolve.

Because choosing a strategic rationale for the next tactical action is a conscious act of creation, the responsible peacekeeper must support it. The exploring officer takes responsibility for the strategic choices of routes and objectives on his journey into the unknown. The routes and actions he takes have a direct impact on the outcomes he seeks. This ability must be created and nurtured always. It's hard work and hard work means an effort must be made to develop the necessary skills of observation employing all your senses.

You then combine these observations with the ability to make tactical decisions implicitly and explicitly considering time, and risk.   You then apply them to the given set of circumstances producing a positive outcome.

An officer who possesses the explorer mindset understands that circumstances dictate tactics and that it's not the other way around. He understands his training and experiences, the procedures and methods he has learned will only help him when things go as planned. He also understands that when the irrational and unexpected unfold he just may have to use his own insight and initiative along with innovative tactical ideas. Possessing the explorer mentality you not only recognize the normal patterns of conflict and behavior but you recognize and adapt to their opposites, buying yourself some critical time, time to choose a tactical option that's effective and safe.

Meet Officers Lewis and Clark-Exploring Situational Awareness
What if the famous explorers Lewis and Clark were police officers?   How would they look at the multitude of situations that cops handle from their viewpoint as explorers?

In the early 1800s they did not have two-way radios, cell phones, GPS, and computers, 6-inch policy and procedure books. They were given a one page hand written instruction from the Secretary of War as to their mission of exploring the new Louisiana Purchase and find a water route to the Pacific Ocean. They had to depend on their natural instincts and look at each exploration from a new and unique perspective observing their surroundings and trying to make sense of every situation. How much better would we be? How much safer on the street? Making headway in competitive situations in complex, unbounded, interactive, and unpredictable human environments, such as any extended business, military, or political endeavor, requires some new critical thinking about some old subjects – tactics, strategy, and operational art -- the art of campaigning.8

All law enforcement and security can benefit from the line of thinking in BG Huba Wass de Czege article.9
The metaphor in the article, *"the early American explorer"* relates to, law enforcement responding to calls for service. Often times in our world due to minimum standards in or lack of consistent training, know how, or the always dangerous "false sense of urgency" there is no exploration, no change in navigation. Instead response to a problem is just a direct route to the problem, like ducks in a row. Our officers use a detailed prescription, the school solution to problems requiring much more.

Street cops follow one another to the problem and attempt resolves it, is all too often the only thought process that goes into it. No observation and orientation taking place when it's necessary. Operational art is a concept foreign to most in our profession. Too much reliance on standard operating procedures, practices and too little reliance on the ability and knowhow of experienced people using their insights, imagination and initiative to solve complex problems.

The logic the explorer must follow is one that will exploit the potential for a successful crossing to the far ocean within the country the expedition is traversing, based on an understanding drawn from partial clues only. This is choosing a strategic logic or rationale to decide what short-term concrete ends are achievable, reflect progress and allow the expedition to learn how to make even more progress. Whatever his strategic rationale of the moment, it is only as good as his current understanding. It is inconceivable that any strategy of ways and means he could formulate at the outset would not require extensive revision as he *progressed and learned more about the country. (Assuming he was not capable of easily overpowering all known and unknown potential difficulties – a very rare case, indeed.)*10

The heavy policy and procedure driven culture stifles the initiative the explorer was forced to rely on. We cops get stuck in decision and action response mode developed out of context of the problems we face. The *"early American explorer"* had to adapt and make his decisions on the fly, based on the current conditions. This ability to decide under pressure makes a big difference in our effectiveness.

Full spectrum cops, in a cohesive learning environment, bound by trust (mutual trust) equals individuals and organizations, capable of campaigning and adapting to, shaping and reshaping the conditions as they unfold. In other words getting things effectively and safely done by adapting and doing! Don Vandergriff often reminds me that cultivation of adaptability requires a vast effort, from the top down as well as bottom up. Good leadership is a key!

*"The explorer's journey into the wilderness is also a purposeful journey of learning. In fact, effective explorers are always improving their scouting. And the expedition's maps are constantly in revision."*11

The numbers of cops getting killed in the line of duty over the last couple of years has escalated dramatically. In 2010 the officers feloniously killed in the line of duty was up 37% and a third of these cops were killed by ambush. In 2011 we already had 43 law enforcement officers killed in the line of duty up 2% from 2010. This is a dangerous trend and I am a firm believer that much of the reason why, lies in our lack of *knowledge and ability* to apply what we now in our heads to the street, known as operational art or *"campaigning"* as the General describes it. Old ways of training and leadership are clashing with the evolving face of crime and losing.

We are making some headway, slow moving but headway, in law enforcement utilizing Adaptive Course Methodology (ACM) and Outcomes Based Training and Education (OBT&E) to help create and nurture problem solvers and decision makers.

In a thread discussing this chapter with Colonel Casey Haskins, Director of the Department of Military Instruction (DMI), which employs ACM as part of OBT&E, of the United States Military Academy, West Point posed an important question:

*How do we develop creative thinkers? Answer: It can't be done in a rigid framework that prizes conforming to pre-approved solutions? A strategic end is conceptual and general; it cannot be specific or concrete. It would be foolish to make it so. A very specific desirable end may be impossible to achieve, while the route to an acceptable one may be readily at hand after some progress. Or, an even better outcome than could be first imagined may become available by a new route not currently exposed. Strategy is moving from one promising position to another, occasionally retracing steps to find a way around obstacles, and following where learning takes it.*12

At times explaining the relationship between Strategies, operational art and tactics can be difficult, as most see them as separate entities and fail to see the crucial relationship one has on the other.

As Col. John Boyd stated in an interview; Machines don't fight wars. People do and they use their minds. Operational art is not a level of war, or the art of generalship. It is what goes on in the explorer's mind, the mediating and balancing interaction between his strategic and tactical reasoning.13

Chapter 14
The Tactical Decision Maker: The Devil is Definitely in the Details

"The pursuit of data, in almost any field has come to resemble a form of substance abuse."
~Gary Klein, author Street Lights and Shadows: Searching for the Keys to Adaptive Decision Making 1

The ability to make quick decisions under pressure is the attribute most often sought in law enforcement, security and military personnel, especially for the front line operative. Such decisions are expected in the heat of rapidly changing and complex circumstances, often under life threatening conditions with limited information.

There is a recent trend in the law enforcement and security community, evidenced by laptops in patrol cars and the proliferation of smart phones that provide internet and social networking website access (such as *Twitter* and *Facebook*) used by agencies to gather more relevant data to improve on the ground decision making. But is this a good way to go? Are we approaching a point in which there is simply too much data supplied to the front line operative to permit critical decision making? Are we approaching the clichéd 'paralysis of analyses?

While law enforcement management is busy gathering and disseminating an ever greater stream of information, does it hamper or enable the operative? Are we doing it because it's available, or because it's wise to do so? Should we be limiting the supply of data to only targeted information, or should we be gathering as much as possible? Let's examine this more closely.

Jacob Bronowski stated, that *"Action depends upon understanding"* and understanding comes from harnessing our senses and searching for an answer as to what's going on. We analyze a situation searching for its meaning that will allow us to make decisions.

Is adding more details the same as expanding understanding of the situation at hand?

In our quest to save lives and stop violence we often set out on a mission to gather all of the information we possibly can. This seems like the right thing to do and it is often done when there is plenty of time to decide and risk is low, such as developing a school emergency response plan. The information gathered for the plan can be explicit and it can be analyzed, honed and tweaked in a way that makes it comprehensive.2

But what happens when a live emergency takes place, such as an active shooter for example. Is the search for details as important in this instance, or can the search for these details become problematic and delay response time? When an active shooter goes into action, the situation we planned for becomes instantly complex and time pressures. Uncertainty in the minds of those responding sets in almost immediately. Time is now scarce and risk is very high. There are lives at stake, and we must take action.

We ask ourselves: What's going on? How many shooters are there? How do I handle it? How should I approach? Which way should I enter? If I am the first responder, should I wait for back-up or enter and engage with the shooter? Is there time to wait or should I go? He was initially in the cafeteria and now there are reports of someone on the roof and in the west wing of the school; where should I go first? There are numerous kids running panicked; could one of them be the shooter? Can this really be happening here, or was the caller mistaken? It is happening here. Now what?

If we tried to answer the questions above "explicitly" we would have no time to respond and stop the ongoing deadly action as we search for answers to each of these questions. There will be more questions once you actually engage with the subject. Will he stop his action? Will he shoot? Should I shoot and eliminate the threat? There are innocent kids in the background; what if I shoot and miss?

A flood of questions will come to mind in the heat of a violent encounter. My point is, the questions will be there but the answers will come in the form judgment -- implicit and intuitive decisions based on your experience and training.

Attention to detail is not the sole answer in the non-linear world of violence. Instead it's paying **attention to detail that has meaning** in the heat of the moment.

In his book, *Street Lights and Shadows: Searching for the Keys to Adaptive Decision Making,* Gary Klein offers some insight into information and uncertainty:

*There are different types of uncertainty. Sometimes we are uncertain because we don't have the information we need. Sometimes we have the information but we don't know if we can trust it. Sometimes we trust it but it conflicts with other information we also believe. And sometimes we believe it but we can't figure out what it means.*3

Too much information can cause our brains to shut down and fail to respond accordingly. Trying to answer, every possible question, until we find explicit understanding, and the optimum solution, in the complex world of violence, is not strategically or tactically sound, operational art. I know this goes against the grain of how we normally think, but we must remember violent encounters despite their constant exploitation in the media are not normal events. Operational art required here is in our ability to gather information and manage it correctly on the fly and extract understanding that leads to effective action.

To be effective we must understand the differences in information, the time verses risk factor and how they relate to decisions we make. Like the shooting debate, is precision sighted shooting the best method or is it close quarter battle point shooting? The answer lies in our knowledge and ability to apply both based on the circumstances. When it comes to decision making, sometimes the devil is in the detail.

Chapter 15
"Friction" Why is the Simplest Thing, So Difficult?

If one has never personally experienced war, one cannot understand in what the difficulties constantly mentioned really consist, nor why a commander should need any brilliance and exceptional ability. Everything looks simple; the knowledge required does not look remarkable, the strategic options are so obvious that by comparison the simplest problem of higher mathematics has an impressive scientific dignity. Once war has actually been seen the difficulties become clear; but it is extremely hard to describe the unseen, all-pervading element that brings about this change of perspective.
~Carl von Clausewitz 1

- Why did you make that decision officer?
- Why did you go in the front door, instead of the back or side?
- Why did you not have the subject come outside to you?
- Why instead did you not set up a perimeter, containing the adversary and attempt to negotiate?
- Why did you do a face to face negotiation, with the subject armed with a knife, you know that is dangerous, don't you?
- Did you have to take him down with force?
- Why didn't you talk him out, use OC spray or Taser him instead?
- Why didn't you take a passenger side approach on that car stop?
- Why did you *walk up* on the vehicle to engage instead of having the subject *walk back* to you?
- Why didn't you see the gun, weren't you watching deadly hands?
- Couldn't you have chosen another option?

- What in the hell were you thinking?
- The bad guy had a gun why didn't you shoot?
- Why didn't you wait for back-up?
- You knew something bad was happening there, why, did you wait, for back-up?
- Why didn't you do this or do that?

These are all questions anyone who has been in law enforcement for any amount of time and has experienced a violent encounter has been asked or has even asked himself. We law enforcement professionals *what/if, if/then, or when/then* ourselves so much in an effort to prepare and become more effective on the streets you cannot help but question the decisions we make. This questioning and reviewing of our decisions is, in the *aftermath* of an encounter helpful to us.

This process of review known as an AAR or decision making critique teaches us valuable lessons helping us to adapt more effective methods and tactics to apply on the street.   **BUT** when in the heat of the moment, face to face with an adversary second guessing ourselves can be dangerous and risk lives, our own, and to those we are there to assist.

Why then, in the moment of decision is it so hard to decide? Why is it our preparation and planning, our policies and procedures come unraveled at the first hearing of the call, the first push, shove, clinch or punch, the first sight of a weapon or the first shot? Why is it, our decision making slows down or as Carl von Clausewitz described it why is there "friction" in our decision making? 2

Friction in Decision Making
"Friction is the only concept that more or less corresponds to the factors that distinguish real war from war on paper."
~ *Carl von Clausewitz* 3

An understanding of friction is necessary. An officer must know friction so he can overcome it on the street when dealing with an uncooperative and potentially violent adversary. Friction can be mental, as in indecision over a course of action. Friction can be physical, as in effective adversary size, strength, firing capabilities location (inside/outside) or an environmental obstacle such as a locked door, barricades or open kill zone, which must be overcome. Population and innocents in the area is a physical factor to consider that creates friction in decision making.

Friction can be external, imposed by adversary's actions, his motive, nature and intentions, is he armed or unarmed? Is it a hostage situation or is it ongoing deadly action and active shooting taking place? The weather or mere chance or uncertainty is another form of external friction.

Friction can be self-induced, caused by such factors as lack of a clearly defined goal, unclear or overly complicated plans, policies or procedures. This self-induced friction can also manifest itself in worry over liability related issues, disciplinary action, dash cams in patrol cars, fear, poor attitude, complacency or being unprepared. Self-induced friction can come from unknowns about your own skills and limitations. Ego can also affect friction in how we make decisions.

Clausewitz says, *this tremendous friction, which cannot, as in mechanics, be reduced to a few points, is everywhere in contact with chance, and brings about effects that cannot be measured, just because they are largely due to chance.*4

While we try to reduce these unknowns by gathering information, we must realize that we cannot eliminate them or even come close. The very nature of conflict makes certainty impossible; all actions in conflict will based on incomplete, inaccurate, or even contradictory information. At best we can hope to determine possibilities and probabilities. This implies certain standard of tactical judgment.

Conflict is a clash between two or more complex adaptive systems, by adaptive systems I mean walking, talking, thinking and planning, deciding and acting people who are at odds with one another. When people meet and their efforts to survive on their own terms collide, "stuff happens!"

As a cop your efforts to deescalate the situation depend upon your adversary complying with you. If the adversary decides he will not comply, the plans you had while responding will have to change based upon the decision and actions of the adversary. An emotionally charged adversary is unpredictable and that unpredictability forces you to adapt.

The simple linear step by step plan you had in mind now becomes more complex in the midst of the unpredictable chaos, an intent on getting his own way adversary, can create. *"Everything in war is simple, but the simplest thing is difficult,"* 5 is how Clausewitz described it. Add innocent victim to the equation and you get even more complexity to the situation.

Competitive challenges as in conflict and violence cannot be truly planned for. Opposing plans from different people collide with results that no one can predict. Those who think that they can foresee exactly how any confrontation will progress are simply wrong.

This factor of two sides conflicting will always be there in law enforcement encounters so we must be knowledgeable of the give and take of conflict and work positioning ourselves utilizing methods and tactics to change the climate, and create friction in our adversary by attacking our adversaries' thought process and shattering his morale and decision making process in an effort, to gain voluntary compliance or catch him off guard and unprepared so we can use appropriate force options.

Carl von Clausewitz offers some very good advice for law enforcement:
An understanding of friction is a large part of that much-admired sense of warfare which a good general is supposed to possess. To be sure, the best general is not the one who is most familiar with the idea of friction, and who takes it to heart (he belongs to the anxious type so common among experienced commanders). The good general must know friction in order to overcome it whenever possible, and in order not to expect a standard of

achievement in his operations which this very friction makes impossible.

Incidentally, it is a force that theory can never quite define. Even if it could, the development of instinct and tact would still be needed, a form of judgment much more necessary in an area littered by endless minor obstacles than in great, momentous questions, which are settled in solitary deliberation or in discussion with others.

As with a man of the world instinct becomes almost habit so that he always acts, speaks, and moves appropriately, so only the experienced officer will make the right decision in major and minor matters, at every pulse beat of war. Practice dictates the answer: 'this is possible, that is not.' So he rarely makes a serious mistake, such as can, in war, shatter confidence and become extremely dangerous if it occurs, often.6

With an adversary who says NO and takes action to thwart our efforts! We will always have to be prepared to use our awareness, insight, imagination and initiative applying the science and art of tactics, operationally while striving ourselves to overcome   the effects of friction, while interacting with an adversary. We must attempt at the same time to raise our adversary's friction to a level that weakens his ability to fight. This interplay is necessary in an effort to shape and reshape the climate of the situation and win without fighting if possible.

Friction is that force which makes the apparently easy difficult. We shall frequently revert to this subject, and it will become evident that an eminent commander needs more than experience and a strong will. He must have other exceptional abilities as well.
~Carl von Clausewitz 7

Chapter 16
Deciding Under Pressure... and Fast: You Need to Understand the Concept of "Coup d'oeil"

This facile coup d'oeil of the General, this simple art of forming notions, this personification of the whole action of War, is so entirely and completely the soul of the right method of conducting War, that no other but this broad way is it possible to conceive that freedom of the mind which is indispensable if it is to dominate events, not be overpowered by them.
~Carl von Clausewitz 1

The success of officers on the street or leaders overseeing operations often centers on our ability to read situations as they are unfolding in real time. Our ability to observe and exploit weakness in an adversary's position or decision making is an attribute many in law enforcement strive to develop, in an effort to improve on their ability to maneuver, in an effort to position, resources and, set up future tactical options. This ability is known in the world of tactical science as "Coup d'oeil" (pronounced koo doy or koo dwee).2

Carl von Clausewitz in his book *On War* describes coup d'oeil in the section of his book titled "Military Genius" "This type of knowledge can only be gained through a talent for judgment and by the application of accurate judgment to the observation of man and matter.3

Today this ability, to recognize the truth, instinctively, using all your senses as you accord with an adversary in uncertainty and the ebb and flow of conflict vary, is also known as Napoleons glance, strike of the eye, strategic or expert intuition and today experts such as Gary Klein and Don Vandergriff among others, use the term, recognized primed decision making.

The idea of coup d'oeil translates well into the law enforcement world and combines the strategic and tactical mindset, and the explorer mentality, enhancing the ability to see openings and exploit opportunities.

Understanding "coup d'oeil" can do wonders in enhancing real time decision making under pressure.4

In his book Field Command, Sid Heal, states, *"coup d'oeil is a French expression which loosely translated means strike of the eye or the vision behind the eye. The closest English translation would be that of "intuition." Intuition is defined as "perceptive insight" or the power to discern the true nature of a situation. It explains the commanders ability to see what the terrain looks like on the other side of the hill, or the floor plan of the inside of a building, coupled with and understanding of the impact they have on an operation. When time is a factor, it might involve envisioning situations which cause the suspect to react in some predictable manner which can be exploited."*5

This implies that officers will be effective in handling crisis situations if braveness to march towards the sounds of the guns is supplemented by good tactics and initiative, and the willingness of leaders and street officers to act independently. This also implies all of us in law enforcement must be experts in our field if we are to reduce the chaos crisis brings. There must be a high degree of self-confidence so we must develop officers who consider themselves experts, leaders who are proud to be part of their organizations and possess a willingness to trust and be trusted so decision making can be fluid and timely.

Sid Heal goes on to say, *"While a commander who possesses coup d'oeil might be considered gifted, it is more likely that his abilities have been developed. Coup d'oeil involves judgment and judgment can be enhanced by a thorough knowledge of the three T s; Tools, Troops and Tactics. The tools of the trade for tactical operations extend far beyond weapons and would include breaching devices, vehicles, communications equipment, diversionary devices and so forth."*6

In addition to these team tactics the street cop, should consider some other tools; tactical response and approaches to include, ongoing deadly action, domestic violence, robbery calls, etc. Vehicles stop tactics, contact cover, subject and prisoner handling, and searches.

A deep understanding of conflict and how humans respond to it is crucial as well, so the street cop must also possess sound social skills and the ability to apply them tactfully and tactically. Coup d'oeil is developed through experience. Experience leveraged from both training and the real world. We must harness every lesson possible taking advantage of tactical critiques in the form of debriefs and after action reviews. We must study tactics with real effort if we are to increase our effectiveness in deciding under pressure. Insight and imagination lead to initiative only if we have the knowhow and are able to gain an understanding of what's going on and have some understanding into how it is to be resolved. Coup d'oeil comes from, understanding these tactical concepts and how to apply them.

"The most formidable warriors are students of their profession."
  ~Al Gray, USMC GEN (Ret.) 7

Chapter 17
What Do OODA Loop's Mean to the Street Cop, and Becoming "World Class" Tacticians?

Three officers respond at 3AM to the call of a disturbance. When they arrive, there are three people present, two males and a female. One male is intoxicated. I will only focus on him for the purpose of this example. Intoxicated male is spoken to by responding officers. They tell him to call it a night and to go to bed and sleep it off. He says he will and turns to go into the house.

The officers continue gathering information for the incident report. While speaking to the other two people involved, the "intoxicated male" comes back outside to talk, he is relaxed but is again told to go back inside or he will be placed in protective custody for the night. The officers spend another 5 minutes gathering information, and are about to leave when they see the "intoxicated male" standing outside the front door waving good bye. The officers decide to bring him to the police station for his safety.

At the station the booking process proceeds, during which the "intoxicated male" talks about police beating up innocent people and asked several times if they were going to beat him up. After booking, the sergeant and one patrol officer went to put the man in a cell for the night and all hell broke loose. A fight broke out in which the subject attempted to escape. He punched, kicked, clawed and scratched three officers inside the station and made his way outside where a fourth officer got involved in the altercation. An attempt on an officer's gun was made by the subject without success. In the end four officers were injured on duty, three were out for over a week, the other returned to duty that morning. In the end we were lucky no one was seriously hurt.

What caught my attention later were the reports filed by the officers involved. Every report, I mean all of them stated "The individual was cooperative throughout contact including the booking procedure until we went to place him in the cell." This statement begs me to ask a few critical questions:

Why did these veteran officers, observe the signs and signals and yet, not orient to the possible dangers?

Why did they use the term "cooperative" when clearly he was not?

How do we develop a better way of exploring unfolding situations so we gather actionable information in real time, so we make sound tactical decisions throughout the encounter?

On the street when danger presents itself in an obvious manner, "we cops know it is a bad set of circumstances we are walking into," a fight with shots being fired, a felony car stop, a violent domestic call turned hostage situation, high risk warrant service. In these types of circumstances, we cops, handle ourselves quite well, most of the time. We control our emotions and put ourselves in "win" positions. We establish command, identify kill zones, set up inner and outer perimeters, we set up command posts and staging areas and bring in all the resources necessary to bring about a successful resolution. In these known dangerous encounters our senses are alive and fine-tuned. We are observant and paying attention to every detail of what's going on which helps us orient to the potential dangers and we make decisions and take actions that allow us gain the advantage and win these types of encounters.

I would like to discuss the unknown risk calls we handle: the disturbance, the car stop or encounter with the unknown individual, the alarm, and the trespasser, the field interview, etc.

These so called "routine" things we do that are getting us injured and killed.

-   Why is it happening?
-   Is it physical skills or lack thereof?
-   Is it training?
-   Is it fear?
-   Fear of getting in trouble with the administration, fear of

being sued, criticized, ridiculed by the media?
- Is it complacency or the "it will not happen here attitude?"
- Is it lack of emotional control and a false sense of urgency?
- What about over confidence or lack thereof?
- Does our mental conditioning have us believing we are better than we actually are, or has our training developed a bias for action, over reflection and tactical problem solving?

Probably all of these contribute some degree to the friction that slows down or effects negatively the decision making process and makes us vulnerable to attack.

I do not want to get into statistics in this chapter but one that has stuck out in my mind, is from the FBI's *Officers Killed in the Line of Duty* publication that states: "in gunfight situations where law enforcement professionals were killed in the line of duty 98% of the time the suspect fired first." 98%! This statistic has scared the hell out of me for years now. I thought why are we in affect being ambushed in 98% of the gunfight situations we handle on the street? What are we missing in the street that allows the bad guy to get the upper hand on us in 98% of the situations?

Law enforcement officers all get physical skills training i.e. defensive tactics, firearms, impact weapons, OC spray, handcuffing techniques, CQB, active shooter, etc. so, why are we still getting caught in disadvantageous positions?1

We are not paying attention to the subtle signs of danger that lurk in the fog, unknown and unpredictability hidden in another's motives and intent, that prohibits us from obtaining accurate information in a timely manner. We cops all too often let our guard down and put ourselves at great risk. We simply have not developed sound tactical habits of looking for the signs and signals of danger.

Oh yah!

We look for the "furtive move" to the waist band or under the seat, the fists that comes up and punch directed towards us or, the emotional person doing something so outrageous we know we got trouble.

But what about the cops being lured into complacency and killed not even getting their gun out of the holster or worse yet getting their gun taken and used against them by the bad guy? What "force multipliers" are we cops missing in our observations and tactical decision making toolbox that put us at a disadvantage and how do we reverse this to significantly increase the tactical advantage?

How Do We Gain The Tactical Advantage?
To be more prepared we must better understand what conflict is and how it unfolds if we are to gain the needed advantage. This is a shortened version of the Marine Corps definition of conflict:

*"The essence of conflict is a struggle between two hostile, independent, and irreconcilable wills, trying to impose itself on the other. Conflict is fundamentally an interactive social process. Conflict is thus a process of continuous mutual adaptation, of give and take, move and counter move. It is critical to keep in mind that the adversary is not an inanimate object to be acted upon."*2

Simply put, having a win mentality is necessary, but so is acknowledging that the bad guy has his own! There are at least two people involved in the conflict and both compete in time through their "observation, orientation, decisions and actions." We cops must never lose sight of this crucial fact that at least two people participate in conflict and both have their own objectives and plans. Our goal as cops as we interact with people on the street is to constantly be observant and explore the situation from first contact until we resolve the situation and clear the scene.

The Boyd Cycle (OODA Loop) and Gaining the Tactical Advantage

"Machines don't fight wars. People do and they use their minds. You must get into the minds of humans for that's, where the battles are won."

~Col. John Boyd 3

So what can we do better to gain the advantage and keep it throughout our interaction with a suspect? How do we continually improve our situation awareness so we can manage things safely and effectively?

The answer lays within the concept known as the OODA Loop aka—the Boyd Cycle. Col. John Boyd discovered that conflicts are competitions between you and the suspect(s) using Observation, Orientation, Decision, and Action. These cycles known as OODA Loops, divides understanding into FOUR processes each feeding the next.4

1) OBSERVATION: what we see through all of our senses, including our, sixth sense,
2) ORIENTATION: your understanding of what's happening NOW,
3) DECISION: what do we DO, and
4) ACTION: behavior or DOING WHAT WE DECIDED.

The idea of the OODA loop is that the advantage goes to those that can complete the decision cycle fastest. It stresses that situational awareness allows you to set the tempo by creating friction, or, slowing down a suspect(s) decision making cycle. This suggests that disrupting a suspect(s) thinking process and improving your own, is the crux to winning.

The OODA Loop is not a onetime thing.   It's continuous throughout your encounters. Because our actions change the situation, the cycle begins anew and repeats itself throughout the encounter.   Simply the O-O-D-A Loop gives us cops the advantage through better SITUATIONAL AWARENESS FROM

BEGINNING TO END!

By observing the obvious AND the all-important subtle signs and signals that manifest themselves in a suspect(s) behavior patterns, body language, facial expressions, what they say and how they say it, etc. we can reasonably predict outcomes and act accordingly. By being alert and aware of the information exchange between "us and them" and our environment, we are able to stay ahead of the "action versus reaction curve" in the mental dimension of conflict allowing us to outmaneuver a suspect with sound tactics.

The big question that Don Vandergriff and I bring to the table is how to develop this ability? More on the OODA loop first. Understanding the "Why" behind the OODA loop, will then allow us to develop cops to better operate at a faster OODA loop than our criminal adversaries.

The goal as Boyd put it is the *"ability to operate at a faster tempo or rhythm than an adversary enables one to fold an adversary back inside himself so that he can neither appreciate nor keep-up with what's going on. He will become disorientated or confused. Unless such menacing pressure is relieved, adversary will experience various combinations of uncertainty, doubt, confusion, self-deception, indecision, fear, panic, discouragement, despair, etc., which will further:*

*Disorient or twist his mental images/impressions of what's happening. Thereby disrupt his mental/physical maneuvers for dealing with such a menace: Thereby Overload his mental/physical capacity to adapt or endure. Thereby Collapse his ability to carry on."*5

In a simple word we "confuse" him with the unexpected. And when the timing is right you move in and control the subject. Make no mistake, like any other skill; outmaneuvering a suspect takes focus of effort to achieve.

Boyd said it best: "Machines don't fight wars. People fight wars and they use their minds. You must get into the minds of humans. That's where the battles are won."6

The interplay of the human mind is the most critical aspect of winning. I am not saying the physical aspect is not critical, it is, you must always be able to do what needs to be done, but if you were Gandhi (communicator), Bruce Lee (hands on DT) and Carlos Hathcock (firearms) all rolled into one, "what a human weapon" you would be.

With all these skills you could handle any situation; verbally, hands on defensive tactics or if necessary deadly force. But if you were not making good observations (using all your senses), that tell you something about the unfolding situation (orientation) then the decisions you need to make and the actions you need to take would not get done because you were not fully aware of your surroundings.

How do you take "initiative" decide and act, if you do not observe and orient to a tactical problem? Understand this! Winning a fight actually has very little to do with what you are armed with and a great deal to do with what you are thinking at the time, hence the importance of the OODA Loop to the street cop.

Using your past experiences as an opportunity to learn and be become "world class" tactician

In an after action review of the example described above, the officers involved (all good cops) stated, "they did not think of his coming out of the house after being told to stay in and sleep it off as a sign of non-cooperation, even after the second time, even when they were bringing him in. When asked why they brought him in? They responded, "He was not doing what he was told." At this point we all began to laugh a little although the circumstances were not funny the responses I got were both funny and alarming. We continued the discussion and agreed the individual was indeed non-cooperative and therefore a possible threat, requiring close "monitoring and control."

Lesson: A fluid OODA loop (continuous and focused attention from start to finish) would have alerted these officers to the potential dangers sooner and help prevent dangerous altercations and injuries through sound tactical decisions and actions.

To be, BETER THAN GOOD cops, takes having a great interest in what we do and developing an understanding of the WHY behind, what we do and the tactics we use. It's important for the street cop to keep in mind that, in tactics, the most important thing is not whether you go left or right, but why you go left or right.

Meaning: why are we doing, what we are doing? The OODA Loop keeps you interested and exploring the tactical encounter from start to finish. It keeps interest and exploring enhances awareness or insight into tactical problems. Insight allows us to activate our imagination as to, how we decide and act in "real time" as we interact with a suspect and focus efforts on gaining the initiative.

After all, what is the aim and purpose of strategy and tactics? Col. Boyd's answer, to improve our ability to shape and adapt to unfolding circumstances, so that we; can survive, on our own terms. We do this by outpacing or disrupting our adversary decision making cycle in real time, real life situations.

The OODA Loop (Boyd Cycle) based on Col. John Boyd's dedicated work and service to this great country is a tool every cop, should know and, understand thoroughly if we are to become better than good and continuously improve our safety and effectiveness on the street. Isn't it time we focus our efforts in developing these skills?

Chapter 18
Character and Tactical Decision Making

"If to please the people, we offer what we ourselves disapprove, how can we afterward defend our work? Let us raise a standard to which the wise and honest can repair."
~General George Washington 1

Now we begin to answer the question on how to use the OODA loop, more specifically, how to develop our cops to use it effectively in their everyday missions. But using the OODA loop, like John Boyd himself, is about developing Strength of Character.

Strength of Character denotes honesty and integrity. Strength of Character means doing what's right based on our beliefs and a belief system set forth by society. Strength of Character is doing what is right when no one is looking, when there is possibility of receiving no credit or reward. Strength of Character is seeking responsibility and taking joy in making and standing by decisions. There are certain things we do and don't do based on this system of beliefs. What's wrong or right in our belief system is where the question often lies, and the answer, too, can at times be clouded by the system of beliefs we value. If we do not possess strength of character and follow our beliefs while carrying out our duties, how can we defend our decisions and actions? 2

The German Army, which practiced *Maneuver Warfare* better than any other Army, sought after most in their leader development the strength of character in its officers. They defined Strength of Character as *The ability, even the joy in seeking responsibility, and in making decisions under all circumstances, in the face of peers, superiors, subordinates and most of all in the face of the enemy. It is the ability to do what is right despite the consequences to one's self or career.*2

This chapter is not to judge others in the moral sense. However it is important to think about strength of character and explain how it applies to tactical decision making in the context of law enforcement, security officer and military personnel working the frontlines or the street.

Strength of character or courage helps us *gain control over ourselves* and to *influence others* in a positive way. Character is part of leading and leadership within a community, organization or unit. Without character you cannot function accordingly in the field dealing with the complexity of conflict and violence.

Strength of Character is an attribute that's critical in implementing strategy and tactics, it's necessary to connect the ends with the means and the moral, mental and physical aspects of conflict and violence. Without it we falter and are perceived by those we serve as just another bully pushing folks around, just another Goliath picking on and bullying David, and we all know how that ended.

Strength of Character influences our decision making because it's the crux of our ability to make decisions fluidly. Strength of Character affects the physiological and psychological responses to conflict, as well. Without character, we struggle even harder to make a decision in conflict, heightening the survival stress response which can spiral out of control, slowing or freezing decision making or lifesaving action from taking place. Strength of Character or lack thereof, has a profound effect on what goes through our minds and how those thoughts play out in our actions.

Let's take the simple example of a basic tactical concept of "contact and cover." You are investigating a suspicious person's call and come upon two people fitting the description. They turn and walk away, you and your partner encounter them, and they hesitantly go along with your requests. This type of situation requires use of the principal of contact and cover. One man's job is to make all contact with a subject, ask the questions, gather all the information and take down notes for a report or to further an investigation.

The contact officer also makes all searches and seizures when warranted. The basic premise of the contact officer is to make contact. The cover man is your back up, your safety officer. His job is to monitor the environment and climate of the situation. He looks for other people, weapons or circumstances that may lead to danger. He is constantly monitoring all that's going on around you and him.   His job is to refrain from talking, or interfering with the contact man unless he sees something threatening; then and only then does he take action or makes contact in an attempt to stop the threat.

Let's say while investigating this scenario, another officer arrives to assist. The officer is standing there arms folded looking the suspicious persons over, laughs at them and makes the statement "what do we have here a couple of **sholes?" One subject says, "I'll show you an **shole!"

The officer responds, "come over here and show me." The subject walks over, as the officer walks toward him they're calling one another names, which turns into a pushing and shoving match that then turns into an all-out physical altercation.   The second subject, feeling his friend is being harassed by the officer who arrived "to ASSIST" gets angry.

As he makes an effort to help his friend, your partner attempts to stop him and a second violent encounter unfolds: your partner is knocked to the ground and an unsuccessful attempt made on his gun.   In the end, the officers prevail, winning the physical altercation and leading to the arrest of both subjects.

Where is the Strength of Character in this scenario?

Who possessed it?

Who did not?

And now that an internal investigation into the alleged excessive force case has begun, who will possess the strength of character to tell the truth about what happened?

Would that truth, be the same if the attempt on the officer's gun was successful and ended up in the death of a law enforcement officer?

Would the officers who witnessed an officer get out of hand and unprofessional possess the strength of character to tell that officer he was an unprofessional officer—a pretender who should not wear a badge?

This type of behavior or lack of character has a direct effect on officer safety, the lack of character on the part of the cop who arrived on the scene led to the escalation of this situation.

Strength of Character is, knowing and doing what's right, no matter how uncomfortable and conflicting it may be. Strength of Character is the bedrock of what we do and don't do on the street. Without character, we fail to make appropriate decisions, and bad outcomes can occur. When we act with character, those we protect and serve will believe in us, they'll trust us and what we stand for, and have confidence in our decision making.

Again, the reader is asking, how do I develop or improve the Strength of Character in my fellow, subordinate officers, even in my superiors? First of all, you have to set the example yourself. That is the most important beginning. Without doing this, nothing else we say in this handbook matters. Once you do this, then you can begin to use the innovative and progressive training and education methods we talk about.

Chapter 19
The 10%er Mindset

Of every 100 men you send to fight, 10 shouldn't even be there. Eighty are nothing but targets. Nine are real fighters, we are lucky to have them, they the battle make. Ah but the one, one is a true warrior and he will bring the others back
~ Heraclitus 1

If you're reading this book and chapter, you are probably in what we call the 10%er mindset or those in law enforcement that are continually improving them both physically and mentally.

This chapter is preaching to the choir, but as members of this proverbial choir your voices need to be heard. You need to sing out loudly to those who are not so concerned about improving themselves as they are jeopardizing your life, the lives in the communities you serve, and the tranquility in a free society that is being torn apart by those that would destroy us. Police officers are the fine blue line between chaos and order. You are our first line of defense.

Today's law enforcement officer can no longer be what has been referred to as a "ROD". That is "Retired on Duty." Those who look at law enforcement as just a paycheck and a career leading to a secure retirement need to be not only shaken, but steered either out of their departments or quickly change their attitude about what it means to be a cop.

The risks today are far too great and too treacherous to have anyone that is not at the top of their game. Any athlete of quality who understands that their performance involves mindset, attitude, skills and long term preparation, would not think of the demands of game day long before game day itself. For cops, every day is game day and being prepared is not just winning, but survival.

In 2011, 162 police officers lost their lives in the line of duty. In 2012, 12 officers were shot in one weekend, 53 officers shot at in the month of January alone and the death toll continues to rise. Those who wear the uniform and badge are more than a symbol of government; they are the people and their community.   Police officers are a virtual target to those who oppose the American way of life be they terrorist, anarchist, gang member, drug cartel or lone wolf.2

We have learned through hundreds of conversations with cops that officers talk a lot about "officer safety." The "talk" stems around safety in numbers or staffing, back-up, contact cover principle, cover and concealment, firearms training, situational awareness, recognizing the signs and signals of crime and danger, reading body language, decision making under pressure, active shooter response, hostage negotiation, barricaded subject response, tactical response and approach to calls, off duty survival and many more tactical concepts as well. Talking about the concepts behind officer survival is great.

BUT IT'S NOWHERE NEAR ENOUGH!

The concepts behind officer survival must be practiced and integrated into every aspect of officer mind set, attitude and personal approach to their duties.

- How many of us apply these officer survival concepts on the street?
- How many of us take short cuts or fall into a complacent mindset and daily routine?
- How many think 'it will not happen to me' or 'it will not happen here?

We ask you this question: is officer survival just a concept or have you internalized these safety principles into your habits every day and on every shift? The need for change is obvious, threats are real and evolving despite the fact that most people would never do harm to us.

There are still those who, for whatever their personal agenda and reasoning, know we as American guardians are, what we as American Law Enforcement do, and they will unleash their rage and fury at us according to that personal agenda.

The fact that few organized aggressors would resort to mass violence, and many more unplanned, opportunistic or event related aggressors act against Law Enforcement is all the more reason we must develop a mindset of heightened superior situational awareness and mental attitude, while simultaneously being approachable and engaged with those whom we serve and interact. This is true no matter where we are and no matter what we are doing.

Talk is cheap and its time we started walking our own talk and applying the concepts we say are so near and dear to our survival. In the end it comes down to **doing the things we talk about; continual learning; and applying what we know to the evolving situation at hand.** This takes effort in leadership ensuring proper realistic training is brought to officers, and that law enforcement personnel be open to ongoing professional development, honing of skills, attitude and preparedness through their own individual initiative.

If each officer took the responsibility for assuring their survival through ongoing developing, training, and evolution; their entire organization is optimized for survival and adaptive response to threats. It's time to stop merely talking and learn to discipline yourself to walk the walk of officer safety by doing what you know is necessary, and by seeking out more training so you consistently strive to nurture what you know and evolve your skills to be adaptable and instinctive.

You do not need to be in formal training class to create and nurture this mindset, indeed it must come from within. It must come from one's own sense of integrity and personal anima and believe system. When this belief system is a way of life, the development occurs as part of an ongoing evolution of a warrior or modern knight.

Several forms of thinking play a crucial role in preparing and readying us for conflict, violence or crisis. These include the **"if –then** or **when-then** thinking; when X happens, then I will do Y".

Positive self-talk and visualizing the situation are positive tools that develop patterns in your mind (like any other form of training) in an effort to anticipate threats as we explore the situation, make an situational assessment and plan an adaptable response to a predator we can't fully anticipate.

We need to become students of human behavior, both normal and aberrant, to rapidly recognize the difference between the two and be ready to instantly respond correctly and accurately. Inherent in this understands the various dimensions of aberrant behavior between deviant, dangerous, suspicious, under the influence, and psychiatric.

A simple and recognized concept is the Boyd Cycle, which includes Observe, Orient, Decide and Act elements. Commonly referred to as "OODA Loops," this is a concept that applies to everything we do. No matter what we are doing this concept is part of how we learn about what's going on, make decisions as to how to handle it and take actions to effectively and safely get it done. Obviously it takes physical skills as well and time must be spent developing these skills, but by and large, it's lack of awareness or complacency and lack of good sound decision-making that gets us killed in the field.

Yes the bad guy has something to do with it, but the fact is we know they are out there stalking the public and cops. The bad guy watches us, learns our habits, and plans his actions and when the opportunity presents itself the bad guy puts his plan into action. His planning and plotting give him an advantage because he is putting an effort forward and walking his own talk. We should be aware of, prepared for and ready to prevent this type of advantage from developing.

We need to be thinking in the same way as the bad guy, and do what we call personal "Red Teaming". This means thinking of how we might be compromised and if you yourself were the bad guy how would you aggress or act in a given situation.

Winning takes constant superior situational awareness and a willingness to step outside the lines of traditional training. It requires each of us to use individual insight and innovation in applying what we have learned in training and through our experiences to what we know.   Applying what we know then takes consistent and constant practice and "practicing what we preach" to our daily duties.

We can no longer be complacent watching cops die, making the same mistakes time and time again. These mistakes are fixable! It's time to call to arms and to wake-up every law enforcement officer to the mindset of survival in the context of where we are now, in a current environment of multiple and chronic threat. It is time to take the mindset that each of us must be one of the 10% who diligently and continually try to improve themselves, optimize our own chances for effective response and survival from threats of all kinds.

That warrior mindset, that approach of the knight guarding the kingdom, needs to be the goal of our profession and obligation to serve.

If you knew that tomorrow you were going to be in a gun fight, if tomorrow your community would be hit with a Mumbai type terrorist attack or your child's elementary school was being attacked by terrorists, how would you train today and how would you prepare yourself for tomorrow? Tomorrow may be sooner than we think. Train hard, be aware, stay oriented, and be safe. Evolve to the every-prepared and evolving state-of-the-art modern knight.

Chapter 20
Recognizing the Signs and Signals of Crime and Danger: The Non-Verbal Factors

Some can struggle to a victory and the whole world may praise their winning. This also demonstrates a limited ability. Win as easily as picking up a fallen hair. Don't use all of your forces. See the time to move. Don't try to find something clever. Hear the clap of thunder. Don't try to hear something subtle. Learn from the history of successful battles. Victory goes to those who make winning easy. A good battle is one that you will obviously win. It doesn't take intelligence to win a reputation. It doesn't take courage to achieve success. You must win your battles without effort. Avoid difficult struggles. Fight when your position must win. You always win by preventing your defeat.
~ Sun Tzu" 1

Your duty requires you to make observations to detect potential threats or criminal activity. As you stand your post or patrol your sector, just what is it you are looking for? What are the things that alert you to wrong doing? Alert you to danger? This post will be the first of two parts and will focus on the signs and signals to look for in the performance of our duties to help us prevent crime and threats from taking place and keep us safe while doing so.

You're on patrol, and the day is sunny, about 55 degrees. All has been quiet thus far during your shift. As you pass by a service station at 30 mph you note a tow truck, a flat bed with two vehicles loaded. You think to yourself, "nothing unusual here, a gas/service station and tow truck, with two vehicles on board. All seems OK?" Then you note there are no markings on the door of the commercial vehicle. "Maybe they forgot to put the magnetic markings on before their service call?" you say to yourself as you pass by. "I am sure its fine?" But, Hell, your intuition, shouts loudly, "I better check it out."

You do and solve a major case involving automobile theft and salvage for profit.

The question here is what linked this officer's mind to the tow truck with cars, on the flat bed, at a gas/service station?

Isn't that normal?

Isn't that where they belong?

Yes they do belong. They fit a pattern of what's normal. The abnormal (no markings on the vehicle) is what triggered this officer's intuition and told him something may be wrong. His response, ultimately prevented this particular crime from taking place, as well as solved numerous open cases in several other jurisdictions. This subtle sign triggered this officer's orientation to criminal wrong doing. A fine-tuned Boyd Cycle, running smoothly and intentionally activated, solved this series of crimes.

The obvious, is just that, "obvious." A smashed window and a man standing next to this tow truck with a crowbar in hand quickly turning away from this officer and hurriedly, fast walking to the driver's door with the apparent intent to leave the area, would have been a more obvious sign that something was amiss. Anybody, cop or not would recognize this second scenario as a probable criminal act taking place.

The same can be said about the person reaching towards their waist band, while shouting "I am going to kill you," would be the great probability of the person in question reaching for a gun. After a high speed pursuit, the man who quickly exits the vehicle and run away is trying to evade capture. The person who gets out of the vehicle, hands held in the boxer's position coming towards the officer, most probably wants to fight.

The obvious signs of danger are indeed clear signs of a particular intent. They are signs we should be able to see and respond to accordingly. These obvious signs are important to observe and respond too. But the obvious signs are often the latter stages in the game. It is the little things or what I call the subtle signs and signals that give us the edge. This gives us the initiative and advantage in dealing with crime and danger.

In past chapters we have talked about the Boyd Cycle and how important observation, orientation, decision and actions cycles are to gaining an advantage. We top it off discussing how critical it is to have officers with Strength of Character as being the final closure to practicing a successful OODA Loop.

The officer that returned to the scene with the unmarked tow truck had the Strength of Character to make that decision and live with its consequences. An officer without that critical Strength of Character would be justified in their mind and others to drive on since there were no obvious signs of a crime being committed.

The Boyd Cycle is about developed patterns, "Patterns of Conflict" as Col. Boyd put it. We develop these patterns or characteristics through individual training and experience. We develop, over time, an intuitive understanding of what is right and what is not. What is normal and abnormal? Then consciously and subconsciously respond accordingly.

Not everything we intuitively sense, through observation, will be a crime taking place or a dangerous set of circumstances.

We must also be inquisitive, look deeper into the circumstances that drew our attention. This inquiry may simply prove what looked wrong was not a crime or danger at all, but may be a person in need of assistance or some other type of service? The persons with tow truck in the above example could have been just doing their job and had forgotten to place the signs on the door.

A quick registry and document inquiry could have proved normal activity. However the initiative driven officer whose initial intent was to stop and advise the markings were not on the vehicle, determined through observations, something was abnormal. What he was seeing, hearing and feeling, during this initial inquiry told him there was more going on. He stated: "eye contact being poor, they seemed to want to leave in a hurry and end the contact. They answered questions before they were asked.

All signs of possible deceptions which upon further review

were indeed deceptive. The officer's inquisitive nature and intuitive understanding of signs and signals related to crime and danger, told him something abnormal was going on.

What is abnormal or suspicious?
This is a question that should be asked more often in our profession that is a question that does have answers.
Abnormal is defined as: "unusual, exceptional, irregular, not normal." as compared to Normal: "regular, standard, usual, and common." The ability to differentiate between the two is critical to our ability to detect, prevent, avoid, defuse and resolve crime, crime problems and threats to do harm. Putting circumstances in context which they occur based on what our individual perception or orientation is telling us is key to understanding, "what's going on?" It is also important to understand that not all things are as they seem.

When we are discussing subtle signs and signals we must expect the unexpected and be prepared, through keen observation, orientation, decision and action skills, to respond accordingly based on the facts and circumstances presented.
Crime and violence do not just happen.

There are signs and signals presented long before the crime is committed or the assault takes place. Seeing a man approach you pointing a gun at you is an obvious sign of danger. A man getting out of a vehicle after being stopped for speeding and angrily demanding to know why you stopped him is a clear sign of high anxiety. When he continues to shout and closes distance with you after repeated commands to get back, is a clear sign of impending attack. After an assault by this man he disengages, goes to his vehicle and retrieves a firearm! The answer to what's about to take place, based on the context of the situation is obvious. This is a worst case scenario of a person about to inflict deadly force and your orientation, decision and action should be clear.

Obvious signs and signals of crime and danger can be clearly seen to the trained law enforcement and security professional.

Yet they all too often go unseen or are seen too late. The most common danger signs experienced, however are subtle feelings, a hunch, you intuitively know something is wrong. The alert observer that listens to his intuition based on facts and circumstances presented at the time can seek advantage and prevent crime and dangerous circumstances from unfolding. The ability to observe these subtle signs and signals and orient to what they are telling you, can give you the clear advantage in dealing with conflict.

My experience spans 28 years between military and law enforcement, with 19 years of that being a front line officer and grunt. I have also spent those 28 years training myself and others in the military, law enforcement and security professions. Don Vandergriff has served for 24 years as a Marine and Soldier, and another 8 years as a contractor with the US Army and NATO on leader development, as well as owner of his leader development business, what we have seen is a lackluster approach to observation skills and decision making training.

We do not say this to be unjustly critical. It's just the way it is. Hell, I am guilty of it myself by focusing mainly on the physical skills required to handle conflict. However, over the last 6-7 years it has occurred to me that if we are serious about officer safety and preventing crime and violence we must fine tune our mental skills. This is where the focus of training should be. The physical skills training is a must also, but our approach has to balance all realms of conflict to be successful. Understanding what to look for the signs and signals is a good place to start.

What are signs and signals of danger or crime? The signals are perceptible signs telling you something bad, illegal is occurring, about to occur or has already happened. Most perpetrators of crime and violence do not tell you their plans beforehand.

To the protection professionals of law enforcement and security, it's important to understand their acts or intended acts will show themselves in body language or non-verbal communication.

Research states that non-verbal communications accounts for

93% of communication. These statistics reiterates the importance of our situational awareness, a smooth functioning Boyd Cycle.2

The Boyd Cycle; a clear understanding of the **observation, orientation, decision and action "OODA Loop"** is a key first step. In the training we conduct through LESC or Adaptive-Leader when we conduct it with law enforcement and security professionals, this tactical decision making and threat assessment tool is a prerequisite that gives us the clear initiative in detecting crime and danger. The Boyd Cycle is a mental tool that helps us first understand how conflict unfolds, as well as, allows us to observe keenly through "all our senses" including intuition.

What is going on?
If we are to understand completely as is humanly possible what the circumstances are telling us, we must understand to effectively employ this concept. To see the subtle signs and signals, understand them and react to them gives us the advantage. This advantage I submit will prevent through "decisive action," most scenarios from escalating to violence. Why, because you took action, early in the situation and gained control—you out-OODA looped your opponent!   The Boyd Cycle in combination with knowing what to look for, paying attention to details, and the little things is the catalyst to successful resolution of crime and violence.

By a man's fingernails, by his coat-sleeve, by his boots, by his trouser-knees, by the calluses of his forefinger and thumb, by his expression, by his shirt-cuffs, by his movements, by each of these things a man's calling is plainly revealed. That all united should fail to enlighten the competent enquirer in any case is almost inconceivable.   ~Sherlock Holmes 3

Above we discussed patterns, the normal and its reverse, the abnormal conditions of conflict. We also discussed how a fine tuned Boyd Cycle can enhance our abilities as protection professionals to orient to our current environment.

To sharpen our skills we must study and learn the subtle signs of danger as well as those obvious to us, if we are to adapt and evolve, to more efficient, preventer's of violence. Subtleness in human conflict comes in the form of "body language." The understanding of non-verbal signs and signals of anxiety, or pre-attack, pre-crime, indicators are crucial to our orientation and safe resolution to dynamic encounters.

Life is predictable most of the time, most people act in certain "normal ways." Obviously we all have differences as well, but most *normal human behavior* is somewhat, predictable.

When it comes to safety and security and those that would do us harm, what is it that we in law enforcement and security should be looking for to help us prevent and resolve violence and crime?

- What's suspicious or telling, that something is wrong or amiss?
- What are the signs and signals telling us?
- How do we synthesize the signs and signals to help us maintain order and control of that small percentage of predators, who wish to do harm?

This chapter also focuses on the non-verbal signs of danger that show, when things are out of the realm of normalcy.

What are the signs and signals, their meanings in context of law enforcement and security encounters?

How to seek initiative and gain the advantage through reading the non-verbal signs and signals of crime and danger?

First things first: If we are to read non-verbal communication (body language) in the context of conflict we must understand that conflict is inevitable. Conflict is part of everyday life and most conflicts are resolved through communication, without ever being brought to the level of violence. However when it does go bad and escalates, the very nature of violence, is chaotic and unpredictable. So it is important to note; the observer of the overall circumstances surrounding a potential violent encounter takes in to consideration the environment he is in, the overall picture and his perception of what's happening. This is based on experience, possessed through the individual officers knowledge of his job, training he has had throughout his life and career as well as any new information presenting itself at the time of the encounter.4

Reading body language is both an art and science and takes training and practice to develop and utilize the skills properly. Nothing when it comes to predicting violence is 100% accurate. Conflict is defined by Don Vandergriff in his book *Raising the Bar* as "a clash between two complex adaptive systems."5 These systems (humans) have their own plans and agendas, moves and counter moves in an effort to get what they want. This must be understood clearly first if we are to seek the advantage we want to control and resolve conflict safely.

The Definitive Book of Body Language describes three rules for accurate reading.7

Rule 1. Read gestures in clusters. This means no one gesture in isolation of other gestures or circumstances is an effective sign of anything. Body language, a gesture can have many meanings and it's based on seeing the whole picture. So look for clusters of gestures to read what the body is telling you.8

Rule 2. Look for Congruence. If you ask a person you've made contact with, a question, his body language must match his verbal response. An example I have seen often in law enforcement and security; are you going to cooperate and comply? The subject answers yes and his head turns left to right, right to left saying no... The body language is incongruent to the verbal response yes and the head gesture, saying no! 9

Rule 3. Read gestures in Context. All gestures should be considered in the context in which they occur. If for example a man was taking an exam rubbing his hands back and forth through his hair it could be a sign of test anxiety or frustration with a question, and means no harm to anyone.

If on the other hand the man was in a police booking room and as part of a cluster of gestures he ran his hands through his hair or across his head, could mean anxiety, related to his freedom being taken away. A potentially dangerous set of circumstances that must be dealt with accordingly, before it escalates. In this article on Recognizing the Signs and Signals of Crime and Danger all gestures should be considered with these three rules in mind.10

The eyes: *The thousand yard stare*, a person looking through or beyond you is a clear sign something abnormal is going on. Whether the person is thinking and putting a plan together, to run, escape, give up, or to assault, is being considered. That look into nowhere is a look inside the individuals mind. He is running through options. The action he chooses is based on "his" orientation of the situation, everything that's going on, taken into consideration. *Gaze avoidance*, or a failure to make eye contact with a uniformed law enforcement or security officer is another form of deception. Looking away or avoiding eye contact is a way of mentally hiding. This goes back to childhood. Remember when, you were a child playing hide and seek? There you are hidden in the obvious spot eyes closed hoping not to be discovered.11

More serious plots bring about the effect of *gaze avoidance* as well. For example; the terrorists that by-passed security in one of the airports on 9-11 withheld eye contact from security officers as they passed by. This was found after reviewing and analyzing security tapes from Dulles International Airport.12 Another example is an officer approaching an individual and gets the proverbial turn and walk away as if you were not seen again avoidance of eye contact. In the interview setting at the point of a critical questioning and a response is warranted, the subject looks down or away, again a sign something maybe amiss, or a possible sign of deception.

When you are up to no good or lying, you divert your eyes

away or down from whom you are trying to deceive. This according to research is a normal human response to deception, guilt, embarrassment and shame. (People who do this well are then considered social paths, lying freely with no shame or remorse—which moves this issue to the next level of problem solving).

Dilated or constricted pupils are a sign of possible drug usage, legal or illegal. Dilated pupils are also a sign of survival stress (High Anxiety) and we should remain alert and prepare to take initiative to control the situation. It is important to note, when face to face with the unknown.

The eyebrows are a sign, what is known as the *eyebrow flash,* could be either a hello or an indication of surprise or fear based on context of the situation. *Furrowed eye brows,* could be a sign of anger or aggression. *Widening of the eyes* shows dominance or possible aggression. Widening of the eyes is an involuntary enlargement of both eyes, which takes place in situations of high stress, and emotion.

Darting eyes could be a sign of just checking out people in a room, looking for an escape route, possible witnesses or for assistance from other criminals. *Blink rate,* is another import sign of anxiety and stress in an individual.

A normal blink rate is approximately 6-10 blinks per minute. As stress and anxiety heighten, so does the blink rate. Slowing of the normal blink rate is less common, but is also a sign of high stress or concentration. In some, the rate almost comes to a complete stop, eyes wide open with the whites of the eyes exposed 360 degrees. Observation of the eyes and an understanding of the involuntary information they give to law enforcement and security professionals is critical, to controlling dynamic encounters.13

The nose and mouth: is a critical location to watch on subjects we deal with in the law enforcement and security professions. We live by bringing oxygen into our system. A normal breathing rate is somewhere between 12 and 20 breaths per minute.

However, when a subject is in a potential conflict, where his freedom may be at stake, a significant increase in breathing rate takes place. You will note flared nostrils or a wide open mouth and the chest rise and fall at a more deeper and rapid pace. This natural effect opens the mouth and the nostrils flare in an effort to get the oxygenated blood to where it needs to go, the gross motor muscles, lungs, legs, and arms to prepare for the perceived potential fight or flight. Lips are another place to watch closely. A subject full of anxiety, lips may curl or tighten in a moment of decision making.

The jaw and neck: When we are fixed on a feat of strength, some of us clinch or teeth or bite our tongue in an effort to perform the strenuous action we choose. This clinching or biting is unconsciously shown, it's right there, plain to see. Think about yourself in the gym, about to lift some heavy weights or remember back to moving a heavy piece of furniture and looking across at your partner with tongue out or teeth clinched in an effort to assist. Someone skilled at deception and who knows himself will attempt to disguise this. The skilled observer can see the jaw moving slightly. This jaw clinching also moves the small muscles in the neck.

Watch also for raising or lowering of the chin. Chin up! Possible flight! Chin down! Possible fight! My experience has been either one of these chin up, or chin down, are accompanied by a slow deep breath and then action! Also the carotid artery is in the neck and when the fight or flight kicks in the pulse rate can be seen plainly, sending out a message anxiety is present, subtle signs and signals presenting themselves.

The Skin: Before we move on to the rest of the body let's talk of the signs and signals the skin gives off. First thing that's noticeable to the observant security or law enforcement officer, is the color of the skin. Is the skin suddenly flushed? Look for sudden redness in the face and ears. A sign survival stress is kicking in, as this happens, blood pressure rises and skin color changes to red or bright pink. This rising of the blood pressure can also result in the area of the face becoming pale colored.

Again survival stress causes this opposite reaction in some. The gross motor muscles need, blood pumped into them to prepare for action and simply the blood run from the small blood vessels in the face into those areas and is obvious to see. You can also note this effect in the neck and upper chest area as well, so be observant and heed the signs. Sweating or perspiration is another sign to watch for. Look in the area of the forehead or brow and the upper lip for drops of perspiration beading up. This is again a result of survival stress and the bodies' physiological response to anxiety and stress.

The Shoulders: The shoulder shrugs you will see take place usually in combination with a lot of head movement right, left up and down. You will also see an overall submissive body position, leaning forward with palms of hands open and facing upward or towards him. This is a sign of uncertainty and helplessness or submission. Be alert for the shoulder shrug as it may be an opportunity to talk your subject into compliance.

Chest: The chest brings us back to breathing rate. Normal breathing in a healthy person is around 12-20 breaths per minute. Under pressure and anxious the breathing rate increases. This breathing rate in combination with an increased heart rate will show itself and the trained observer who pays close attention will note this change. The chest will rise and fall at a more rapid pace. The heart rate in the warmer months can be seen beating through a tee-shirt of a would-be attacker or person committing a crime you come in contact with. Take note as to whether or not the chest of the individual you have made official contact with is squared off. Facing someone when you have nothing to hide is normal upper body positioning. If the subject is bladed or positioned at an angle, deception, attack or distance away from you are possible objectives.

Legs, Feet and Overall Body Positioning: Watch the legs and feet. Positioning of the legs squarely the subject is not in a good balanced position, for an assault. He can assault but it's not the best position.

Most would be attackers will stand as long as they can flat footed and squared off in an effort to lull you into complacency. When the survival stress kicks in and you begin to see the subject moving his feet and legs into a bladed, balanced "Fighters Stance" with hands either moving up into a boxer's position or held down along his sides with finger extended out, more than normal, the potential for attack is prevalent.

The more obvious is bladed body hands up in boxer's position. The more subtle gesture is the extended fingers at his side. This is done in an attempt to deceive you. In most cases where I have seen this cluster of gestures the fight comes suddenly and furiously. You must be alert, and take initiative quickly through decisive action to regain control.

Watch for *"happy feet"* the continued bouncing up and down rapidly on the balls of feet, is a sign of anxiety and stress as well as the high likelihood of fleeing. Assault could also be the motive behind this signal. You will see this signal in clusters with darting eyes and chin up with the subject leaning in the direction he wants to go accompanied by a slow deep breath at the moment of decision.

Distance and relative positioning are keys to staying safe. How you control the subject and approach, if approach is necessary, will be paramount to you seeking advantage. You want to control the subject, not the other way around. So be alert for a subject who closes distance with you. This closing of distance could be done quickly in an overt attack, or it could be done subtly and slowly and then attack, once the subject has gained the advantage of closing distance. Do not get lulled into complacency! Turn Boyd on and pay close attention to all subject's movements and immediately keep him in your control.

The Hands: Last But Not Least. The hands known in the law enforcement and security realms as "Deadly Hands", hold the tools that can cost you your life, or cause injury to you. The hands grip firearms, knives, clubs or any other object that can be turned into a dangerous or deadly weapon.

The hands and arms contain personnel weapons such as fists, fingers, edge of hand, arms and elbows can cause serious damage by a committed assailant.

You must break all you have been taught when it comes to eye contact, while speaking to others. What mom and dad taught as a sign of respect can get you seriously hurt or killed. I know this seems simple but the informal parental training and life experience from birth to present, of doing the respectful thing (eye contact) can be a hard habit to break. But it can and must be done.

An example of not seeing "Deadly Hands" from training: This scenario was a force on force free play exercise, using sim-munitions! I played the bad guy. My role was a man with a gun emotionally disturbed. The lesson was to get the responding officer to see the gun and respond accordingly. The responding officers were told they had a suspicious person acting strangely, and given a brief description. No mention that I was armed! 14
A single officer responded and made contact with me. The gun was in my right hand from the start, concealed behind a leg or crossed armed, under an armpit. As soon as contact was made and conversation began officers immediately made eye contact. I was role playing an emotionally disturbed person so I started talking and shouting and at the same time exposing the gun (a full size 45 colt). The first exposure was about hip level, and then a little higher and higher, thirty percent of the officers did not see the gun and respond until it was almost shoulder height. A smaller percentage did not see the gun until I fired upon them!

Most did not visually observe the gun until the second exposure to it.

The lesson: We must scan the hands first and make sure they are free from any weapons. Then once we initially see free hands and open palms, scan the rest of the body constantly and efficiently up and down, all around, throughout the contact. This is your Boyd Cycle working. Observe, orient, decide and act constantly to insure, no weapons get into the hands of the subject. This takes serious training.

We say serious training, but training comes in many forms. This can and should be done on every contact you make. Constantly scan and observe, every contact looking for weapons, location of hands, are they wearing rings, watches etc. are they carrying anything soda, beers, tools, keys, anything. This will enhance your ability to fine tune this skill as well as become better at reading body language as discussed throughout this article. One more key thing when it comes to *deadly hands.*

You must clear *"both hands"* If you find a weapon in one, you must make sure there is no weapon in the other, an obvious, yet often overlooked tactical consideration.

More signs and signals from the hands: It is important to note that the hands are one of the most expressive body parts. The hands show emotion, ideas and point to things of interest. Those things of interest can be internal thoughts to do harm. The hands hold more signs and signals than obvious weapons. Watch for *drying of the hands.* A subject may be nervous and begin to get sweaty palms and subtly dry them on his clothes, usually the thigh area of his pants or the front of his shirt. This drying of the hands could be simply removing the sweat from the palms or the drying could be to prepare to grab and assault. Look for *hand gestures to the face* another sign of nervousness and anxiety. *Hands to the head* or running the *hands through the hair* in what is called *"grooming" or self-stimulation."* This is a sign of high anxiety when we become fearful or deceptive. *Knuckle popping, stretching fingers,* is a sign of loosening up for potential attack.

Placing hands on hips elbows out and looking or turning away, is known as the *"Confrontational Gesture."* This person is in a NO mindset and will need to be watched closely with officer initiated, strategy and tactics to maintain control. The confrontational gesture is also in some cases accompanied by a cessation of communication and completely ignoring you.

Watch the hands for *rolling up shirtsleeves* or removing *hats from the head* and placing it in an *"I do not want my hat ruined during the fight location"* a sure signs of a physical confrontation. *Arms folded across the chest* is a sign of defensiveness, Its used as a subconscious form of protecting one self and gives the internal feeling of "I'm safe" or "you cannot get me." Watch for the hands rubbing arms or any other area of the body, again this is self-stimulation and is used as a form of comforting one's self in stressful situations.

The palms of hands send signals, the obvious being they should be empty of any weapons. More subtly they give a bigger picture of what's going on. Open palms facing up are a sign of submission. Open and turned towards him, means he is upset mostly with himself although still anxious. Palms open and facing you accompanied by questions like; why are *you* doing this to me? What are *you* going to do now? These are signs the subject is angry and upset with you. If the subject simultaneously closes distance, it could mean impending assault.

As we discussed the hands and arms naturally move a lot. The reversal of that and a key that something is amiss is *lack of movement or sudden cessation, of the hands and arms.* This is important to note as the *lack of movement* could be used to mask a hidden weapon, or it's an attempt by a street smart, experienced criminal to control his body language. A *sudden cessation* of movement means decisions are being made, *"fight, flight or give up?"* Make note of "nothingness when it comes to non-verbal communications, especially the hands. It is just in most cases not "NORMAL!"

Short choppy gestures: When you see hands and arms moving in short choppy gestures accompanied by a verbal barrage of anger directed at you, be prepared for an assault to take place. This is a form of psyching oneself up for ACTION! When you see this, ACT and take control of the subject. An impending attack is highly likely.

The Killing Gesture: When it came to eye contact I was little hard on mom and dad and their early training to always make eye contact. I will give them an A+ when it comes to "Pointing" as it has always been taught by mom and dad as being rude.

In the context of law enforcement or security officer contact, it is known as the "Killing Gesture." The index finger pointed towards an individual already emotionally aroused will indeed illicit a hostile verbal or physical assault.

We must be careful in utilizing this gesture and in reversal we must prepare to remain mentally calm when it's directed towards us. I have seen the pointing gesture used all too often by officers in an effort to gain control. I have also seen it brought to a heighten level of "Declaring War" by tapping the index finger on the chest of an unruly subject. Avoid the "Killing Gesture" *unless there is a good tactical reason for doing so.* If it's a habit, break it!

Tactical use of the Killing Gesture: To get a response in an effort to see if you have an assaultive person or not. Example if you have a person who is violently directed verbally, talking about how he is going to harm you. Your verbal communications has not curtailed his verbal attack and you are unsure of his true intent. Is he all bark and no bite, or is he about to assault?

You determined you need to take action to control the individual. You may want to simultaneously point towards the subject, use a more stern voice and demeanor, and move towards the subject, in an effort to show you will tolerate no longer the escalation of his behavior. "Turn and place your hands behind your back," Sit down on the ground," something to that effect. Based on the reaction, you control him for your safety, or if he raises the bar and becomes assaultive *use reasonable force* or *disengage* and wait for back-up.

I have seen this work in our favor on occasion ending with the verbally abusive subject giving up before it escalated out of control. Nothing is 100% guaranteed in conflict, so you must base it on the circumstances taking place.

Obviously if you can wait for back-up you do so. If no back up is available you have to make judgments as to your actions. You base this judgment on experience and the *fingertip feel (Fingerspitzengefühl)* and presence of mind you have.15

Taking into account the unfolding circumstances, environment and your equipment, skills, training, verses his. This is critical and you must adapt and make the judgments necessary for successful resolution.

The Killing Gesture I focused on the tactical use of because it is often over used as I mentioned above. If you are going to use it, make sure it's thought out.

Knowing Thyself: Sun Tzu said, in the Art of War *"Know yourself and know your enemy you will be safe in every battle. You may know yourself but not the enemy. You will then lose one battle for every one you win. You may not know yourself or the enemy. You will then lose every battle."*16

We have covered the signs and signals of crime and danger and what they mean in context of law enforcement and security. I want you to keep in mind that we need to control and use our own body language as well, if we are to seek the advantage we are looking for in an effort to control danger and violence.

The obvious method of working on this is through training ourselves to control our responses to remain mentally calm in the face of adversity. We are human and this takes practice, like any other skill we want to develop. The first step is to train yourself not to take things personal.

I know it is easier said than done, but it can be done, through self-analysis and an honest assessment of our strengths and weaknesses and making changes to improve. Most of the people we deal with are looking to get control of their lives back. We are the professionals and must first keep ourselves safe, and then attempt to resolve conflict, not encourage it out of some miss-guided sense of ego we possess.

If we can do that, we put ourselves in control of our own emotions. And our tactical judgments and actions are not made from a reaction of fear or anger, but instead, of sound judgment based on implicit and explicit information obtained from the environment we are in at the moment.

Recognizing the signs and signals of crime and danger and being able to interpret them, in context with the environment and circumstances, takes commitment on the part of individual law enforcement and security professionals. The subtle signs are the signs we as professionals must see, to seek advantage and maintain control. It's my belief that seeing the signs and signals early in an encounter will prevent the escalation of violence.

How?

By not allowing situations through lack of observation and orientation get out of control. Seeing the subtle signs and signals, understanding them, gives law enforcement and security the advantage necessary via decision making, to maintain control through initiative. Body Language is 5 times more valuable than the verbal communications. As professionals it's time we refocus our efforts more intently on this valuable information.

Chapter 21
Developing "Fingertip Feel" Shaping and Reshaping Dynamic Encounters to Gain the Advantage

"When the fight starts you do not have time to stop and think about the fundamentals." ~Chet Richards, Certain to Win 1

Chet Richards wrote an interesting piece "Developing the Touch", in which he asks the question, **if Fingerspitzengefühl (fingertip feel) can be taught, why do so few people have it?** He goes on to make two key points:

First, Fingerspitzengefühl is a skill, so although most people can get better at it, some are going to get a lot better.
Second, it's a strange kind of skill, not for performing complicated or even dangerous tasks mystically well, but for sensing what is going on among groups of people in conflict and then influencing what happens.2

Chet's points got me to thinking about, why is it we in law enforcement often times have difficulty applying what we know to a given situation?

How do we get better at it?
The answer lies in creating and nurturing our abilities in "Operational Art" taking what you know and being able to apply it to a given set of circumstances to affect your strategy and to bring an end to a potentially violent occurrence using appropriate tactics.
To do this takes awareness, discipline, adaptability, skill development and strength of character to focus our efforts on the task at hand to meet our overall intent. You cannot learn this by sitting in some training class listening to an instructor give you a checklist formula on how to solve a particular set of

problems. As Chet states:

*The first problem in learning Fingerspitzengefühl is that you can't learn it by yourself. You have to have at least two groups of people to practice with — your team and some opponents.*2

Our training must involve interaction with an adversary, red teaming comes to mind. Red Teaming is an approach to understanding our adversary and the methods they use. To develop a fingertip feel and maneuver we must possess numerous skills and be able to apply those skills individually and collectively if we are to be as effective as we need to be, to win. Winning requires knowing many things, including an understanding of the environment, the climate of the situation, psychology, physiology, decision making, social skills, combative skills, firearms skills, and leadership and how they apply to the overall mission or intent. Understanding the *whole of conflict and violence* allows us to get a better feel for the situation and allows us to, use attributes and ability to apply tactics in an effort to deceive, appear confusing to our adversary who generates disharmony or surprise, panic.

This allows us to seize and keep the initiative and hence exploit weaknesses and opportunities to gain compliance or utilize reasonable force options. Training must have this focus in mind. Use scenario based training and experiential learning with tactical decision games, being the foundation of your training. Include free play exercises to include force on force exercises with Sim-munitions to help create and nurture fingertip feel.

In an engagement all these factors combine in a synergistic way and require interaction with your adversary(s), fellow officers and the community. Interaction with your adversary(s) allows you to gather actionable information to employ in your efforts to solve whatever strategic and tactical problem you face. Information you have gathered only becomes actionable if you have the ability to take what you know and apply it in a way that accords with the circumstances and your overall intent.

You must always keep in mind that it is impossible to control exactly how the adversary(s) will respond to your actions. So the goal is to control the adversary's mindset with both direct and/or indirect action which takes decision making and adaptability.

Interaction, Insight and imagination are needed to adapt tactics and apply them in an initiative driven way to the particular problem at hand. The ability to apply these attributes in a violent encounter help to put you in a position of advantage. You can then seize the initiative on your terms. You control the tempo of things with interaction--moving in, tactically loitering, tactically swarming, tactically retreating, communication, negotiation, deception, and reasonable force options, etc. A balance of persuasion and force options focused on preventing or resolving the problem. This ability or *fingertip feel* to sense the environment and climate of the situation via the decision making cycle is known as *"operational art"* a much needed concept to understand if we are to connect our endgame (strategy) with how we play the game (tactics).

Learning the *art of operations* and develop the *fingertip feel* for applying tactics during interplay between adversaries, you can see is crucial to our success. This interplay teaches us that interaction leads to maneuver and maneuver opens up opportunities to exploit weaknesses. Then through superior situational awareness and insights you develop innovative ideas as you accord with an adversary. This leads to well thought out and/or intuitive decisions and actions to meet our strategic goals, whatever those goals may be.

In essence a highly developed *fingertip feel* allows us to shape and reshape the circumstances and conditions. We are not merely responding we are setting up the situation or as Sun Tzu stated:

*"Therefore it is said that victorious warriors win first, then go to war, while defeated warriors go to war first, then seek to win."*3

When having to perform effectively in the complex circumstances conflict and violence offer, we must strive to overcome obstacles and focus on exploiting weaknesses and avoiding adversarial strengths. This takes ability to intuitively feel the climate of an ongoing and rapidly changing situation and then adapt accordingly.

The ability and or timing of adaptation can be fleeting as opportunities present and close often times very quickly.

Developing fingertip feel so that we can rapidly transition fluidly as the circumstances require is critical. Boyd called these fast transient Maneuvers.

Generate a rapidly changing environment (quick/clear observations, orientation and decisions, fast-tempo, fast transient maneuvers, quick kill). Inhibit an adversary's capacity to adapt to such an environment (cloud or distort his observations, orientation, and decisions and impede his actions) simultaneously compress own time and stretch-out adversary time to generate a favorable mismatch in time/ability to shape and adapt to change. **Goal:** *Collapse adversary's system into confusion and disorder causing him to over and under react to activity that appears simultaneously menacing as well as ambiguous, chaotic, or misleading.*4

Law Enforcement Misfortunes: Developing a Fingertip Feel to Reduce:

We understand that conflict is a "clash between two adaptive systems"5, so when dealing with adapting adversaries you cannot predict exactly what's going to happen next, because there are things going on that you cannot see, or hear. For example: the numerous thoughts going through an adversaries mind: *"I will do what I am asked," "I will not do what I am asked," "I will escape," "I will fight," "I will assault," "I will kill," "I will play dumb until...," "I will stab," "I will shoot," "he looks prepared I will comply," "he looks complacent I will not comply,"* etc.

It is important to remember that the adversary has his own objectives; also, they have plans that conflict with the friendly side, therein creating further conflict and hence the need for adaptation.

If one side pauses to try and figure out (analysis) what's happening or gather more explicit (precise) information, it could be over with unfavorable results. Therefore, the obvious need for conditioning tactical judgment or implicit guidance and control is absolutely necessary. Both direct and indirect experiences come into play here.

To adapt to a walking, talking and thinking adversary takes training cops how to make decisions and take actions based on the situation verses the traditional training that is focused on policy and procedure, checklists or canned responses telling cops what to do. What to do in one set of circumstances can get you hurt or killed in another. It is time we open our eyes to this reality.

Law Enforcement history: Newhall, Waco, Ruby Ridge, Columbine, Virginia Tech, Trooper Mark Coates, Constable Lunsford, Officer Kyle Dinkheller, Oakland PD (2009), Pittsburg (2009), Okaloosa County Sheriff's Office, FL (2009), Seminole County Sheriff's Office, Ok (2009) Lakewood WA (2009), the 43 officers killed in the line of duty just in 2010 and the countless other lesson learned from law enforcement history we should heed and adapt accordingly.

To answer the Chet's question **If Fingerspitzengefühl (fingertip feel) can be taught, why do so few people have it?** I submit law enforcement spends too much time developing policies and procedures that stifle initiative and the ability to use interaction, Insight and Imagination.

These attributes are the building blocks of police operational art and we spend little time, if any developing them. What we need to do is develop a sense of mission and high morale. This takes leadership that knows how to develop people and use people and their ideas in a positive way that leads to developing individual, unit, shift and organizational discipline to train and prepare.

Presence of mind and superior situational awareness should alert our sense of urgency that we must not focus on the physical aspects of conflict only. Performing in extreme situations requires developing a *fingertip feel* to manipulate the *moral, mental and physical dimensions of conflict*.

Knowing this and how to apply the appropriate methods at the appropriate time takes fine-tuned and honed skills, a fingertip feel for Police operational Art!

Have you developed yours?

Chapter 22
Positive Leadership: Invest in People Building a Culture of Innovation

"THE BASIS OF COURAGE IS INDIVIDUAL INITIATIVE. IF WE CANNOT ACT ALONE, WE CANNOT ACT TOGETHER."
~JOHN MAXWELL 1

For a law enforcement organization to run smoothly it needs positive leadership. Positive leadership is when a leader interacts with the frontline. Interaction is not just getting to know those a leader works with and serves, although knowing your people is an important component to leading. Interaction is as well to continually develop and train and develop not only ourselves but those the leader serves in an effort to build a common outlook. In the end positive leader understands that a strong common outlook between the top and frontline establishes trust, or even better mutual trust. The leader's true work: BE WORTHY OF HIS OR HER CONSTITUENTS' TRUST. Positive leaders know the side with the stronger group feeling has a great advantage.2

Strong trust encourages delegation and reduces the amount of information and tactical direction needed at the top or strategic level. With less information to process and a greater focus on strategic issues, the decision making cycle at the top accelerates and the need for policies and procedures diminishes, creating a more fluid and agile organization. Mutual trust, unity and cohesion underlie everything.

Positive leaders give objective driven orders. Orders that give a commander's intent or end state of operations over methods. The commander expresses his or her desires in the form of an end state or outcome. This allows the subordinates to figure out the "how to." This reduces the need for explicit communications (micro-management) between command and the frontline.

This causes little overlap of responsibility and good economy of effort evolves throughout the organization, allowing the strategic, tactical and operational elements to influence the environment, and enabling decision making to be much more fluid in handling conventional and unconventional problem(s).

Tactics are not mandated from above but are developed and implemented at each level by those closest to the problem. In other words decisions are made by those reading and feeding off the scene as events unfold. This allows individual insight, innovation and initiative at solving problems, resulting in greater morale and engagement throughout the organization. These factors combine and increase the probability of rendering effective solutions to a vast array of law enforcement and safety and security related problems.

Positive leaders give the frontline broad authority, hence allowing initiative to be the driving factor behind solving problems, by continuously interacting with the environment allowing a fast and fluid decision making cycle on the frontline. Information flows from the bottom, up and influences the organization strategic and operational elements in accordance with the overall commander's intent.

What I am talking about here is that positive leadership offers s true decentralized control throughout the organization. This decentralized (BOTTOMS/ UP) approach allows freedom to decide at the strategic, operational and tactical levels of a law enforcement mission. The intuitive decisions are made at the tactical and operational levels while the slower strategic decisions are made at the top. Decision makers working cohesively at all levels enhance successful operations.

Positive leadership takes hard work on the part of all in an organization. Positive leaders focus on developing both themselves and those they lead making themselves the type of person people want to follow and at the same time developing others to be effective at their jobs. A Positive leader let go of their egos and lead to serve others and not for personal gain.

Positive leaders build positive relationships in an effort to influence others which in the end "influencing others" is what leadership is all about.

It takes a complete understanding that, *leadership is a day to day thing and not an event driven thing!* Day to day interaction, training and developing in an effort to prepare and ready all in an organization for any event we may face.

Positive leadership is about sharing whatever power you have throughout an organization, not keeping all you know to yourself. You must teach those you lead what you do and they will become better at what they do! Positive leadership inspires, imitative and action as well as continued learning, unlearning and relearning always striving to be better and more effective at what we do. Positive leaders breed positive attitudes and DOERS.

"Good character is more to be praised than outstanding talent. Most talents are, to some extent, a gift. Good character, by contrast, is not given to us. We have to build it piece by piece, by thought, choice, courage and determination."
~John Luther 3

Chapter 23
What Represents a High Level of Professionalism?

The essential thing is action. Action has three stages: the decision born of thought, the order or preparation for execution, and the execution itself. All three stages are governed by the will. The will is rooted in character, and for the man of action character is of more critical importance than intellect. Intellect without will is worthless, will without intellect is dangerous.
~Hans von Seeckt 1

Law enforcement demands professional competence among its leaders. As law enforcement professionals charged with protecting and serving communities, law enforcement leaders must be true experts in the conduct of policing. They must be individuals both of action and of intellect, skilled at "getting things done" while at the same time conversant in the law enforcement art. Resolute and self-reliant in their decisions, they must also be energetic and insistent in execution.

The law enforcement profession is a thinking profession. Every cop is expected to be a student of the art and science of conflict, crime and justice. Leaders are expected to have a solid foundation in police theory and, knowledge of law enforcement history and the timeless lessons to be gained from it.

Leaders must have a strong sense of the great responsibility of their position; the resources they will expand in conflict or crisis are human lives.

The United States policing style of dealing with conflict and crisis requires intelligent leaders with a penchant for boldness and initiative down to the lowest levels. Boldness is an essential moral trait in a leader for it generates power beyond the physical means at hand. Initiative, the willingness to act on one's own judgment, is a prerequisite for boldness.

These traits carried to excess can lead to rashness, but we

must realize that errors by frontline street cops stemming from over boldness are a necessary part of learning.

We should deal with such errors leniently; there must be no "zero defects" mentality. Abolishing "zero defects" means that we do not stifle boldness or initiative through the threat of punishment. It does not mean that leaders do not council subordinates on mistakes; constructive criticism is an important element of learning. Nor does it give subordinates free license to act stupidly or recklessly.

Not only must we not stifle boldness or initiative, but we must continue to encourage both traits in spite of mistakes. On the other hand, we should deal severely with errors of inaction or timidity. We will not accept lack of orders as justification for inaction; it is each police officers duty to take initiative as the situation demands. We must not tolerate the avoidance of responsibility or necessary risk.

Consequently, trust is the essential trait among leaders in effective organizations. Trust by leaders in the abilities of their frontline and by frontline in the competence and support of their leaders. Trust must be earned, and actions which undermine trust must meet with strict censure. Trust is a product of confidence and familiarity built through rigorous professional development. Confidence among fellow officers results from demonstrated professional skill. Familiarity results from shared experiences and a common professional philosophy.

Relations among all leaders from street cop to chief should be based on honesty and frankness regardless of disparity between ranks. Until a leader has reached and stated a decision, the street cop should consider it their duty to provide honest, professional opinions even though these may be in disagreement with leadership's opinion. However once the decision has been reached, frontline personnel must support it as if it were their own.

Leaders must encourage candor among the ranks and must not hide behind their rank. Read y compliance for the purpose of personal advancement, the behavior of "yes-men" will not be tolerated.

We adapted this short chapter from the United States Marine Corps manual, Warfighting.2

We think it is fitting to strive for in law enforcement.

Chapter 24
In Mastering Tactics Shouldn't We Be Blending Policy and Procedures with People and Ideas?

In complex settings in which we have to take the context into account, we can't codify all the work in a set of procedures. No matter how comprehensive the procedures, people probably will run into something unexpected and will have to use their judgment.
  ~Gary Klein 1

Much of this chapter comes from an outstanding book, *Streetlights and Shadows: Searching for the Keys to Adaptive Decision Making*, written by Gary Klein. Klein is a leading researcher on recognized primed decision making and experiential learning that has culminated in two other books, *Sources of Power* and *Intuition at Work*, as well, as, countless research papers.2

The information in this topic of decision making and how to create and nurture it, is beneficial to every cop in their quest to mastering tactics and tactical decision making and are a must read for every cop wanting to be more effective and safe on the street. My purpose is to get cops thinking about this critical question: *In mastering tactics shouldn't we be blending policy and procedure with people and ideas?*

It should be understandable that teaching people, procedures helps them perform tasks more skillfully doesn't always apply. Procedures are most useful in well-ordered situations when they can substitute for skill, not augment it. In complex situations, in the shadows of the unknown, uncertain and unpredictable and complex world of law enforcement conflict, procedures are less likely to substitute for expertise and may even stifle its development.

Here is a different way of putting it as Klein explains: *In complex situations, people will need judgment skills to follow* *procedures effectively and to go beyond them when necessary.*3

For stable and well-structured tasks i.e. evidence collection and handling, follow-up investigations, booking procedures and report writing, we should be able to construct comprehensive procedure guides. Even for complex tasks we might try to identify the procedures because that is one road to progress. But we also have to discover the kinds of expertise that comes into play for difficult jobs such as, robbery response, active shooter and armed gunman situations, hostage and barricade situations, domestic disputes, drug and alcohol related calls and pretty much any other call that deals with emotionally charged people in conflict.

Klein states, *"to be successful we need both analysis (policy and procedure) and intuition (people and ideas)."*4 Either one alone can get us into trouble. Experts certainly aren't perfect, but analysis can fail. Intuition isn't magic either. Klein defines intuition as, *"ways we use our experience without consciously thinking things out"*. Intuition includes tacit knowledge that we can't describe. It includes our ability to recognize patterns stored in memory. We have been building these patterns up all our lives from birth to present, and we can rapidly match a situation to a pattern or notice that something is off, that some sort of anomaly is warning us to be careful.5

Here is where we must *trust our gut* and go beyond the policy, adapt and innovate to be successful. There is a science and art to policy and procedures. The *science* is where the best practices, policy and procedures come from and are developed around. The *art* is where people, ideas, insight, innovation and initiative come as we interact and attempt to resolve law enforcement problems.

Like all tools, procedures have strengths and weaknesses.

Although I have been describing their limitation, we certainly shouldn't discard them. Here is what Gary Klein says they buy us:

- They are training tools. They help novices get started in learning a task.
- They are memory aids. In many jobs they help cops overcome memory slips.
- They can safeguard against interruptions.
- They reduce workload and make it easier to attend to critical aspects of the task.
- They are a way to compile experience and historical information. Procedures are useful when there is a lot of turnover and few workers ever develop much skill.
- They help less experienced cops do a reasonably acceptable job. They can walk a skilled marksman through the steps of handling a pistol or rifle malfunction. They can help a crime annalist troubleshoot a tricky crime trend.
- They can help teams coordinate by imposing consistency. If the people on the team know the same procedures, they can predict one another's next moves.
- The last advantage is particularly important for ad hoc teams that don't have a chance to practice and train together regularly.6

The downside to procedures is that they usually aren't sensitive to context. In complex situations we may not know when to start and end each step. The people making procedures usually try to substitute precision and detail for tacit knowledge. People sometimes make up procedural guides to capture what they think experts are doing. That's a noble intent, but procedural guides really can't explain the tacit knowledge that people acquire over decades of experience. We must be careful in the policy and procedure development process.

Procedures help when you need people to reliably follow the same steps. However, that's different from needing reliable outcomes. For example, on the range or on the street a shooter must place the round down range to the center of available mass, shot after shot, yet we don't care if the arc of the gun, the foot placement, movement, the bend in the shooters knees, is the same each time. And it isn't the same. Even the experienced shooter alters the arc of the gun, his stance, position, his posture in order to get an accurate shot.

Getting procedures right is not just a matter of getting them to be accurate or efficient or updated or covering all the needed contexts, which may well be both impossible and prohibitively expensive in time and money. **It is also a matter of getting the organization to have the right attitude toward procedures.**

To put procedures into prospective, Gary Klein gives this example:

Consider the difference between directions and maps. When we have to travel to an unfamiliar destination, we sometimes get directions, a sequence of actions (e.g., go straight for two blocks, then turn left). Other times we get a map showing where we are, where we want to be, and the terrain in between. The directions are easier to follow, but if anything goes wrong (say, a street is blocked off) we are stuck. A map demands more of us but makes it easier for us to adapt and can be used for other routes in the same area. We have the guide but we still must use our judgment.7

Think about this in terms of the types of calls we in law enforcement respond too. Is everything always the same on that domestic or a car stop or are their mismatches that create confusion and a need to bypass certain policies and procedures and we must resort to real time innovative tactical problem solving to resolve the situation more effectively?

Klein goes on:

For many types of complex work we need both procedures and the judgment to interpret and work around the procedures. In a 2007 study (Hockey, G.; Sauer, J.; Wastell, D. "Adaptability of Training in Simulated Process Control: Comparison of

Knowledge- and Rule-based Guidance under Task Changes and Environmental Stress, Human Factors, Vol.49) found, "people trained to understand the way a system worked were more flexible, and did a better job of spotting and fixing unfamiliar and complex problems, than people trained to follow rules and procedures. However, they also take longer to do the work, and they were more affected by a stressor, noise, than people who had been trained to follow procedures." This clearly states to me, there is a need for "blending policies and procedures with people and ideas. 8

How?
Developing effective policies and procedures and implementing them with effective training. Ongoing training that builds the foundation and the ability to adapt when necessary!

Teaching procedures
When we want to teach some procedures, the typical way is to present the standard procedures and make everyone memorize and practice them. Not good enough!
   Here is another way to teach procedures. Setup scenarios for various kinds of challenges and let cops go through the scenarios. If the procedures make sense, then cops should get to see what happens when they depart from the optimal procedures. When procedures are taught in a scenario format, people can appreciate why the procedures were put into place and can also gain a sense of the limitations of the procedures.
This scenario format works better than having people memorize the details of each step. The scenarios provide a good counterpoint for learning the steps of complicated tasks. Moreover, the scenarios can help people acquire some of the tacit knowledge they need in order to apply procedures effectively.

Why Does Blending Policy and Procedures with People and Ideas Matter?

It matters because when we emphasize procedures over skills we set a standard of mediocre performance. The standard procedures become a basis for evaluating job performance, making people even less likely to adapt or improvise and more careful to comply with the rules. In unpredictable settings (law enforcement setting), the standard procedures can impede progress because cops may have to explore the situation and experiment and not be told what to do every step of the way.

It matters because too often we issue procedures in order to change behavior even though there may be simpler and more effective ways to do that.

We cannot take all the guesswork out of law enforcement decisions by providing procedures to follow and clear criteria for how to move on to each step. *Teaching people procedures helps them perform tasks more skillfully.* This statement reflects our desire to break complex tasks into step by step procedures. Dr. Gary Klein ran into this attitude in initial research on recognized primed decision making, working with firefighters.

"I asked them how they made their decisions and they explained that they rarely if ever, had to decide anything. 'We just follow the standard procedures,' they explained. But when asked to see the procedures they told me they weren't written down. Firefighters just knew what to do. Even when faced with a complex situation, the commanders could see it as familiar and know how to react.

The commander's secret was that their experience let them see a situation, even a non-routine one, as an example of a prototype, so they knew the typical course of action right away. Their experience let them identify a reasonable reaction as the first one they considered, so they did not bother thinking of others. They were not being perverse. They were being skillful. We now call this strategy recognition-primed decision making."10

Klein says, "the *Recognition-Primed Decision Making Model* fuses two processes: *the way decision makers' size up the situation to recognize which course of action makes sense, and* *the way they evaluate the course of action by imagining it. It is important to keep in mind that decisions evolve with circumstances. While some decisions are made simply, with more time to decide, other decisions require quick if-then thinking in order to achieve results."*11

The focus here is how to prepare members of the law enforcement profession to make those rapid decisions that need to be made under pressure. Blending people and ideas with policy and procedures is the way to that outcome.

This is a challenging task, which will take hard work and a coactive effort by all members of policing. After careful consideration, and reassessing and reshaping my own ideas on the value of policy and procedures, is a task I believe worth undertaking, when balance out by allowing people (cops) and their ideas, their skills to evolve when dealing with real time rapidly changing circumstances if we are to move our profession forward toward full spectrum and effective responses.

Chapter 25
Tactical Decision Games to Increase Speed and Maturity of Problem Solving: The Lessons Learned

Confronted with a task, and having less information available than is needed to perform that task, an organization may react in either of two ways. One is to increase its information-processing capacity, the other to design the organization, and indeed the task itself, in such a way as to enable it to operate on the basis of less information. These approaches are exhaustive; no others are conceivable. A failure to adopt one or the other will automatically result in a drop in the level of performance.
~Martin van Creveld, Command in War 1

The ability to solve emerging problems, both those day to day issues that we encounter in normal work, and those complex emergencies that hit us without warning, are pivotal to our personal and organizational survival in difficult economic times. *Tactical Decision Games* are short, pointed exercises to increase the speed and maturity of problem solving. Used regularly and thoughtfully, tactical Decision Games will train individuals and teams to shorten the time needed to recognize and successfully overcome emergent problems of any type.

EXL Pharma is an emerging leader in developing innovative and educational events that serve the healthcare community and allied professionals. On Wednesday March 19 2012, Dr. Terry Barnhart and Fred Leland facilitated a workshop Tactical Decision Games to Increase Speed and Maturity of Problem Solving. There were 17 workshop participants from the pharmaceutical profession, all leaders in Lean Six Sigma with strong backgrounds identifying and setting up frameworks to solve problems.2

The workshop consisted of 4 tactical decision games that included typical Pharma research and development problems as well as leadership and workplace violence scenario.

Participants used problem solving tools such as; critical question mapping, A-3s, thought mapping, 6 hats methodology and each exercise included an after action review. The goals of the workshop was to develop both rapid and rational methods of decision making and to learn from experiencing novel and unconventional problems how to use experience, intuitive and logical thinking to create and nurture people who are comfortable in uncertain conditions, building confident decision makers who understand their options when solving problems.

The lessons learned from the workshop were many. The use of tactical decision games induced stress levels that created initial confusion and uncertainty, even among these experienced problem solvers; however the problem solving tools helped create and nurture quickly the ability for strangers to form groups or teams and develop unit cohesion in a rapid manner. Through their experience and socials skills they identified the problems presented through robust conversation and a willingness to collaborate that led all groups to successfully identify paths to outcomes they sought. They were able to engage pretty broadly on very complicated problems in 5 -20 minutes depending upon the scenario. They began to understand the power of human attributes such as; strength of character, decisiveness, seeing and testing assumptions, identifying the power of interaction and the value of incorporating other people's ideas into more effective outcomes.

That said, none of the groups were able to come to successful outcomes in all scenarios, displaying an inability to convert their problem structuring into a course of action. This could possibly be from **bias towards reflection** as Lean Six Sigma leaders in the pharmaceutical industry have strong training at identifying and setting up problems due to their lean training (and typical academic training as scientists).

By contrast most cops, security and military teams appear to have a greater **bias towards action**, but struggle with identifying and setting up problems.

Taking this thinking into Boyd's OODA model for decision making, we observe that some groups (like researchers and Lean Sigma experts) will have a propensity to get stuck in the observation and orientation (OO) phases, while others (e.g. cops) will have the propensity to decide and act (DA) in the absence of a good orientation. These examples show different overemphasis in our thinking and learning cycles, disaggregating a balanced thought processes and potentially leading to failure. With this in mind, it is apparent that when training better decision making into any profession, one focus of effort should be on how we engage in improving the entire OODA Loop or thought process so that we balance a bias for reflection with the bias for action based on the unfolding conditions, time and risk.3

I attended this conference because I saw it as a great learning opportunity and I expected to see vast differences in how research and development people from the pharmaceutical industry as compared to those of us in law enforcement. The main difference was the bias for reflection versus the bias for action mentioned above, but most everything else I observed over the four days was very much similar and centered on the human element. Throughout the conference including the other classes I attended was a big emphasis on the human side of decision making and the barriers that stifle it.

Communications and ensuring the flow of information is *flowing up/down/sideways* in a robust way ensures that mission and intent is understood and allows for all to possess a common outlook allowing parallel execution throughout the organization. What we reward, tolerate and punish is what people will base their execution on or put another way; "*people train and execute to the test.*

So it's important for leaders to acknowledge resistance toward any new method, policy, procedure or initiative sought by the organization to help manage the mindset of all in the organization. This will help enhance the common goals, mission and intent so important to execution in any organization.4

What does this mean for future workshops and our training? We will look for a bias for action or reflection and if detected engage the team in overcoming that bias. This understanding of what bias, reflection or action is important to identify as it could be detrimental to fluid, effective and ongoing observation, orientation, decision and action cycles. Law Enforcement questions; how will this help us police better? How do we add value to the methods and tactics we use? What cognitive biases do we have that we need to be aware of and work around to become better real time decision makers? Then how do we reshape our culture so we become an organization that can really see and solve our problems and make that culture stick?

To share a comment from a fellow conference member and Pharma professional I feel was quite insightful in our efforts to continually learn, unlearn and relearn and breed the culture of a learning organization, "we need to prepare the ground, plant the seeds and replant the seeds" so the root of sound decision makers and state of the art problem solvers takes hold and does not wither away.

Then he told them many things in parables, saying. "A farmer went out to sow his seed. As he was scattering the seed, some fell along the path, and the birds came and ate it up. Some fell on rocky places, where it did not have much soil. It sprang up quickly, because the soil was shallow. But when the sun came up, the plants were scorched, and they withered because they had no root. Other seed fell among thorns, which grew up and choked the plants. Still other seed fell on good soil, where it produced a crop-a hundred, sixty or thirty times what was sown. He, who has ears, let him hear.
~Mathew 15:5-9 5

Chapter 26
Adaptive Leader Methodology: An Alternative for Better Outcomes

Adaptive Course Model (ACM) offers the first responder a better alternative to the traditional "input-based" or "competency theory" philosophy that currently governs their training programs at all levels.1

ACM is perhaps best described as "developmental training," i.e., the development of the individual within the training of a first responder's or leader's task. It emphasizes teaching the "why" behind actions through an emphasis on the fundamental principles that should guide future actions and decisions. ACM is best suited to nurture innovation and adaptability, the characteristics that are absolutely essential on today's complex streets and in handling crisis situations. The recurring question, however, is this: how does one teach in an ACM environment? What are the "how to" aspects of implementing the theory behind ACM? Perhaps most importantly, how does a trainer approach leader development using this philosophy?

This last question is of particular importance to homeland security (law enforcement, emergency medical, fi re and security) in entry-level, advanced and continuing education and training programs. It is easy to proclaim the need to build adaptive leaders during a PowerPoint briefing, but it is quite another matter to achieve the desired outcome.2

The Adaptive Course Model provides a "how to" guide for leader development and instruction within today's environment. This methodology emphasizes nurturing, effective decision-making and adaptability through experiential learning. In keeping with an outcomes-based approach to training, ACM focuses on the fundamental principles of the exercise and encourages experimentation and innovation when exploring solutions. Aspiring leaders are allowed to try, and sometimes fail, as they struggle to solve increasingly complex tactical problems.3

Each individual's strength of character is tested through a crucible of decision-making exercises and communication drills that require the students to brief and then defend their decisions against focused criticism from their peers and instructors.

As a Lieutenant in the Walpole Police Department and the founder of a law enforcement consulting firm (LESC, Inc.), I have been part of a determined collective effort to improve how we develop law enforcement professionals. I have implemented this approach within our department, and as a central aspect of the training courses I offer through LESC, Inc. With ACM serving as the guiding philosophy, retired Army Major Don Vandergriff has implemented instruction based on the ACM model within the Army, and is now starting to spread it outside the Army to law enforcement, businesses and academic organizations.4

It was clear to us that the old briefing and lecture-based methods of teaching—called the "competency model"—were falling well short of where the Army wanted to be given the complex environments its leaders and soldiers are facing; a change was necessary. ACM was their guide as courses redesigned their curriculums to grow the individual while achieving task proficiency. Beginning in 2007, several courses, including the United States Military Academy's Department of Military Instruction (DMI), captain, lieutenant and non-commissioned officer courses throughout the Army put ACM into practice, learning some valuable lessons along the way. The effort continues, and changes continue to be implemented based on the feedback from the initial term.5

As we write this handbook, several programs are enjoying unprecedented success and receiving enthusiastic feedback from our students. The purpose of this article is to outline the Army's efforts to implement ACM within the framework of a homeland security and first responder environment, and to communicate their lessons-learned from this exciting period of execution.6

Teaching with ACM

As stated above, ACM emphasizes nurturing effective decision making and adaptability through experiential learning. Experimentation comes first through the execution of Tactical Decision-Making Exercises (TDEs) followed by student briefings of their decisions, plans or orders. After the student explains himself and responds to criticism from his peers and instructor, the group executes an intense instructor-facilitated After-Action Review (AARs).7

The instruction is accomplished through AARs as the students discover for themselves the concepts and principles included in that lesson's learning objectives. Only after this has occurred, is the theory or doctrine involved formally introduced by the instructor. The students generally find themselves saying: "Wow! That's what you call it!" There are no preparatory reading assignments or lectures prior to the execution of the TDE. Instead, the readings follow the exercises, allowing the students to more effectively absorb the information within the context that they already established during their experimentation in the classroom.8

The Tactical Decision-Making Exercise (TDE) is the basic tool that is used in ALM based classes regardless of the focus. If it is a decision making scenario where an individual or a team must solve a problem, then each TDE consists of a scenario summary and a map with graphics.

The instructor has the option to either hand out a printed copy of the scenario or to issue it verbally to his students, requiring them to listen closely and take notes. The TDEs in ALM based classes are generally of two types: (1) immediate decision exercises that give the students a range of time, usually from 30 seconds to a few minutes, to make a decision and (2) planning exercises that are longer in duration and culminate in the briefing of orders.9

In either case, the students are given both limited time and limited information to make their decisions and complete their plans.

This induces stress and allows them to discover for themselves that delaying decisions until one has "perfect intelligence" is both unrealistic and ineffective.

As in combat, or dealing with crisis ever-changing situations are the norm as instructors issue fragmentary orders (FRAGOs) or changes that require the students to make new decisions. In this way, TDEs nurture adaptability and flexibility as chaos becomes commonplace.10

A specific area of emphasis for instructors is the examination of how students use the information at their disposal. Can they distinguish between information that is pertinent in making decisions and that which is insignificant? Can they do so quickly? Are they then able to translate why that information is important and determine how they should use it? This is the essence of the Boyd Cycle, a 4-step theory of decision-making that was first articulated by Col. John R. Boyd following his study of fighter pilots in combat during the Korean War.11

Commonly known as "OODA" (observation, orientation, decision, action), the Boyd Cycle is a useful framework for the assessment of students throughout any course using ACM. In ACM based courses and our workshops we focus on the critical step of "orientation" because this is where the students attempt to make sense out of the information at hand. The decision that the student makes is important, but how they arrived at that decision is equally significant. Although some might be tempted to draw parallels between OODA and the methodical, process-oriented focus of the Army's Military Decision-Making Process (MDMP) or known as the "analytical approach" in business and first responder circles, these two concepts are extremely different. The

MDMP is "a linear and analytical decision-making approach" while OODA is a guide for how to think that allows for creative thought and innovation without the restrictions of a rigid step-by-step procedure.12

It is also important to understand that ACM instructors do not "teach" the Boyd Cycle. There is no block of instruction or reading assignment devoted to the academic aspects of the OODA Loop. Instead, the Boyd Cycle is an intellectual framework for ACM instructors as they guide the execution of TDEs. Students in an ALM based course exercise their OODA Loops without knowing that they are doing so.13

This practical, hands on approach to teaching often inspires anxiety in the minds of those who have grown comfortable with traditional methods of instruction. The most common complaint is "the basics should be taught first!" After all, the critics argue, how can we teach any student how to plan a tactical operation before we teach them the organization and technical aspects of their respective organization?

What these critics fail to understand is that students learn much more effectively by experimenting and making mistakes than by having the "answers" spoon-fed to them beforehand.14

With ACM, students learn through immersion in a scenario. For example in an Army course using ACM, by executing a TDE that requires them to employ an air assault infantry platoon with the mission of conducting an ambush, a student will learn not only the principles behind planning an ambush, but they also learn about the assets at their disposal. Such is the same for law enforcement: executing a TDE that requires a response to an active shooter in the workplace, shopping mall or school. Again the student will learn to plan and execute a tactical response and approach to stopping the ongoing deadly action and rescue the injured, while also developing an understanding of what resources they have available to assist in such a dynamic response. Without a single PowerPoint slide or lecture, students learn several complex tactical concepts.15

Vandergriff and I, as well as many Army instructors, have seen that the immersion scenario keeps students mentally engaged in the class, and invariably results in higher levels of enthusiasm for the training and better results when applied in real life scenarios.16

The Theory of Maneuver Warfare: A Unifying Framework

Diversity is important in ACM-based courses. Army focused tactical scenarios involve many different types of units as well as a wide variety of operating environments. Homeland security professionals including police, fire, EMS, and others can apply the same approach. Students solve problems within the context of high-intensity combat, peacekeeping operations, and counter-insurgency (COIN). This diversity is well suited to the intent of a course as it makes students adapt to the tactical situation of the moment. With each lesson, future leaders'—regardless of specialty—"comfort zones" grow ever larger. While this diversity is absolutely essential, it remains important to keep everyone (instructors as well as students) moving in the same direction. In order to achieve this, the course requires a "conceptual azimuth" to guide our efforts.17

William S. Lind's theory of Maneuver Warfare offers a unifying framework that binds our lessons together through a common set of themes, and we have discovered this also applies to any organization that relies on each of its members to demonstrate adaptability as it operates in a high intense and ever-changing environment.18

First, students learn to approach their analysis of the terrain (or tactical environment) and the opponent (man-made or natural crisis) with the objective of identifying that which they can use to their advantage.19 With respect to the enemy (criminal, terrorist element or Mother Nature), we teach our students to identify enemy strengths (which they must avoid) and weaknesses (which they must exploit).20

Rather than strictly focusing on producing a product such as an enemy course of action sketch, the cadets seek to gain an understanding of the enemy that is useful for future decision-making. This approach is applicable in any type of operating environment but especially so when facing the complex problems of counter-insurgency or dealing with today's transnational crime or terrorist action.

With counter-insurgency, it is often more difficult to identify the weaknesses of today's criminals, criminal gangs and terrorists, and a greater challenge to find ways to exploit them. However, the reality of our current conflicts shows that finding creative ways to defeat an asymmetrical threat is essential for our tactical leaders.

Secondly, it is vital that students understand the long term consequences of their immediate actions. This requires the ability to operate within the framework of their higher headquarters "Commander's Intent."21

In order to reinforce this concept, students see orders as "contracts" between senior and subordinate. The higher commander assigns a mission (the short term contract) with the understanding that the subordinate leader will be allowed maximum latitude in figuring out exactly how he will accomplish that mission. The only stipulation is that the subordinate leader's "solution" must not violate the Commander's Intent. This intent constitutes the long term contract between senior and subordinate.

Ethical conduct and adherence to the Rules of Engagement (ROE) are always part of the Commander's Intent, and this serves to emphasize the often strategic-level consequences of actions at the lowest levels. We have found the U.S. Army lessons from their current wars in Iraq and Afghanistan apply to everyday problems that law enforcement encounters.22

Thus, the way ACM is used by the Army also has applications in developing first responder's to deal with the conventional and unconventional threats they face. The final unifying theme in ACM-based courses is that they focus on the way that "tactics" are defined. In ALM based courses, instructors describe tactics as unique "solutions" to specific problems, not tasks or drills that must be executed through doctrinal formulas or set procedures.23

Following fixed rules not only results in predictability, it quickly becomes an excuse for not thinking. Since courses using ACM focus on "how to think" about tactical problem-solving, while developing an individual's competence and confidence, anything that discourages creative thought has no place in its curriculum.

Assessments and Grading

Developing an effective plan for assessing students is the most difficult challenge for courses applying ACM as part of their Program of Instruction (POI). The reason for this is the tendency to seek easily quantifiable methods of assessment. In most course environments so much depends on a student's class rank and the number of people a course graduates that there is often a burning desire to remove judgment from instructors in favor of a rigid, mathematical grading rubric. In short, there is a natural fear of subjectivity and a longing for the safety and presumed reliability of numbers and checklists. However, is it "safe" to quantify the intangibles of leadership and adaptability? How can one assign a number to creativity and initiative?

Despite these questions, one thing is certain: fill-in-the-blank and multiple choice tests are woefully inadequate for measuring our effectiveness in achieving the desired outcomes for our military science program. Since the ability to memorize information is not a good indicator of one's decision-making skills while in conflict, there is no reason to use this criterion as a basis for testing.24

Instead, an ACM based examination focuses on things that are much more difficult to quantify, placing a great deal of the responsibility and trust in the individual instructor. Some ACM based tests are of the short-answer variety. These examinations place students in a specific tactical scenario and require them to make decisions. They must then explain the reasons behind their decision in writing. For example, a student might be told that he is the commander for a convoy of vehicles that must travel to an assigned destination within the next several hours.25

After being presented with information about the composition of the convoy, a map, the nature of the enemy threat, and the specifics of the mission and Commander's

Intent, the student would have to determine which route he will take and then explain why that route was selected. The instructor then assigns a grade on the approach used to solve the problem using the information at hand and how well the reasoning was communicated. This gets to the point of examining "how" the student is thinking, but not "what" he is thinking.26

Another and more common, assessment technique that ACM instructors use is a "graded TDE." Just like the short-answer tests, these are scenario-based and require students to make decisions on the fly. This technique is virtually identical to a standard in-class TDE with the exception that students are required to write out or brief their solutions to their instructors who, in turn, grade those solutions. In many cases, these examinations require students to produce a concept sketch with short hand-written notes concerning exact guidance for individuals, their teams, the sequence of events, and most importantly the purpose behind various actions.27

Regardless of the technique or format of the assessment, the tactical scenario must allow for multiple correct ways to solve the problem. For the assessment to be truly effective, students must have the freedom to actually make a decision on their own and formulate a plan rather than being forced to regurgitate a pre-determined template. If tests fail to allow room for creativity, students become focused on identifying the approved solution rather than thinking for themselves.

In order to permit freedom of thought, scenarios must have a significant amount of ambiguity. The situation must be such that one could reasonably interpret the available information in multiple ways. Of course, this does not preclude the existence of wrong answers.

Violations of the Commander's Intent, unethical conduct, poor communication, or an unrealistic course of action all constitute an automatic failure. Additionally, if the student is unable to make a decision within the time and information constraints of the test, the student is assigned a failing grade.28

These automatic failure criteria are absolutely essential in communicating to students that they cannot achieve success in the class by going through the motions of employing a template or checklist to the problem.29

The intentional ambiguity in the scenarios necessitates other efforts to keep everyone on the same path when it comes to grading. It is vital to ensure consistency across the board in this area without imposing an overly-restrictive grading scheme that would hinder freedom of judgment from the instructors. In order to effectively calibrate the grading criteria, all instructors must participate in a free exchange of ideas regarding the key concepts that are the focus of the upcoming assessment.30

In ACM-based courses, these group discussions are referred to as Faculty Development (FD) sessions. Not all FD sessions focus on grading, but those that do begin with the instructors actually taking the test followed by an open discussion regarding the content of the exam and how to approach grading. At the end of this exchange, the Course Director compiles the applicable notes from the session into a short set of general guidelines. Because these guidelines are the product of a collective effort, they keep grading consistent among all instructors.31

Conclusion

One of the essential principles of outcomes based training is the requirement to treat the trainee like an adult. This encourages them to take ownership of their development and training. Not surprisingly, students at all levels from entry level to senior executives respond accordingly. If the expectation is that they cannot be trusted to do anything without micro-management, then students will fail without extensive guidance.

However, if from the very beginning the expectation is that they must think on their own and take responsibility for their own training, they will almost always conduct themselves responsibly.

We have applied this principle in our workshop "Deciding

under Pressure and Fast"32 workshop over the past three years, which inspired a surge in enthusiasm from students from several Army courses. What they seem to enjoy most is the fact that they are actually allowed to make decisions and figure things out on their own. Rather than being asked to regurgitate lists of information, they are required to think creatively under pressure. Many of students took the time to voice their opinions either through the automated end of course survey and via personal emails to us after our workshop or the courses were completed.

Their comments on the method of instruction (ACM) were almost uniformly positive with statements like these from BPD police officers who attended the workshop in 2010:

We had never in any of my previous so called professional courses within the department, been treated like professionals. My voice was heard, but not for the sake of being heard, but as interaction. I learned as much from my fellow students—a variety of officers from all aspects of the department—as I did from the teachers, who we called the facilitator. The exercises drove these discussions and were not limited by state requirements of one way to do it, but 14 other students all pitching trying to solve the problem. The facilitators, also fellow police officers but on the list to make lieutenant, guided us through the exercises and encouraged us to solve the problem. They could have stepped in and taken over as I have seen in every course inside and outside the department, but they did not. It was outstanding!!

Another student, a sergeant with 12 years in the police force stated,

After the first day, I looked forward to coming back, and this enthusiasm grew each day. For the first time in my life, I was sorry that the course was over. I learned so much because we were encouraged to learn more and get better through a series of more complex but achievable exercises. Finally was easy, we did a series of Active Shooter exercises, followed by intense AARs that wore me out. I realized how bad shape both mentally and physically I had become.

The previous classes seemed to be merely checking the box. 'Okay here is a situation and here is how it was resolved. Study it and know it.' I didn't like that approach very much. I enjoy the way we did it this in your workshop because it was really my plan or decision that failed or succeeded. Courses in the past have been monotonous and boring. The approach this new course required us to take an interest, make a call, and put ourselves in the shoes of a real leader on the street."33

I think the class discussions were the best part of the course. We went over alternate solutions for TDEs, and we had to defend ourselves against criticism. This made me more confident in myself, but it also showed me other perspectives and made me work on dealing with criticism.

Putting ACM into practice in our homeland security disciplines will take a large amount of time and work on the part of many instructors. It will be a collective effort executed within the overarching framework of an outcomes-based training environment. Although there are always improvements to make, it is clear that Army instructors using ALM in coursework results in resounding success, and students and instructors alike enjoy the experience. Most importantly, the level of performance in the classroom has increased from previous courses.

The results speak from themselves: ACM is an effective tool for teaching and developing adaptability regardless of the environment. It is here to stay in the Army, and hopefully take hold in protecting the homeland.

Chapter 27
Mastering Tactics with Decision Making Exercises and Critiques

"Only those who have challenged themselves with countless tactical situations in peacetime, only those who have refined their ability to make decisions and communicate clearly with subordinates, are prepared to command in war."
~GEN Paul K. Van Riper 1

On the job training and experience is often stated as *"the way"* to learn the job of policing. What does this mean to us cops? Does it mean with time on the job we'll get better at what we do, automatically, or magically from working shift after shift and handling call after call?

Every time we race to the scene and charge towards the sounds of danger and come out safe with suspect in custody, mean that we have somehow gotten better just by being there and participating in the dangerous encounter? Or is there something more to this concept of "on the job training" we should be doing to leverage every experience no matter how small or big to improve our performance?

When I think of on the job training I do not envision an environment where you show up for work and fly by the seat of your pants and hope things work out as you think they should. No, what I envision by *on the job training* is that you learn from every experience and focus on leveraging the lessons learned to make you better at the job. Law enforcement officers are members of a profession that does not routinely practice its tactical skills.

Only constant violent conflict and violent crime, a condition to objectionable, to even contemplate, would allow such practice. Thus the honing and developing of law enforcement peacekeeping skills must be achieved in other ways.

An understanding of tactical theory is an important foundation for mastering tactics, but theory alone will only take you so far. The use of the decisions making exercises and decision making critiques are a couple of ways for officers to gain experience and learn to translate tactical theory to the street, that otherwise could not be gained.

Research has shown that the most important principle of skill performance is that skill depends on knowledge base. In general, the more practice one has had in some domain, the better the performance, and from all indications, this increase in expertise is due to improvement in the knowledge base. This same principle holds true for tactics as well and this is where decision making exercises otherwise known as tactical decision games come into play.

Using Decision Making Exercises aka Tactical Decision Games to Master Tactical Decision Making

"The problem is to grasp, in innumerable special cases, the actual situation which is covered by the mists of uncertainty, to appraise the facts correctly and to guess the unknown elements, to reach a decision quickly and then to carry it out forcibly and relentlessly."
   ~Helmuth von Moltke 2

In his book *Mastering Tactics* MAJ John Schmitt states *Tactical decision games (TDGs) are a simple, fun, and effective way to improve your decision making ability and tactical acumen, to improve your mastery of the art of war.3*

In law enforcement tactical decision games improve the art of operations or what I like to call police operational art or our ability to take what you know, be able to adapt and then apply it to a given set of circumstances to affect your strategy on the street, bringing an end to a violent occurrence using appropriate tactics.

MAJ Schmitt goes on to say, *"like most skills, you can improve tactical decision-making ability through practice."* The idea behind TDGs is to put you in the role of a cop facing a tactical problem, give you a limited amount of time and information, and require you to develop a plan to solve the problem. Maj Schmitt explains, by repeatedly working through problems like these you will learn not only to make better decisions, but you will also learn to make decisions better, that is, more quickly and efficiently. You will learn to look at a situation and instantly take in its essential feature and cut right to the heart of the problem.4

We have been using tactical decision games (solitary, group and free play) in our training in law enforcement and the military for two decades, and they work very well at building confidence in military personnel and law enforcement officers—if they are taught or facilitated correctly. Here are some techniques when employing TDGs:

Solitary play-is exactly like, *if then/when then thinking,* only you write your tactical response (how) and rational (why) down in response to a scenario you have been given.

In group play TDGs-you work the tactical problem as a shift or unit using pen, paper and a map. You, again explain your response (how) and rational (why). The benefit of group play is as you work the problem collectively you see different perspectives from different players and alternatives and options to your own way of thinking about the problem become clear. In short you realize there is more than one workable tactical option to a situation. You also learn to communicate plans and options better with one another when using group play, which is quite a powerful and much needed effect. Group play also generates discussions on tactical concepts and creates a heightened interest in tactics overall.

Free Play TDGs- is a role playing with Sim-munitions or if you have no Sim-munitions use red or blue guns. With free play you combine both the cognitive and physical skills needed to solve the problem in an as close to real life encounter.

When the free play scenario is completed both blue team (officers) and red team (adversaries) critique the response and action taken. The power of free play is that you have to walk, talk, think and do while you accord with an adversary(s.) This conditions the mental and physical aspects of real life tactical decision making and action.

Solitary, group and free play are all effective ways to conduct TDGs with both solitary and group play being an easy cost effective way to get your repetitions in. You can conduct solitary and group play TDGs in a short time span with only pen and paper during roll call or some other time on shift when there is down time.5

Free play force on force takes a little more coordination but with effort and cooperation from all, it also can be done while working a shift. The question comes down to how much does officer safety and tactical effectiveness mean to you? Getting to the level you want takes walking your talk! Force on force gives you big pay off, but it requires a lot of preparation, starting with first defining your outcome. What do you want it to accomplish? We recommend that you first start with TDGs, then advance later to force on force free play exercises and then live fire exercises.

The biggest lessons learned from using TDGs are, they teach officers *HOW TO THINK* verses telling them what to think. TDGs in all their forms create and nurture tactical problem solvers. Officers also learn there is no one single solution to a tactical problem and hence they learn to blend their thoughts and ideas with departmental policies and procedures allowing for better decision making and adaptable, safe and effective responses to the host of problems police officers face. The feedback I have received from all who participate in the decision making exercises feel much more confident in their abilities as a result of using TDGs. They begin to understand the WHY behind the tactics they use verses just blindly following a checklist of techniques.

Chapter 28
Train the brain: Using decision making critiques to leverage lessons learned:

"To learn as quickly as possible, we must be more deliberate, more disciplined, and more thorough in our approach in order to squeeze as much as possible from each experience, as with everything else about mental conditioning there is no magic here."
~ Gary Klein1

In the previous chapters, we examined how tactical decision games (TDGs) can be a simple, fun, and effective way to improve your decision making ability and tactical acumen. We explored how the different forms of TDGs — solitary, group, and free play — work to build confidence in officers.

These chapters set the foundation from which the following discussion will flow. Okay, with that administrative stuff out of the way, let's consider the decision making critique (DMC) — or after action review (AAR) — as another critical component to developing decision makers.2

The DMC/AAR is conducted after the decisions are made and actions taken. You can use the after action review process after a TDG and should regularly use them after an actual event officers handled on the street. A candid, frank and open discussion takes place amongst the group involved in the TDG or actual incident to bring out lessons learned.

The goal of the DMC/AAR is to focus on key aspects of the incident, such as, were the decisions made in a timely manner? What was the rationale of the individual or group in making their decision? Could we have done something better, safer, and more effective? Focus on every aspect from communications (both friendly and adversarial), tactical response and approach, perimeter set up and containment, entry techniques or the ruse, surprise and/or deception you may have used to help you gain control.

You should also examine arrest and search techniques and anything else you or other member of the shift or team, feel was strength or weakness that lessons can be learned from.3

Time Tested Methods
The powerful lessons that are learned from reviewing and critiquing a crisis situation you were personally involved in is a better than most formal training you can get. Why? Because you were there and experienced the circumstances first hand and then sat down and discussed the strengths and weaknesses of the response. From these lessons learned you develop a better plan for next time. A key component to conducting a DMC/AAR is a candid open dialog, anything less and you are only fooling yourself.

Police operational art places high demands on the intellect and skill set of police officers. To master our skills which include decision making ability we cannot be afraid to use tactical decision games and after action reviews as a catalyst to mastery.

I want to conclude with the fear factor and its importance. It has been my experience many police officers and administrators are afraid to use these techniques. They believe it's an admission of guilt to wrong doing on their part.

To those of you who fear or are leery of these methods of training and learning I say this, nothing we do is routine, nothing! Conflict and violence are riddled with complexity and unknowns and no two situations unfold identically, there is always something novel, be it, the people involved, or the location we find ourselves in. Even if it is the same location and the same people involved their intent, motives and emotions may be different from one day to the next. Risk and time are also factors to consider.

As Carl von Clausewitz said, "countless minor incidents, the kind you never really foresee, combine to lower the general level of performance, so that one always falls short of the intended goal."4

We can't get it perfect despite our best efforts because there are just too many variables when human adversaries collide. What we can strive for, is a better and more desirable execution. Learning from falling short of the intended goal is what a learning organization is all about and law enforcement is or should be a learning organization. We owe it to ourselves and to those we protect to harness every lesson possible.

The basic concepts behind good decision making and tactics are not all that complex, nor are they particularly hard for the average police officer to understand and comprehend. The difficult thing is in applying those concepts to a specific tactical problem. It is here where the development and mastery of decision making and tactics come in. Understanding the essence of conflict is a struggle between two hostile, independent, and irreconcilable wills, trying to impose itself on the other.

Conflict is a process of continuous mutual adaptation, of give and take, move and counter move. It is critical to keep in mind that the adversary is not an inanimate object to be acted upon but an independent and animate force with its own objectives and plans. While we try to impose our will on the adversary, he resists us and seeks to impose his own will on us. Appreciating this dynamic interplay between opposing human wills is essential to understanding the fundamental nature of conflict and hence the difficulty in getting it correct while adapting tactics.

Human conflict is an extreme test of will. Friction, uncertainty, fluidity, disorder, fear and danger, moral, mental and physical forces are its essential features. We never eliminate these features completely so we must learn to take "effective action" despite them.

In law enforcement there is no substitute for experience, no substitute for the intuitive experience that comes from repeated practice.

Decision Making exercises and critiques are the practice field for the tactical leader and officer. If we as individual officers and as a profession are not willing to collectively learn from our own on the job experience and history in an effort to continually educate ourselves to, improve safety and effectiveness, we will have failed to protect ourselves and the communities we have sworn to protect.

I will close with this great message from MAJ John Schmitt; "Experience is a great teacher. Unfortunately, ours is a field in which experience can cost us dearly."5

As Field Marshall Sir William Slim wrote of taking over British forces in Burma in 1942 "Experience taught a good deal, but with the Japanese as instructors it was an expensive way of learning. We are professionally obligated to do whatever we can to gain whatever experience we can without paying the full price. That is precisely why we study past campaigns and precisely why we should play tactical decision games." Now it's time to master your decision making and tactical skills.6

Chapter 29
Shift Debriefings: Becoming More Deliberate, More Disciplined, and More Thorough in our Approach to Learning

As cops we often cry loudly about the lack of training in our profession (I am guilty of it myself). However while we complain and whine about the seemingly lack of interest in ongoing training we also miss the opportunities to train and learn from the everyday lessons available to us. Those lessons that come from every call we respond to and every shift we work.

The uses of training tools such as; tactical decision games and after action reviews still are rare occurrences in our profession and seemingly only used when some catastrophic or unconventional crisis has occurred i.e. a cop killed in the line of duty or a deadly force scenario that leaves the public calling for an explanation. We should be doing more to harness the wisdom of the street cop and what he learns from each and every day on each and every shift. The shift debriefing is a *training tool* we can and should utilize to develop full spectrum cops capable of making sound decisions and employing sound tactics to resolve crisis situations and record and report them accurately in the aftermath.

"Only those who have challenged themselves with countless tactical situations in peacetime, only those who have refined their ability to make decisions and communicate clearly with subordinates, are prepared to command in war."
~GEN Paul K. Van Riper [1]

Police departments by their very nature are learning organizations and eventful or not, every shift yields fruit in the form of lessons learned. Hence, some effort needs to be made to "harvest" knowledge that can be used in bettering future shifts.

While methods may vary, they usually take the form of a debriefing. A debriefing is a facilitated discussion focused on gaining understanding and insight regarding specific actions, taken on shift and involving those people who were personally involved.

Because lessons learned by police personnel play such important role, it is necessary that a system be in place to insure that such lessons are properly and correctly recorded. Experience is a powerful teacher, but experience by itself is not the most efficient way to learn. The process can often be painful and time-consuming. To learn as quickly as possible, we must be more deliberate, more disciplined, and more thorough in our approach in order to squeeze as much as possible from each experience.

As with everything else about better execution there is no magic here.

Shift Debriefing System

A debrief includes a careful examination of the tactics, techniques and procedures, decision and actions that took place on shift; and is focused on improving performance. While there are no rules for conducting debriefings, the focus of a shift debriefing is on fact-finding, not fault-finding. Open discussion facilitated by the supervisor is nearly unlimited in scope as long as the focus remains on the shifts operations. Consequently, any person is allowed to introduce any subject for discussion and recommendations.

Shift debriefs are an opportunity to discuss incidents that took place on shift and the tactics, techniques and procedures, utilized as well, as, the need for ongoing investigations and to ensure evidence and information have been gathered and reported and acted upon. The shift debrief allows for early resolution of incidents where mistakes may have been made and an early identification of officer safety, work practices, policies and procedures and other issues that arise on shift and effect department wide execution.

Examples:
- Was there a sound tactical response and approach to an incident?
- Were the decisions made in a timely manner?
- What was the rationale of the individual or shift in making their decisions?
- Could we have done something better, safer, and more effective?
- Was communication effective?
- Were there any officer safety or innocent by-stander concerns?
- Were the proper tools, troops, tactics, techniques and adaptable procedures utilized?
- Were the outcomes sought met? If not why not and how do we adapt?
- Were there any novelties, rare occurrences, methods and tools used by the subjects involved that effected decision making and our overall response to a specific operation that we need to develop new tactics for?
- Were complainant, witness, victim and suspect information gathering completed?
- Was property and evidence gathering completed and documented?
- Did the narrative report include officer observations, orientation, decision and actions, to include probable cause and elements of the crime?
- Is a follow-up investigation necessary and if so who is conducting follow-up investigation (patrol/detectives)?
- Were there any new training and equipment needs discovered?

Shift Supervisors should facilitate shift debriefs to ensure tasks have been completed and updated with the outcome of each task.

The examples listed above are just some of what may be covered in a shift debrief and are normally associated with tactical responses and safety related issues but those things so crucial to a successful operations such as the dreaded but all important paperwork process (listed above) needs to be included in the debriefs as well.

Supervisors should meet with their personnel prior to the end of the shift for a debriefing, where the shift's events and reports will be reviewed. The Shift debriefing should *ideally occur* at the end of a tour of duty although this may not always be practical. Supervisors should view debriefing as an ongoing process that should take place at the first available opportunity. The shift debriefing process will become a routine and essential part of everyday policing, if we take an interest and make a habit of doing them daily, much like roll call.

The shift debriefing is one of the ways through which shifts and individual officers will know how successful they have been and a way in which all will learn from specific planning, tactics, techniques and procedures as well as the decision making process utilized. The shift debriefs also enables supervisors to properly access assigned tasks, which evolved during their shifts, that they have been completed and processed properly in accord with the departments overall mission and intent.

Item, Discussion and Recommendation

The Item, discussion and recommendation (IDR) format is great for recording shift lessons learned. The IDR format is a simple, three-step process for identifying and describing issues, items or ideas with their related recommendations after a shift.2

1) The *item*, issue or idea step identifies the particular subject and provides a brief but precise description of the concern. It also serves as the title of the subject and as such is normally just a few words and never longer than a single sentence.

2) The *discussion* is the second step and is a short summary explaining why the concern is relevant. It provides sufficient information to convince an uninformed reader of how the problem was manifested and in what circumstances and context. When more than one contributory cause is identified, they are all listed if they can be addressed by a single recommendation. The discussion component may be several paragraphs to as long as a single page. Those items that require longer explanations and descriptions are normally reserved for more formal reports.

3) The *recommendation* is the last step and is a short statement suggesting a corrective course of action, countermeasure or remedy.

Shift debriefs are normally informal discussions as described above, however at times the problems identified and there solutions require documentation and follow-up on lessons learned. Follow-up can include policy and procedure review and or revisions, training and equipment needs assessments. Either in discussion or written form, the IDR format is a great tool to facilitate the, debrief and document lessons learned.

As stated above and, it bears repeating; to learn as quickly as possible, we must be more deliberate, more disciplined, and more thorough in our approach in order to squeeze as much as possible from each experience, as with everything else about mental conditioning there is no magic here. If our goal is to be better than good we must focus our efforts to get there. The shift debrief is one way of doing just that!

I adapted much of this piece on shift debriefings, from two sources; Sid Heals, *Field Command*, and Don Vandergriff's, *Raising The Bar: Creating and Nurturing Adaptability To deal With The Changing Face of War* both are great books and a must read for any cop. 3

Chapter 30
Baltimore Police Sergeants Training Using Adaptive Leadership Methodology

The final chapter deals with application of all the things mentioned in the previous 29 chapters. For 18 months from late 2009 through early 2011, Don Vandergriff was brought on as a consultant to the Baltimore Police Department to reform their training. He has also attempted to apply the principles of the Adaptive Course Model and a Mission Command Culture throughout the Army with some success and some failures; and he continues to do so in the Army, the Marine Corps and he brought these methods to a modern metropolitan police department specifically the Baltimore Police Department.

Don applied the principles of Mission Command and ACM to how the reformed their training. First he taught the trainers, the leaders hand-picked by Baltimore City Police Department Commissioner Fred Bealefeld, whom had been a police man for 27 years.

From the beginning, Don had "top cover" from the Police Commissioner in reforming police development. After Don certified the hand-picked instructors (all police men and women who the Commissioner knew had a future in the department) in ACM through two workshops, he left them for three months to design the entire Program of Instruction (POI) for the new Sergeant's Leaders Course. The outcome was that the 334 Sergeants of the department would attend and be exposed to the latest methodology in adaptability development using policing situations as the vehicle to teach adaptability.

This also sent out a strong message to the rest of the department that professional development was important. When Don returned in mid-August 2010, he was briefed on the POI that the instructors developed. As of note, he changed nothing they recommended.

They also briefed the Police Commissioner with the same outcome. He felt his handpicked instructors were meeting his desired outcome, so nothing in their recommended POI was changed.

Don's recommendation to the cadre of the new course was simple. First, the Commissioner stated it would be no longer than five days a week, for four weeks (and within police union guidelines, 8 hours a day without over time). Class size would be kept to 15 officer cohorts until all 334 Sergeants attended and graduated (some did fail). Two cohorts would be conducted every four weeks, facilitated by 20 sergeant and lieutenant teachers. Students would be involved in the learning as much as possible. It was also desired to leave time for the students to study, while avoiding cramming every moment with required tasks from the Maryland board of policing.

The course POI would abide by the principles of ACM and Mission Command. There would be no lectures. All classes would be taught through the use of TDGs. Group seminars and problem solving was paramount. Also, at least 50% of the course would be spent outside in problem solving exercises. Additionally, the students were to be treated like professionals, with all subjects taught to outcomes not time. Also, leaders were designated for each day and during each exercise with leadership constantly critiqued by students and the teachers. Additionally, outside observers, such as Don were brought in to also evaluate the program, the teachers and student conduct during exercises.

Also, every class and problem solving exercise that the students would be asked to do, the teachers had to do themselves under similar conditions.

They spent the summer of 2010 going through every class, TDG, team exercise, be it on the Climbing Tower or the obstacle course, at the BPD training facility where free play exercises would be conducted or at the marksmanship training facility at Gun Powder Springs Maryland (just north of Baltimore City), where there was also a leader development course with the facilities to do 8 team building and solving exercises simultaneously (this would be a week 4 problem solving exercise along with rappelling from a little used tower also at Gunpowder Springs).

Finally, the students were to get to critique the course at the end of each day using the AAR format mentioned earlier in this book. No one was exempt during the critique. Also, the students were to development a list of recommendations on how to improve the department to be briefed to the Commissioner at the end of each course, by the students themselves.

There were two additional subjects that the Commissioner did ask to be conducted within the POI, but were ones that the instructors of the course were also contemplating as well. One, he asked to come to the first morning of the course and address each class on why the department was doing this course. This was something that was encouraged anyhow because it was important for each officer to see directly where the idea originated from and why.

Secondly, the instructors decided, with the Commissioner's concurrence, to begin each day with the students conducting a proper roll call (an example of a free play exercise, but with the outcome of showing what "right looks like" as just explained in Chapter 29), and the team leader for that day conducting a class relative to what sergeants needed to know.

The 20 teachers did an incredible job setting up and facilitating this course (an article on this course was written by LT Parker Elliott, course director and Don Vandergriff appearing in the 2012 spring edition of CATO magazine called "Adaptive Leader Methodology: An Alternative for Better Outcomes").

The first day of the course began with the Commissioner speaking to the students, followed by a course lay out by the course director LT Parker Elliott (who in my opinion had the best grasp of ALM, so was chosen as the course director for the 18months).

Don's work have been applied through the courses I have designed and applied in trainings through the Massachusetts Municipal Police Training Committee in Basic Sergeants School and in use of force workshops during In-service training. Don's ideas and his mentorship have been instrumental in these teachings. I believe this is how we should be leading and training law enforcement if we truly want to raise the bar of professionalism and perform with excellence in handling the problems and crises we deal with.

Criminals are evolving and the threats they pose are much more serious and asymmetrical. Hybrid forms in methods of operations, technology and the reasons why "motive" and "intent" behind why criminals do what they do are all the more prevalent creating an atmosphere where the frontline street officers and leaders must adapt more quickly if we in law enforcement are to gain the advantage.

Adaptive Course Model and Outcomes Based training is CHANGE from law enforcement's normal way of leading and training and with change comes some descent but the feedback and buy in from the top and from the rank and file have all been outstanding and mostly positive, especially once cops experience it firsthand.

Open minds are important to creating and nurturing a learning organization.

Learning organizations are key to dealing with adversaries who through history have shown and continue to show they learn and adapt daily. Its law enforcements job to set the tempo and climate within their jurisdictions through proactive and coactive policing. Here is the way of getting this done.

The Vandergriff After Action Review

TO: Police Commissioner Frederick Bealefeld, Lieutenant Parker Elliott, Facilitators of Baltimore Police Department Sergeants Leaders Course, Sergeant Dennis Raferty
CC: Mr. Adam Walinsky

SUBJECT: Vandergriff Review of Baltimore Police Sergeants Course, review of course of action, discussions with cadre, and observations of leader development during fourth and fifth cohorts three days of course November 14-22, 2010.

1) **Purpose:** Mr. Vandergriff provide feedback in assisting Baltimore Police Commissioner and cadre in creating and evolving an innovative sergeants course that prepares officers of character to police in a 4th generation environment.

2) **Findings:** The Sergeants Course is clearly having a positive impact on the near term and long term health of the Baltimore Police Department. The sergeants attending the course are beginning to show competence and confidence in 21st Century policing. It is hard to believe how few of the sergeant students have had this quality of problem solving development prior to this course. Almost every one of the students I talked to in this session responded with how much they were getting from this course, particularly the training offered in week 3. A lot of senior sergeants told me that, "I wish I had this when I made sergeant." In order to be successful in dealing with policing in the 21st Century against the varied threats, individual officers must be developed and become confident and competence in dealing with complex problems.

a) **Summary:** Observing the 3rd week saw the beginning of a cultural change with the application of a new leader development model in place of the "competency" learning model techniques being used today in both learning institutions and most organizations.

The Adaptive Course Model (ACM) is cultural rather than a prescribed list of procedures and exercises. The facilitators were clearly developing adaptability using the experiential learning model to teach the Rapid Decision-Making (RDM) process focused on development of strength of character, specifically moral courage while using complicated individual and team tasks as the vehicle. All sessions closed with good AARs, and student feedback on the subjects taught.

b) Observations: Lieutenants Hyatt and Schludergerg are outstanding teachers and did a great job over the three day period (they were not present for the last day, the 24th, but other Sergeant Course facilitators did a great job overseeing the training). Instructor attitude and knowledge, confidence, are outstanding, and it is easier to learn how to facilitate from this prospective than not being knowledgeable and confident. The students actually were motivated by his enthusiasm.

1) **Monday 22 Nov-Tactical Situations and Barricades (classroom phase).** Lieutenants Hyatt and Schludergerg did an outstanding job with this classroom period, and used the Case Study Method by having the students learn from both good and bad examples of other police forces. They ended the day's class with situational exercise allowing the students to learn through doing. Their approach had many layers. Thus, when it is taught well, each student will naturally find the layer that appeals to him and thus, regardless of his level of preparation or familiarity with the subject, will find something of value.

The ability to make good decisions is, in part, a function of having a stock of mental models that a decision-maker can compare to the problem in front of him. (Psychologist Gary Klein calls this a "repertoire of patterns.") Whatever else is being taught, a well-taught case will add to the "repertoire of patterns" in each student's mind.

Marshall Mcluhan was right: "the medium is the message." Thus, as the case method is a medium that celebrates storytelling and decision-making, its use sends the message that these things are important features of a Police culture.

(a) Whatever the subject at hand, a good case well taught also fosters the following virtues:
(b) Enthusiasm for learning, whether in or out of the classroom
(c) Curiosity and the habit of seeking out information
(d) Empathy
(e) Humility
(f) "Joy in taking responsibility" (the willingness to make a decision that serves the common good, particularly in an ambiguous situation.
(g) An understanding of history
(h) Judgment
(i) Critical thinking
(j) Self-awareness
(k) The ability to explain the rationale behind one's decisions

2) **Tuesday 23 Nov-Room Clearing and Building Cover Exercise.** Here the students got to master the basics—clearing a building and a room, as well as learning the "move or hold" method. These fundamentals that build toward tools to use in decision making. I got to observe every team go through every aspect of this and was impressed with the one-on-one mentorship shown by the facilitators. Lieutenant Schludergerg brought in SWAT personnel to assist in the development, and this greatly enhanced learning with a low instructor to student ratio, usually one to four. What is good about this is the interaction between special units and patrol, building a bridge between the two.

3) **Wed 24 Nov-Active Shooter and Free Play Force on Force exercise:** This period was made more intense with the use of SIM-MUNITIONS.

(a) **Active Shooter Free Play:** Sections of four students, with a TAC officer went through an Active Shooter drill several times, while also applying the tactical approach of "move or hold." It was good that the students were able to learn from their mistakes because initially most stuck to "hold" prior to the TAC pushing them through. The TAC also improved the training by adding the use of a "chalk talk" prior to and after each team ran through their problem. This approach uses a chalk board drawing where the TAC walks the team through what they might do, seeing a picture speaks a thousand words. The facilitators changed the conditions each time in order to challenge the students and keeping it from being a rote process. Every student team improved throughout the morning. The Sergeants also are learning, not just here, but throughout the entire Sergeants Course, the value of teamwork and lateral communications with other professionals in order to solve the complex problems they face.

(b) **Team Force on Force Free Play:** The students learned two valuable lessons, communication and teamwork. In addition, the need for a solid physical fitness program was brought up by several students after only one iteration. I loved the use of competition during this phase as well. At the end of the day, there was a clear winner and loser, with each understanding why they won or lost. I would recommend an AAR after each iteration, instead of one after the entire period. Though, I observed several students standing to the side after they had fought, going over what they did right or wrong.

(4) After Action Reviews. Improved throughout the period of observation. The one that ended the training on Tuesday and Wed were outstanding. I also saw outstanding uses of mentorship, particularly by Lieutenant Hyatt toward students during the room clearing exercises.

a) Evolution: Officers are discovering how much more they need to know to be successful, while gaining more confidence. They have also discovered that they need to stay on a disciplined regime of physical fitness. Many of the officers were exhausted after the Tuesday and Wed training sessions, and remarked how they had to get back to doing physical training and stop some bad habits, such as smoking.

5) **The way ahead (these are works in progress):**

a) Strategic Information Plan must be created and executed to show off the course, the Commissioner should meet weekly with the cadre and with the students at the end of the course to update this plan and talk about the way ahead. This is the Commissioner's course and the main effort on how he is going to evolve the culture of his organization. This includes articles written or signed by the Commissioner and Lieutenant Parker (or anyone who wants to do it in the course), and published in a professional journal.

b) Develop a follow up plan to see how the Sergeants who have graduated from the course also use what they learned to be better. This approach should now reach into other areas of the Police Academy, to include the police recruit training as well as in-service training.

c) After the Sergeants, then run all Lieutenants through the course, and eventually the majors and members of staffs.

d) Develop graduations standards to select an honor graduate as well as deal with non performing students. After this session, I believe more than ever, that the facilitators and course director should be able to identify non-performing and weak sergeants, allowing the department to take action to keep them from leading people.

e) **Bring in guest speakers,** ensuring that they will reinforce what you are trying to produce through the course.

f) **Add Physical Training and Nutrition instruction to POI.** I know police officers work long hours, but physical fitness has to be part of the whole person concept in regard to strength of character parallel to critical thinking (mental cognitive skills). Physical fitness and eating right must become part of one's daily routine. I would recommend that innovative physical fitness be done for one hour every other day. The U.S. Army Physical Fitness Center of Excellence at Carlisle Barracks, PA (home of U.S. Army War College) provides excellent material on this subject. It is surprisingly easier than we realize. I went through the course in November 2009.

6) **Conclusion:** In the three days I attended the training, students were always in a situation conducive to the development of personal initiative and adaptability. Everyone took an active role in the course. This consisted of learning how to evaluate their peers through other student's leadership and team work in the exercises where adaptability was or was not demonstrated. This served two objectives: demonstrated experiential learning and kept students actively and positively engaged in all aspects of the course.

We have proven that it can be done

The significance of the Baltimore City Police Department Sergeant's Leaders Course is that it applied some aspect of everything discussed in this book. More importantly the surveys taken from each class were overwhelmingly positive. The only negative comment, if it could be called that, was why was this course not given earlier in an officer's career, particularly when they made sergeant? Also mentioned is why had the leaders of the department, and law enforcement in general not adapted this methodology for all policemen.

Also significant was how almost to a man and a woman, the police officers said they were treated like adults and professionals and truly took ownership of their learning. If the students reached the approved outcomes for a given class or problem, they were allowed to AAR and leave early (this happened a couple of times with the students initially confused about not training to time!).

One officer asked, will we get in trouble for leaving early.
Finally, this could not have been done without the leadership of Police Commissioner Frederick Bealefeld. He was involved with the details without telling us how to do it. His outcome was to produce more adaptive and confident police officers with the latest training and education methodologies. He sent a strong message to the department by hand-picking each instructor, then detailing them from their divisions for 18 months.

We also highly recommend the article "Adaptive Leadership Methodology: An Alternative For Better Outcomes," written by LT Parker Elliott and Don Vandergriff about this course, and published in the spring 2012 edition of *CATO* magazine.

ENDNOTES

Preface
1 Ronald Heifetz, Alexander Grashow, Marty Linsky, *The Practice of Adaptive Leadership: Tools and tactics for Changing Your Organization and the World* (Harvard Business Press, 2009)
2 Ronald Heifetz, Alexander Grashow, Marty Linsky, The Practice of Adaptive Leadership: Tools and tactics for Changing Your Organization and the World (Harvard Business Press, 2009)

Chapter 1
1 Donald Vandergriff, Path *to Victory Americas Army and the Revolution in Human Affairs,* (Amazon Digital Services, updated edition, 2013)
2 Donald Vandergriff, *Path to Victory Americas Army and the Revolution in Human Affairs,* (Amazon Digital Services, updated edition, 2013)
3 Donald Vandergriff, Path *to Victory Americas Army and the Revolution in Human Affairs,* (Amazon Digital Services, updated edition, 2013)
4 Massachusetts Municipal Police Training Committee (MPTC) firearms training curriculum 2011 update
5 See FBI uniformed crime reports, adapted to report Violent Encounters a Study on Felonious Assaults On law Enforcement (2006)
6 Donald Vandergriff, Path *to Victory Americas Army and the Revolution in Human Affairs,* (Amazon Digital Services, updated edition, 2013)

Chapter 2
1 Gary Gagliardi, *Sun Tzu's The Art of War Plus: The Warrior Class 306 Lessons in Strategy* (Clearbridge Publishing 2004 edition)
2 Gary Gagliardi, *Sun Tzu's The Art of War Plus: The Warrior Class 306 Lessons in Strategy* (Clearbridge Publishing 2004 edition)
3 See, email correspondences between author and Edward Beakley purveyor of the website Project White Horse (2009)
4 Col. John Boyd's Briefing *Patterns of Conflict* (1980)
5 Massachusetts Municipal Police Training Committee recruit training standards and personal discourse with police instructors from across the United States (2000-2013)

6 Massachusetts Municipal Police Training Committee veteran officer in-service training standards and personal discourse with police instructors from across the United States (2000-2013)

7 Massachusetts Municipal Police Training Committee recruit training standards and personal discourse with police instructors from across the United States (2000-2013)

8 Generals Zeb Bradford and Frederic Brown, *America's Army a Model for Interagency Effectiveness* (Praeger 2008)

9 Robert Coram, *Boyd the Fighter Pilot who Changed the Art of War*, (Little, Brown and Company, 2002)

10 See Destruction and Creation, Col. John R. Boyd, September 3, 1976

Chapter 3

1 Gary Gagliardi, *Sun Tzu's The Art of War Plus: The Warrior Class 306 Lessons in Strategy* (Clearbridge Publishing 2004 edition)

2 Donald Vandergriff, *Raising the Bar: Creating and Nurturing Adaptability to Deal with the Changing face of War*, (Amazon Digital Services, updated kindle edition 2013)

3 Donald Vandergriff, *Raising the Bar: Creating and Nurturing Adaptability to Deal with the Changing face of War*, (Amazon Digital Services, updated kindle edition 2013)

4 Nassim Nicholas Taleb, *the Black Swan: The Impact of the Highly Improbable*, (Random House, 2007)

Chapter 4

1 See the Strategic Corporal Leadership in the Three Block War, Marines Magazine, January 1999
by Gen. Charles C. Krulak
http://www.au.af.mil/au/awc/awcgate/usmc/strategic_corporal.htm

2 See Destruction and Creation, Col. John R. Boyd, September 3, 1976

3 See notes from Adaptive Leader Symposium the United States Military Academy West Point, Department of Military Instruction 2010

4 Donald Vandergriff, *Raising the Bar: Creating and Nurturing Adaptability to Deal with the Changing face of War*, (Amazon Digital Services, updated kindle edition 2013)

5 Donald Vandergriff, *Raising the Bar: Creating and Nurturing Adaptability to Deal with the Changing face of War*, (Amazon Digital Services, updated kindle edition 2013)

Chapter 5

1 Gary Gagliardi, *Sun Tzu's The Art of War Plus: The Warrior Class 306 Lessons in Strategy* (Clearbridge Publishing 2004 edition)

2 Gary Gagliardi, *Sun Tzu's The Art of War Plus: The Warrior Class 306 Lessons in Strategy* (Clearbridge Publishing 2004 edition)

3 H. John Poole, *Phantom Soldier: The Enemy's Answer to U.S. Firepower,* (Posterity Press, 2001)

4 Gary Gagliardi, *Sun Tzu's The Art of War Plus: The Warrior Class 306 Lessons in Strategy* (Clearbridge Publishing 2004 edition)

5 Gary Gagliardi, *Sun Tzu's The Art of War Plus: The Warrior Class 306 Lessons in Strategy* (Clearbridge Publishing 2004 edition)

Chapter 6

1The United States Secret Service and United States department of Education, *The Final Report and Findings of the Safe School Initiative: Implications for the Prevention of School Attacks in the United States* (2002)

2 See, Homeland Security Television, *Are Police Officers Ready for the Next Generation of Active Shooters? (HSTV 2010)*

3 See, http://en.wikipedia.org/wiki/North_Hollywood_shootout North Hollywood shootout

4 See, email correspondence with William Barchers, President of Hard Tactics (2010)

5 NYPD, *Active Shooter Recommendations and Analysis for Risk Mitigation* (2010 & 2012 editions)

6 The United States Secret Service and United States department of Education, *The Final Report and Findings of the Safe School Initiative: Implications for the Prevention of School Attacks in the United States* (2002)

7 Frans P.B. Osinga, Science Strategy and War: The Strategic Theory of John Boyd (Routledge 2006)

Chapter 7

1 United States Marine Corps, MCDP 1-3, *Tactics* (1997)

2 United States Marine Corps Doctrinal Publication 1, *Warfighting,* (Wildside Press, 2005)

3 United States Marine Corps Doctrinal Publication 1, *Warfighting,* (Wildside Press, 2005)

4 See, *National Strategy for Combating Terrorism* (2003)

https://www.cia.gov/news-information/cia-the-war-on-terrorism/Counter_Terrorism_Strategy.pdf

5 John Arquilla, David Ronfeldt, *Swarming and the Future of Conflict*, (Rand Corporation, 2000)
http://www.rand.org/pubs/documented_briefings/DB311.html

6 John Arquilla, David Ronfeldt, *Swarming and the Future of Conflict*, (Rand Corporation, 2000)
http://www.rand.org/pubs/documented_briefings/DB311.html

7 John Arquilla, David Ronfeldt, *Swarming and the Future of Conflict*, (Rand Corporation, 2000)
http://www.rand.org/pubs/documented_briefings/DB311.html

8 John Arquilla, David Ronfeldt, *Swarming on the Battlefield: Past, Present, and Future* (Rand Publishing 2000)
http://www.rand.org/pubs/monograph_reports/MR1100.html

9 The United States Secret Service and United States department of Education, *The Final Report and Findings of the Safe School Initiative: Implications for the Prevention of School Attacks in the United States* (2002)

10 Carl von Clausewitz, *On War*, translated by Michael Elliot Howard and Peter Paret, (Princeton University Press 1989)

Chapter 8
1 See, *Holy Bible: New Living Translation* (Tyndale House Publishers, 2006)
2 Gary Gagliardi, *Sun Tzu's The Art of War Plus: The Warrior Class 306 Lessons in Strategy* (Clearbridge Publishing 2004 edition)
3 Edward T. Luttwak, *the Grand Strategy of the Byzantine Empire*, (Belknap Press of Harvard University Press, 2009)

Chapter 9
1 Frans P.B. Osinga, *Science Strategy and War: The Strategic Theory of John Boyd* (Routledge 2006)
2 Edward T. Hall, *Beyond Culture*, (Anchor Books 1976)
3 See After Action Review adapted to tactical decision game, of an actual Police incident, Walpole Massachusetts, 2006
4 Miyamoto Musashi, *the Book of Five Rings* (Bottom of the Hill Publishing 2010)

Chapter 10

1 Dr. Gary Klein, *Intuition at Work Why Developing Gut Instincts Will make you Better at What You Do*, Doubleday 2003

2 Dr. Gary Klein, *Intuition at Work Why Developing Gut Instincts Will make you Better at What You Do*, Doubleday 2003

3 Donald Vandergriff, personal email communication, July 10th 2008

4 Col. John Boyd, Patterns of Conflict (1976)

5 Dr. Gary Klein, *Intuition at Work Why Developing Gut Instincts Will makes you Better at What You Do*, Doubleday 2003

Chapter 11

1 Donald Vandergriff, *Raising the Bar: Creating and Nurturing Adaptability to Deal with the Changing face of War*, (Amazon Digital Services, updated kindle edition 2013)

2 Donald Vandergriff, *Raising the Bar: Creating and Nurturing Adaptability to Deal with the Changing face of War*, (Amazon Digital Services, updated kindle edition 2013)

3 Donald Vandergriff, Raising the Bar: Creating and Nurturing Adaptability to Deal with the Changing face of War, (Amazon Digital Services, updated kindle edition 2013)

4 Diane Zahm Using Crime Prevention Through Environmental Design in Problem-Solving http://books.google.com/books?id=DBEIfNS-iYwC&pg=PA64&dq=SARA+Police+Problem+solving+COPS&hl=en&sa=X&ei=UYO4UuadFvXJsQS9u4CgDQ&ved=0CDIQ6AEwAQ#v=onepage&q=SARA%20Police%20Problem%20solving%20COPS&f=false (2007)

5 Donald Vandergriff, (RET MAJ U.S. Army) *How to Create Adaptive Leaders, How to teach-facilitate-mentor, Handbook for Instruction of Adaptive Leaders* (2005)

6 Donald Vandergriff, *Raising the Bar: Creating and Nurturing Adaptability to Deal with the Changing face of War*, (Amazon Digital Services, updated kindle edition 2013)

7 The Murder of Kyle Dinkheller; (Wikipedia), http://en.wikipedia.org/wiki/Murder_of_Kyle_Dinkheller

8 Carl von Clausewitz, On War, translated by Michael Elliot Howard and Peter Paret, (Princeton University Press 1989)

9 Donald Vandergriff, *Raising the Bar: Creating and Nurturing Adaptability to Deal with the Changing face of War*, (Amazon Digital Services, updated kindle edition 2013)

10 Donald Vandergriff, Raising the Bar: Creating and Nurturing Adaptability to Deal with the Changing face of War, (Amazon Digital Services, updated kindle edition 2013)

Chapter 12
1 Donald Vandergriff, *Raising the Bar: Creating and Nurturing Adaptability to Deal with the Changing face of War*, (Amazon Digital Services, updated kindle edition 2013)
2 Donald Vandergriff, *Raising the Bar: Creating and Nurturing Adaptability to Deal with the Changing face of War*, (Amazon Digital Services, updated kindle edition 2013)
3 Donald Vandergriff, *Raising the Bar: Creating and Nurturing Adaptability to Deal with the Changing face of War*, (Amazon Digital Services, updated kindle edition 2013)
4 Donald Vandergriff, *Raising the Bar: Creating and Nurturing Adaptability to Deal with the Changing face of War*, (Amazon Digital Services, updated kindle edition 2013)
5 Donald Vandergriff, *Raising the Bar: Creating and Nurturing Adaptability to Deal with the Changing face of War*, (Amazon Digital Services, updated kindle edition 2013)
6 Donald Vandergriff, *Raising the Bar: Creating and Nurturing Adaptability to Deal with the Changing face of War*, (Amazon Digital Services, updated kindle edition 2013)
7 Donald Vandergriff, *Raising the Bar: Creating and Nurturing Adaptability to Deal with the Changing face of War*, (Amazon Digital Services, updated kindle edition 2013)
8 Donald Vandergriff, Raising the Bar: Creating and Nurturing Adaptability to Deal with the Changing face of War, (Amazon Digital Services, updated kindle edition 2013)
9 See Roll Call Training/Fast Learning, Tactical Decision Games Walpole PD 2002-Present
10 Donald Vandergriff, *Raising the Bar: Creating and Nurturing Adaptability to Deal with the Changing face of War*, (Amazon Digital Services, updated kindle edition 2013)
11 Donald Vandergriff, Raising the Bar: Creating and Nurturing Adaptability to Deal with the Changing face of War, (Amazon Digital Services, updated kindle edition 2013)
12 Col. John Boyd, *Patterns of Conflict* (1976)
13 Donald Vandergriff, From Swift to Swiss Tactical Decision Games and Their Place in Military Education (Performance Improvement •

Volume 45 • Number 2, 2006)
http://www.lesc.net/system/files/vandergriff_2_2_06.pdf
14 W. Edwards Deming, *Out of the Crisis* (The MIT Press, 2000)
15 Dandridge M. Malone, *Small Unit Leadership*: A Commonsense Approach, (Presidio Press, 1983)
16 Donald Vandergriff, *Raising the Bar: Creating and Nurturing Adaptability to Deal with the Changing face of War*, (Amazon Digital Services, updated kindle edition 2013)

Chapter 13
1 See, Law Enforcement and Security Consulting, Program of Instruction, *Handling Dynamic Encounters* 2000-Present)
2 United States Marine Corps, MCDP 1-3, *Tactics* (1997)
3 William Duggan, *Napoleon's Glance the Secret of Strategy* (Nation Books, 2004)
4 Gavin de Becker, *The Gift of Fear and Other Survival Signals that Protect Us from Violence* (Dell, 1999)
5 William Duggan, Strategic Intuition: The Creative Spark in Human Achievement, (Columbia University Press, 2007)
6 Gen. Huba Wass de Czege, *Thinking and Acting like an Early Explorer: Operational Art is Not a Level of War* (Small Wars Journal 2011)
http://smallwarsjournal.com/blog/journal/docs-temp/710-deczege.pdf
7 Gen. Huba Wass de Czege, *Thinking and Acting like an Early Explorer: Operational Art is Not a Level of War* (Small Wars Journal 2011)
http://smallwarsjournal.com/blog/journal/docs-temp/710-deczege.pdf
8 Gen. Huba Wass de Czege, *Thinking and Acting like an Early Explorer: Operational Art is Not a Level of War* (Small Wars Journal 2011)
http://smallwarsjournal.com/blog/journal/docs-temp/710-deczege.pdf
9 Gen. Huba Wass de Czege, *Thinking and Acting like an Early Explorer: Operational Art is Not a Level of War* (Small Wars Journal 2011)
http://smallwarsjournal.com/blog/journal/docs-temp/710-deczege.pdf
10 Gen. Huba Wass de Czege, *Thinking and Acting like an Early Explorer: Operational Art is Not a Level of War* (Small Wars Journal 2011)
http://smallwarsjournal.com/blog/journal/docs-temp/710-deczege.pdf
11 Gen. Huba Wass de Czege, *Thinking and Acting like an Early Explorer: Operational Art is Not a Level of War* (Small Wars Journal 2011)
http://smallwarsjournal.com/blog/journal/docs-temp/710-deczege.pdf

12 Gen. Huba Wass de Czege, *Thinking and Acting like an Early Explorer: Operational Art is Not a Level of War* (Small Wars Journal 2011)
http://smallwarsjournal.com/blog/journal/docs-temp/710-deczege.pdf
13 Gen. Huba Wass de Czege, *Thinking and Acting like an Early Explorer: Operational Art is Not a Level of War* (Small Wars Journal 2011)
http://smallwarsjournal.com/blog/journal/docs-temp/710-deczege.pdf

Chapter 14
1 Gary Klein, *Street Lights and Shadows: Searching for the Keys to Adaptive Decision Making* (A Bradford Book, 2009)
2 See, Lessons Learned from developing emergency response plans for schools, colleges, universities and workplaces.
3 Gary Klein, *Street Lights and Shadows: Searching for the Keys to Adaptive Decision Making* (A Bradford Book, 2009)

Chapter 15
1 Carl von Clausewitz, *On War*, translated by Michael Elliot Howard and Peter Paret, (Princeton University Press 1989)
2 Carl von Clausewitz, *On War*, translated by Michael Elliot Howard and Peter Paret, (Princeton University Press 1989)
3 Carl von Clausewitz, *On War*, translated by Michael Elliot Howard and Peter Paret, (Princeton University Press 1989)
4 Carl von Clausewitz, *On War*, translated by Michael Elliot Howard and Peter Paret, (Princeton University Press 1989)
5 Carl von Clausewitz, *On War*, translated by Michael Elliot Howard and Peter Paret, (Princeton University Press 1989)
6 Carl von Clausewitz, *On War*, translated by Michael Elliot Howard and Peter Paret, (Princeton University Press 1989)
7 Carl von Clausewitz, *On War*, translated by Michael Elliot Howard and Peter Paret, (Princeton University Press 1989)

Chapter 16
1 Carl von Clausewitz, *On War*, translated by Michael Elliot Howard and Peter Paret, (Princeton University Press 1989)
2 Charles "Sid" Heal, *Field Command* (Lantern Books, 2012)

3 Carl von Clausewitz, *On War*, translated by Michael Elliot Howard and Peter Paret, (Princeton University Press 1989)
4 Carl von Clausewitz, *On War*, translated by Michael Elliot Howard and Peter Paret, (Princeton University Press 1989)
5 Charles "Sid" Heal, *Field Command* (Lantern Books, 2012)
6 Charles "Sid" Heal, *Field Command* (Lantern Books, 2012)
7 Charles "Sid" Heal, *Field Command* (Lantern Books, 2012)

Chapter 17
1 See FBI uniformed crime reports, adapted to report Violent Encounters a Study on Felonious Assaults On law Enforcement (2006)
2 United States Marine Corps Doctrinal Publication 1, *Warfighting*, (Wildside Press, 2005)
3 Robert Coram, *Boyd the Fighter Pilot who Changed the Art of War*, (Little, Brown and Company, 2002)
4 Robert Coram, *Boyd the Fighter Pilot who Changed the Art of War*, (Little, Brown and Company, 2002)
5 Col. John Boyd, *Patterns of Conflict* (1976)
6 CNN Tape Project on Government Oversight (POGO) web site, Nick Schwellenbach, "Air Force Colonel John Boyd's House Armed Services Committee Testimony", March 26, 2011, file: http://pogoblog.typepad.com/pogo/2011/03/air-force-colonel-john-boyds-1991-house-armed-services-committee-testimony.html

Chapter 18
1 President George Washington, As President of the Constitutional Convention of 1787, Washington gave this advice to his fellow Delegates:
2 Martin van Creveld, *Fighting Power: German and U.S. Army Performance*, 1939-1945 (Praeger; First Edition, 1982)

Chapter 19
1 David Grossman, *On Killing: The Psychological Cost of Learning to Kill in War and Society* (Back Bay Books, 1995)
2 National law Enforcement Officers Memorial, Law Enforcement Officers Deaths (2010) http://www.nleomf.org/assets/pdfs/reports/2010_Law_Enforcement_Fatalities_Report.pdf

Chapter 20

1 Gary Gagliardi, *The Art of War Plus The Warrior Class*: (Clearbridge Publishing 2004)

2 Janine Driver, *You Say More Than You Think: A 7-Day Plan for Using the New Body Language to Get What You Want* (Harmony, 2011)

3 Alan & Barbara Pease, the Definitive Book of Body Language, (Bantam Dell, a Division of Random House 2004)

4 Col. John Boyd, Patterns of Conflict, (1976)

5 Donald Vandergriff, *Raising the Bar: Creating and Nurturing Adaptability to Deal with the Changing face of War*, (Amazon Digital Services, updated kindle edition 2013)

6 Alan & Barbara Pease, *the Definitive Book of Body Language*, (Bantam Dell, a Division of Random House 2004)

7 Alan & Barbara Pease, *the Definitive Book of Body Language*, (Bantam Dell, a Division of Random House 2004)

8 Alan & Barbara Pease, *the Definitive Book of Body Language*, (Bantam Dell, a Division of Random House 2004)

9 Alan & Barbara Pease, *the Definitive Book of Body Language*, (Bantam Dell, a Division of Random House 2004)

10 David Givens, *Crime Signals How to Spot a Criminal before You Become a Victim*, (St. Martin's Press 2008)

11 David Givens, *Crime Signals How to Spot a Criminal before You Become a Victim*, (St. Martin's Press 2008)

12 Steven Rhoades, Detecting *Danger* Part 1 and 2, Line of Duty Inc.

13 Tonya Reinman, *the Power of Body Language How to Succeed in Every Business and Social Encounter* (Pocket Books a Division of Simon & Schuster 2007)

14 MPTC Sim-munitions Instructors Class (2009)

15 Chet, Richards, Certain to Win: The Strategy of John Boyd, Applied to Business, (Library of Congress 2004)

16 Gary Gagliardi, *the Art of War plus the Warrior Class*: (Clearbridge Publishing 2004)

Chapter 21

1 Chet Richards, *Certain to Win* (Xlibris 2004)

2 See Chet Richards Blog Post, *Developing the Touch* (2010)
http://slightlyeastofnew.com/2010/08/17/developing-the-touch/

3 Gary Gagliardi, the Art of War plus the Warrior Class: (Clearbridge Publishing 2004)

4 Col. John Boyd, Patterns of Conflict (1976)

5 Donald Vandergriff, *Raising the Bar: Creating and Nurturing Adaptability to Deal with the Changing face of War,* (Amazon Digital Services, updated kindle edition 2013)

Chapter 22
1 John Maxwell, *Leadership Promises for Every Day,* (Thomas Nelson 2003)
2 James M. Kouzes and Barry Z. Posner, *the Leadership Challenge,* (Jossey-Bass 2008)
3 See Think Exist
http://thinkexist.com/quotation/good_character_is_more_to_be_pra ised_than/212105.html

Chapter 23
1 Martin van Creveld, Fighting Power: German and U.S. Army Performance, 1939-1945 (Praeger; First Edition, 1982)
2 United States Marine Corps Doctrinal Publication 1, Warfighting, (Wildside Press, 2005)

Chapter 24
1 Gary Klein, *Streetlights and Shadows: Searching for the Keys to Adaptive Decision Making* (The MIT Press 2009)
2 Gary Klein, *Streetlights and Shadows: Searching for the Keys to Adaptive Decision Making* (The MIT Press 2009)
3 Gary Klein, *Streetlights and Shadows: Searching for the Keys to Adaptive Decision Making* (The MIT Press 2009)
4 Gary Klein, *Streetlights and Shadows: Searching for the Keys to Adaptive Decision Making* (The MIT Press 2009)
5 Gary Klein, *Streetlights and Shadows: Searching for the Keys to Adaptive Decision Making* (The MIT Press 2009)
6 Gary Klein, *Streetlights and Shadows: Searching for the Keys to Adaptive Decision Making* (The MIT Press 2009)
7 Gary Klein, *Streetlights and Shadows: Searching for the Keys to Adaptive Decision Making* (The MIT Press 2009)
8 Gary Klein, *Streetlights and Shadows: Searching for the Keys to Adaptive Decision Making* (The MIT Press 2009)
9 Gary Klein, *Streetlights and Shadows: Searching for the Keys to Adaptive Decision Making* (The MIT Press 2009)
10 Gary Klein, *Streetlights and Shadows: Searching for the Keys to Adaptive Decision Making* (The MIT Press 2009)

11 Gary Klein, *Streetlights and Shadows: Searching for the Keys to Adaptive Decision Making* (The MIT Press 2009)

Chapter 25
1 Martin van Creveld, *Command in War* (Harvard University Press 1985)
2 EXL Pharma Lean Six Sigma conference Philadelphia, PA, workshop; *Tactical Decision Games to Increase The Speed and Maturity of Decision Making,* facilitated by Dr. Terry Barnhart and Fred Leland (March 2013)
3 EXL Pharma Lean Six Sigma conference Philadelphia, PA, workshop; Tactical Decision Games to Increase The Speed and Maturity of Decision Making, facilitated by Dr. Terry Barnhart and Fred Leland (March 2013)
4 EXL Pharma Lean Six Sigma conference Philadelphia, PA, workshop; Tactical Decision Games to Increase The Speed and Maturity of Decision Making, facilitated by Dr. Terry Barnhart and Fred Leland (March 2013)
5 See, Holy Bible: New Living Translation (Tyndale House Publishers, 2006)

Chapter 26
1 Fred is an active Lieutenant, with the Walpole PD and a former United States Marine. He is an accomplished and accredited trainer with more than 25 years of experience teaching Law Enforcement and Security. He is a graduate of the FBI National Academy Class 216, where he specialized in terrorism related topics, leadership and management. Fred is a student of the late modern day Strategist Col. John Boyd and the Ancient Strategist Sun Tzu. He founded Law Enforcement and Security Consulting, Inc (LESC) in 2006 with the focus of bringing these principles to law enforcement and security.
2 In the United States and all over the world, Vandergriff has served in numerous troop, staff and education assignments, retiring in 2005 after 24 years of active duty as an enlisted Marine and Army officer. In 2003, he was named ROTC Instructor of the year, and in 2004 he was runner up for the same title. He teaches at Georgetown University in Washington, D.C. and continues to certify Army instructors in Adaptive Leader Methodology, which is a leader development model he created based on the concepts of Col. John Boyd.
3 See WILLIAM HAYES, THE FUTURE OF PROGRESSIVE EDUCATION (2008); W. ROBERT HOUSTON, EXPLORING COMPETENCY BASED

EDUCATION (1974).

4 The Adaptive Course Model (ACM) is the product of the efforts of MAJ (ret.) Don Vandergriff, a well-known and influential thinker in the area of leader development, is also a contractor in support of Army Capabilities Integration Center Forward (ARCIC Forward). Initially, this instructional method was known as the "Adaptive Leader Course" (ALC). However, because of the confusion generated by the many questions regarding the location of "that adaptive leader," the name was changed to more clearly reflect that this is an approach/methodology rather than an actual course of instruction at a schoolhouse.

5 See Major Vandergriff's website at http://www.adaptive-leader.com

6 See NORTHWEST REGIONAL EDUCATIONAL LABORATORY, COMPETENCY-BASED EDUCATION: BEYOND MINIMUM COMPTENCY TESTING, (eds. Ruth Nicksee, Larry McClure, 1981).

7 ACM lessons learned include: Improving one's ability to make decisions quickly and effectively; making sense of new situations, seeing patterns, and spotting opportunities and options that were not visible before; becoming more comfortable in a variety of situations; developing more advanced and ambitious tactics; becoming more familiar with weapons and equipment capabilities, employment techniques, and other technical details.

8 See MCO 1500.55, MILITARY THINKING AND DECISION MAKING EXERCISES (Dept. of the Navy, 1997); BEN J. M. ALE, RISK: AN INTRODUCTION: THE CONCEPTS OF RISK, DANGER AND CHANCE (2009).

9 See A LEADER'S GUIDE TO AFTER-ACTION REVIEWS: TRAINING CIRCULAR 25-20 (Dept. of the Army, 1993).

10 DONALD E. VANDERGRIFF, RAISING THE BAR: CREATING AND NURTURING ADAPTABILITY TO DEAL WITH THE CHANGING FACE OF WAR 77-111 (2006). Chapter 3 of this book outlines the Program of Instruction (POI) for a course that employs ACM-based instructional methods. Vandergriff's approach is also supported by the latest learning theory of Dr. Robert Bjork of UCLA.

11 See VANDERGRIFF, supra note 8.

12 Jeffrey B. Hukill, Maligned and Misunderstood, ARMED FORCES J., Mar. 2009, available at www.armedforcesjournal.com/2009/03/3873827.

13 See CIRCULAR 25-20, supra note 9.

14 Wayne Barefoot, Keys to S2 success at JRTC, MILITARY

INTELLIGENCE PROF. BUL., Jan. 1, 1998, at 48.

15 Gary Klein, Ph.D, INTUITION AT WORK (2003) discusses his experiments and study on how first responders make decisions under pressure and utilize the Recognition-Primed Decision Making Process.

16 John R. Boyd, Patterns of Conflict (Dec. 1986).

17 ARMY PLANNING AND ORDERS PRODUCTION: FIELD MANUAL 5-0 (Dept. of the Army, 2005).

18 Id. at 47-49.

19 See Boyd, supra note 16; see also Aaron A. Bazin, Boyd's O-O-D-A Loop And The Infantry Company Commander, INFANTRY MAG., Jan. /Feb. 2005.

20 See WILLIAM HAYES, THE FUTURE OF PROGRESSIVE EDUCATION (2008); W. ROBERT HOUSTON, EXPLORING COMPETENCY BASED EDUCATION (1974).

21 WILLIAM S. LIND, MANEUVER WARFARE HANDBOOK (1985).

22 Id. at 73-89. Lind describes these concepts as enemy "surfaces and gaps."

23 See generally DAVID GALULA, COUNTERINSURGENCY WARFARE: THEORY AND PRACTICE (2006); Frank G. Hoffman, Complex Irregular Warfare: The Next Revolution in Military Affairs, 50 ORBIS 395-411 (2006).

24 Colin S. Gray, Thinking Asymmetrically in Times of Terror, 32 PARAMETERS (2002).

25 Lawrence G. Shattuck & David d. Woods, Communication of Intent in Military Command and Control Systems, in THE HUMAN IN COMMAND: EXPLORING THE MODERN MILITARY EXPERIENCE 279-292 (Carol McCann & Ross Pigeau, eds., 2000).

26 LIND, supra note 21, at 13-15. Lind describes the Commander's Intent as a "long term contract" between the Commander and his subordinate leaders. The immediate mission is what the Commander wants done, but he allows his subordinates the latitude to exercise creativity and initiative in determining exactly how they will accomplish that mission.

27 James C. Duncan, The Commander's Role in Developing Rules of Engagement, 52 NAVAL WAR COLLEGE REV. (1999).

28 ANTHONY H. CORDESMAN, THE IRAQ WAR: STRATEGY, TACTICS, AND MILITARY LESSONS (2003).

29 LIND, supra note 21, at 12.

30 EDUARDO SALAS & GARY A. KLEIN, LINKING EXPERTISE AND NATURALISTIC DECISION MAKING (2001).

31 *See* VANDERGRIFF, *supra* note 10.

32 Fred Leland, *Deciding Under Pressure...and Fast Workshop Success and Evolutionary Adaptability*, LAW ENFORCEMENT & SECURITY CONSULTING WEBSITE, at http://www.lesc.net/blog/deciding-under-pressurehellipand-fast-and-evolutionary-adaptability (03/28/2009).

33 These comments were taken from the anonymous end-of-course surveys that students and participants completed after the conclusion of the workshop "Deciding under Pressure and Fast" which teaches how to apply ALM in existing POI.

Chapter 27

1 John Schmitt, *Mastering Tactics*, (Marine Corp Assn Bookstore, 1994)

2 John Schmitt, *Mastering Tactics*, (Marine Corp Assn Bookstore, 1994)

3 John Schmitt, *Mastering Tactics*, (Marine Corp Assn Bookstore, 1994)

4 John Schmitt, *Mastering Tactics*, (Marine Corp Assn Bookstore, 1994)

Chapter 28

1 Dr. Gary Klein, *Intuition at Work Why Developing Gut Instincts Will make you Better at What You Do*, (Doubleday 2003)

2 Dr. Gary Klein, Intuition at Work Why Developing Gut Instincts Will make you Better at What You Do, (Doubleday 2003)

3 John Schmitt, *Mastering Tactics*, (Marine Corp Assn Bookstore, 1994)

4 John Schmitt, Mastering Tactics, (Marine Corp Assn Bookstore, 1994)

5 John Schmitt, *Mastering Tactics*, (Marine Corp Assn Bookstore, 1994)

6 John Schmitt, *Mastering Tactics*, (Marine Corp Assn Bookstore, 1994)

Chapter 29

1 Charles "Sid" Heal, *Field Command* (Lantern Books, 2012)

2 Charles "Sid" Heal, *Field Command* (Lantern Books, 2012

3 Donald Vandergriff, *Raising the Bar: Creating and Nurturing Adaptability to Deal with the Changing face of War*, (Amazon Digital Services, updated kindle edition 2013)

25486755R00145

Made in the USA
Middletown, DE
01 November 2015